UNDER THE HARROW

Also by Suzanne Gordon

A Talent for Tomorrow

UNDER THE HARROW

LIVES OF WHITE
SOUTH AFRICANS TODAY

Suzanne Gordon

WILLIAM HEINEMANN
LONDON

William Heinemann Ltd
Michelin House, 81 Fulham Road, London SW3 6RB

LONDON   MELBOURNE   AUCKLAND

First published in 1988

British Library Cataloguing in Publication Data

Gordon, Suzanne
    Under the harrow: lives of white South
    Africans today.
    1. South Africa. White persons. Social life
    I. Title
    968.06′3

    ISBN 0 434 30247 3

Printed and bound in Great Britain by
Richard Clay Ltd, Bungay, Suffolk

For Christopher, Sarah, Milo,
Dashiell and Caitlin

CONTENTS

Foreword by Christopher Hope   xi

Preface   1

Zulu du Toit   7

Carlos Garçaõ   27

Kidger Hartley   45

Emily Kok   68

Dalene Moore   91

Gabriel Nothnagel   109

Bill Wilson   126

Maria Elizabeth van Niekerk   157

Samuel Goldblatt   174

Sue Drummond   191

Johann Frederick Farrell and
     Jacobus Daniël Farrell   218

Tony Ardington   243

Glossary   265

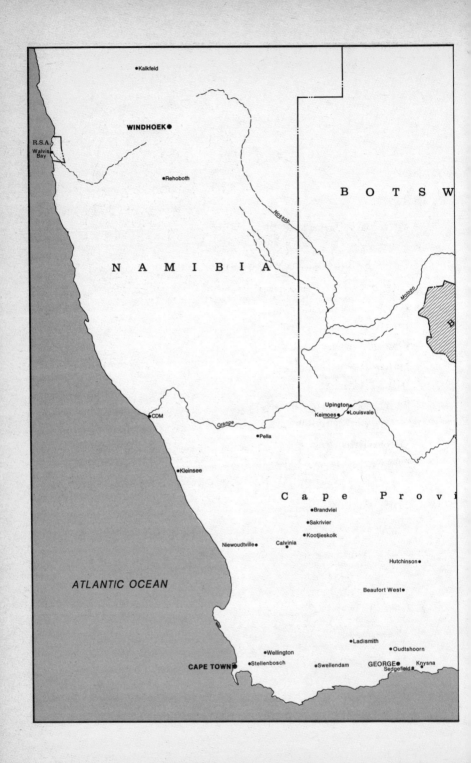

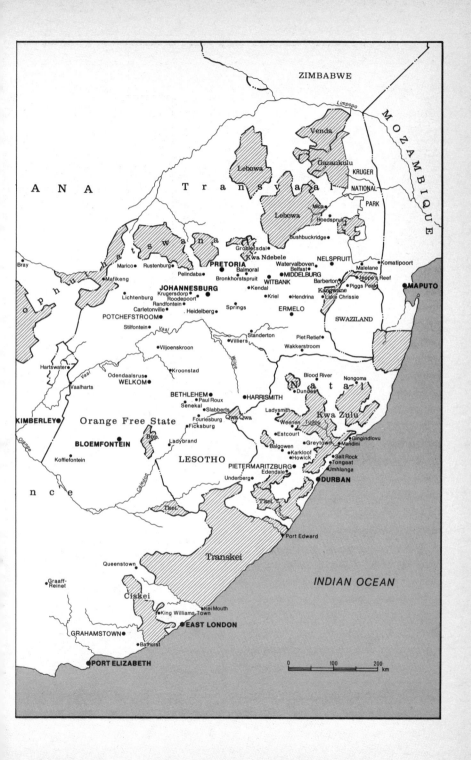

FOREWORD

My INTEREST IN the work of Suzanne Gordon was first kindled when I read her interviews with black household servants in South Africa, published under the appropriate, and prophetic, title *A Talent for Tomorrow*. This absorbing and moving document shows that what had until then been regarded an area of little concern, small lives dimly lit, too obscure to be noticed, too inarticulate for consultation, were vivid existences full of warmth, tragedy, humour and courage. Mrs Gordon found a way to encourage cooks, gardeners, housemaids and nannies to speak for themselves and, more difficult still, she listened to what they had to say. Both activities required degrees of tact and sympathy so rare within the South African context as to be acts of the most delicate and refined subversion. It seemed to me that no one was better placed to record the stories of white South Africans, English- and Afrikaans-speaking, left, right and centre – nor anyone as likely to persuade them to allow her to do so.

I have always thought it remarkable how little of South African life is regarded as a proper field for study. So many areas are off-limits not only because they might be politically inflammatory but for quite the opposite reason – because they are regarded as too 'ordinary', too unexceptional to warrant attention. There are a variety of reasons for this neglect. Chief among them are the political policies directed towards building walls between people of different races, cultures, languages and ethnic backgrounds. This compulsory enclosure of people within cultural and racial pens has meant that voices raised within the group have been faint, except when speaking for some well-established position endorsed by the group. The free expression of personal opinion is almost as novel, say, as the idea that every individual should have a vote. Except in private political debate solitary opinions are not encouraged and single voices seldom heard except when they are raised in some official capacity in support of some communal point of view. This is something to be expected among the perpetrators of racial policy but it is also to be detected among opponents and victims where calls and counter-calls for solidarity drown out individual voices, the 'big' issues take precedence and policies and positions are more important than the fears, failings, loves, dreams and tragedies that go to make up the life stories of ordinary people.

And then the way the outside world sees South Africa further limits the way we see ourselves. It is customary for observers abroad to view South Africa with a mixture of fascination and repulsion and it is seldom necessary for them to revise their traditional views of the country and its people. Nor, I suspect, would they wish to do so. Certainly South Africa is expected to continue to provide sensational examples of racial antagonism which foreigners find essential. A South African abroad, by contrast, fascinated by familiar forms of discrimination and race hatred in European countries will find that the natives do not share his fascination. One might almost say that if South Africa did not exist it would have to be invented. It is a well of self-righteousness to which the world comes to drink because by focusing on the racial policies which South Africans practise so brazenly in public they can forget their own discriminatory habits which flourish in private.

Strapped in the political strait-jackets which rigidify so much South African life, the leaders of the country do their best to maintain this state of affairs by behaving with the clumsy brutality by which the world recognizes them. And in recognizing them it seldom hears from anyone else. What comes out of South Africa are official responses drawn from a small number of representatives of the groups contending for power. Foreigners could be forgiven for thinking that South Africa is populated by spokesmen, and that ordinary people are not able, or willing, or permitted to speak for themselves.

This is something which Suzanne Gordon has begun to remedy. If one of the things she achieves in her record of the testimonies of black domestic servants is the revelation that they observe their white masters and mistresses with a sharpness tinged with pity as much as anger, then her safari through white South Africa reveals a wide range of attitudes and political beliefs. Those she meets are at once better and worse than the stereotypes suggest. The people who tell their stories in *Under The Harrow* are not all bigots or heroes or the ugly South Africans now passing into folklore. And where they express views whether bizarre, brave, comic or tragic, they reveal themselves to be strange in ways not portrayed in the easy caricatures of white South Africans. For the people who speak to Mrs Gordon, be they familiar or frightening, are nobody but themselves. There is the Afrikaans farmer who believes in a multi-racial federation; a Portuguese fugitive from Mozambique who now organizes a feeding scheme for black migrant Mozambican workers in South Africa; a mining boss who hovers between pride and embarrassment at the thought that it took his company almost a century to appoint its first black foreman; a nurse recounting a visit to her husband's relations in Northern Ireland where she discovered that Catholics in Ulster are victims of discrimination more poisonous than anything she encountered between blacks and whites at home; an idealistic liberal doctor working in Zimbabwe who was shocked by atrocities visited on dissidents by government troops and came home to work with victims of township violence and police brutality; a pensioner recalls how she learnt from her 'boys' of the electric shocks administered by the police – and sends an old friend along to ask for the same treatment for his rheumatics. This elderly lady believes blacks to be contented with their lot. Yet her granddaughter, liberated and politically informed, wonders if the violence will ever stop. Through it all we hear the authentic South African voice, a strange and sometimes eerie blend of faith, paternalism, anger and fear ranging across the spectrum from the unabashed racialism of conservative supporters of the Afrikaner Resistance Movement to the anguish of the English-speaking liberal unable to affect political policies yet unwilling to accept defeat.

If Suzanne Gordon's record of the lives of black servants was a difficult venture requiring tact, skill and a most sensitive degree of judgement, her task in persuading white South Africans to feel sufficiently relaxed to confide in her is still more remarkable. Her method leaves little room for interventions or for colouring the responses of those she meets. Apart from a few brief remarks by which the speaker is placed within his or her context, the respondent is at the centre of each story. Beneath her unobtrusive scrutiny her subjects reveal themselves to be a threatened species and it is indicative of her gift for imaginative sympathy for people irrespective of their official designations that she has enabled Afrikaans farmers, a Portuguese immigrant, a Jewish businessman, anglicized Afrikaners and English nationalists to speak openly and freely of themselves.

And this at a time when whites are becoming less communicative – in part because the country grows ever more violent and confusing and also because people are quite simply more afraid. It is perhaps not known to outsiders and it may surprise them to learn that white politics has always been debated fiercely, openly, exuberantly in South Africa and until recently no one would hesitate to express the most extreme opinions whether for or against government policies without fear or favour, no matter who might be listening. But as the political crisis deepens, the state of emergency becomes a permanent fact of life, remaining opposition groups are suppressed and press censorship strangles the rebellious spirit which once distinguished some newspapers – opinions are moderated, people think twice before they speak, conversations become guarded and fear closes mouths. Or, masquerading as anger, it gives way to slogans and threats. And in South Africa slogans are increasingly threats cloaked in political respectability.

The histories collected in *Under The Harrow* confirm and confound all the usual thinking about white South Africans. The voices we hear are stubborn, defiant, obtuse – but they are also resilient, determined, hopeful and generous. A consistent theme among many of these South Africans is that they belong to the country and would not leave under any circumstances. Many of those interviewed harbour a poignant belief in a community of interests binding blacks and whites which the bravest souls look to for salvation, if only people will talk to each other. In the face of much contrary evidence such hopes seem insubstantial grounds for progress yet they are undoubtedly genuine and are perhaps best summed up by the white farmer quoting the black worker who told him that 'we are all flowers of Jesus'. Well, that may be so, but as these testimonies make clear the South African garden contains some less than lovely blooms. It is another farmer, more clear-sighted, from the sugar-growing area of Natal, who faces the likelihood that things will get worse before they get any better and concludes that: 'We are probably going to have the harrow go over us.'

Christopher Hope

PREFACE

THE IDEA OF compiling a collection of oral histories of white South Africans was put to me by Christopher Hope when we met in London in late 1985. I returned to Johannesburg and some months later, despite the pitfalls inherent in the undertaking, resolved to take up the challenge. I accepted the contract offered by William Heinemann Ltd and, sustained by Christopher's faith in the project, set to work.

Both in the interviews which I recorded on tape and in the subsequent writing I have endeavoured to be objective, but there is an unavoidable subjective element in the processes of selecting informants and editing their statements. In order that the reader may appreciate the personal lens through which people and events have been observed I offer a little of my own background.

My mother was born in the south of England in 1886. When she was still a baby her parents were divorced; her father went to South Africa and her mother to Japan where her second husband, an American, was in business. My mother was left in England to be brought up by a paternal grandmother, the severity of her life relieved by seaside holidays and visits to the pantomime with her cousins. In 1909 she joined her mother and stepfather who were then living on the Hudson River. It was there that she met my father. He had been born in New York City in 1885 and raised at a time when its inhabitants were often almost overwhelmed by and resentful of successive waves of immigrants. Among the ways in which their hostility was expressed was the pejorative naming of such groups: Yids, wops, polacks and dagos.

They married in 1910. My father appears to have had no regular job so they came to South Africa in response to an invitation from my mother's father to join him on his cattle farm at Hammanskraal, north of Pretoria. However, the primitive and isolated way of life in the midst of apparently unending low bush held little appeal for my parents and after a year they went to Johannesburg where my father first worked in and then eventually acquired a small motor spares business which he developed over the years.

During the late 1920s and 30s I grew up with my two older brothers in a comfortable middle-class home in the outer northern suburbs of white Johannesburg. In my early years there was a white nanny whom I disliked and later on mothers' helps, white women, generally elderly, who lived in so as to be there when my parents were out. My mother, assisted by two or three 'garden-boys', worked each day in our four-acre garden and by the time I entered my teens she was playing bridge on many afternoons. There was a 'houseboy' and a succession of black cooks, driven out as a rule by my father's violent outbursts when a meal was not to his liking.

I adopted my parents' attitude of regarding 'the natives' merely as those to whom one gave orders, and recall my first deviation from that orthodoxy. When I was about seventeen years old I took a manservant who was going on leave to the bus. When he got out of the car, for some reason that escapes me, I shook his hand. It was the first time that I was conscious of touching a brown skin and I remember being pervaded by a strange succession of feelings.

In 1940, aged nineteen, I married a Jewish lawyer, Nat Gordon. We had four children, the last of whom was born in the month following the elections which brought the National Party to power. We had listened through the night to the disastrous loss of one United Party seat after another, including even that of Smuts, the revered wartime leader. Although, of course, discrimination had been very much in place before 1948, as the new Nationalist government set to work I began dimly to understand the malevolent power of racism.

Impelled perhaps by the need for something more meaningful in my life, I joined the newly formed, non-racial Liberal Party when it was founded in 1953. Never an active member, I was proud to be associated, even in such a tenuous manner, with the Party and remained a member until in 1968 its dissolution was forced by government legislation against political parties with racially mixed membership. In 1954 I enrolled at the University of the Witwatersrand, initially in a rather dilettantish fashion, for I had been a drop-out at school. However, I was intrigued by the possibilities of learning and went on to a post-graduate degree in English. During the years at university I attended political meetings and joined in protest marches. My indignation against the government grew.

In 1960 my husband was discovered to have cancer. He had neglected his legal practice in favour of various business ventures and these were hit by the financial slump that followed Sharpeville. I found a job teaching English at an Asian school in Fordsburg where many Indians were still living at that time. My husband died in 1962 and I moved to a large college in the city where the pay was better.

In 1971 I abandoned teaching to work at the South African Institute of Race Relations. Here I developed the Domestic Workers and Employers Project (DWEP), aimed at improving wages and working conditions of the almost one million South African domestic servants. DWEP was instrumental in initiating over a hundred Centres of Concern throughout the country; these were generally based in church halls and became places where domestics might come to acquire skills such as dressmaking, literacy, first aid and so on. They were also social centres. DWEP organized leadership courses and events to 'conscientize' the domestics. It was the leaders from these Centres of Concern who constituted the nucleus of the S.A. Domestic Workers Association when it was formed in 1981 and which led to the present

S.A. Domestic Workers' Union. My first book, *A Talent for Tomorrow*, is a collection of oral histories of domestic servants.

With considerable eagerness and a degree of excitement I began the research for this book. My aim was to find rural and urban people, both English- and Afrikaans-speaking. A friend, Tim Couzens, advised me to talk to everyone I met about the work I was doing and said I'd be surprised at the results. He was quite right. Unlikely encounters often led to a rewarding discovery. In order to draw from as many social groups as possible, but not with the intention of furthering any stereotypes, I have included amongst the sample a member of the Jewish community and one of the Portuguese-speaking community. An attempt at regional coverage has been made. I sought, too, people of a variety of political opinions, though in the end these extended to neither the far right nor the far left. I can't remember how many times over the past eighteen months I have apologized for my Afrikaans as being *''n bietjie swak'* (a little weak), a considerable understatement, and this limited my access to many people who held, even by South Africa's standards, extreme right-wing views.

I must emphasize that I try to respect the uniqueness of the individual and do not consider any of my informants to be representatives of their regional, religious, language or political group.

The historian Charles van Onselen was remarkably tolerant of my temerity in undertaking such a task for which I was so ill-equipped in terms of theoretical background. I read some books he recommended on the rise of Afrikanerdom and began my travels around the country. Meeting and getting to understand something about Afrikaners was a new experience for me; their hospitality was open and warming. I began to appreciate something of the complexities of differing viewpoints. Staying with the people who lived some distance from Johannesburg had the advantage of enabling me to get to know them better, but the concomitant moral obligation presented difficulties with regard to criticism. I have consistently tried to be as fair and as objective as possible, but this is an element of which readers should be aware.

The use of terminology within and about South Africa is a problem. I have quoted certain terms which I am aware are offensive but which are in current usage by the majority of white South Africans and, incidentally, many black South Africans. They convey the flavour, both historical and contemporary, of the attitudes of the speakers. Some examples are 'native' (black only), 'coloured' (in reference to a person of 'mixed race'), 'boy' and 'girl' (in reference to adults), 'homeland', 'kaffir', 'piccanin', 'hotnot' and so forth. In order to avoid a text peppered with quotation marks they have not been enclosed in this way.

Names of a number of the countries and towns of southern Africa have been changed over the past twenty years. The name used by the speaker has not been updated. Examples are Basutoland, now Lesotho; Nyasaland, now Malawi; Northern Rhodesia, now Zambia; Southern Rhodesia, now Zimbabwe; Salisbury, now Harare; South West Africa, now generally referred to as Namibia; Lourenço Marques, now Maputo.

Certain of the people interviewed are not mother-tongue English speakers. In order that their speech should not convey an impression of intellectual inferiority their grammar has, where necessary, been corrected.

There has been no State censorship, but white South Africans, like most people, are prisoners of the present as well as the past and the fear and the tensions within the society are reflected in a number of people's withdrawing statements they have made concerning military service, in relation to themselves or to members of their family. Suppression has, however been imposed from other sources. An informant holding a fairly senior managerial position in a large non-governmental organization withdrew permission to publish the interview as a result of censorship by his superiors of some of his statements, and subsequent implicit pressure.

In only one instance have the names of people been changed. The case is that of a doctor working in the municipal service who feared that if she were too easily recognizable it might affect her job. This reveals another aspect of the pervasive fear of authorities disinclined to brook any dissenting views.

This book could never have been written without the encouragement and support of a number of people. Firstly Christopher Hope who put the idea to me, introduced me to his publisher at William Heinemann, and who has over the eighteen months during which I have been writing given me continuous encouragement and occasional most valuable advice.

I am also deeply indebted to Charles van Onselen for his reading of the text and for his scrawls that often filled the margins and which, when deciphered and coupled with his verbal advice, provided leads as to how I should remedy defects and make good omissions. I fear that the finished product still falls short in many respects of his standards. I am also grateful to him and to Tim Couzens for allowing me to work as a Research Associate within the African Studies Institute of the University of the Witwatersrand. Furthermore I am most appreciative of the grant given to me by The Chairman's Fund Education Trust of the Anglo American Corporation of South Africa Limited and De Beers Consolidated Mines Limited. Without it the research for this book could not have been undertaken.

I spent countless hours and days during the first year of work at David and Josie Adler's house, using their computer, consulting their library and enjoying their continuing warm welcome as well as many meals with them. Furthermore, without David Adler's intervention I could not have reached several of my most important informants. Verna Hunt read the greater part of the original manuscript and her astringent comments were immensely valuable. Other people of whose help in various aspects of the undertaking I am most appreciative are Eleanor Anderson, Tony Brink, Guy Butler, Herman Hüsselmann, Cobus Farrell, Margaret Jonsson, Brian and Peter Kane-Berman, Isaac Make Moephuli, Dalene Moore, Mark Orkin, Richard Reese, Mary Slack, David Stubbs, Mona Worthington and the late David Snaddon.

Suzanne Gordon
Johannesburg
January 1988

ZULU DU TOIT

THE STREETS OF Middelburg, Transvaal, like those of most South
African towns of an earlier era, are wide enough for an ox-
wagon to turn. It is a small town, with low buildings, serving
chiefly as a trading centre for farmers. Stale-smelling cafés sell
coffee, cold drinks and hot pies to the many passing motorists.
Standing on the eastern horizon are the huge cooling towers of
Arnot, one of the world's biggest coal-fired power stations.
Wealth is not confined to the rich coalfields; in the centre of the
town twelve grain elevators, only one of several such massive
clumps in the area, store maize.

Twenty kilometres eastward along the road to the lowveld is
the turnoff onto a gravelled road where the town motorists wind
up the windows against the dust of passing farm vehicles. At the
sign, 'Kwaggafontein: Zulu du Toit', a long tree-lined drive leads
past paddocks with fine young horses, potential show jumpers.
There are also a few ostriches, and a lone zebra, perhaps a reminder of the *kwagga*, the zebra-like animal that was once abun-
dant in the area and from which the farm derives its name. The
bungalow dwelling, sprawling comfortably from additions over
the years, nestles amongst herbaceous beds and shrubberies.

Zulu du Toit strides out as the tires scrunch the gravel; he is a
taut man of middle size, fit and lean. A friendly man with whom
one is at once on first-name terms, he leads the way into the
living-room with its comfortable deep chairs and sofas. Low

teak-framed casement windows afford a view of the lawns and garden. Beyond is the roof of the squash court and a swimming-pool.

But why Zulu? The name hardly seems appropriate for a white man in such a conservative area, especially when coupled with an Afrikaner surname like Du Toit. 'Well, you see, I was named Gerrit Johan, but when I was small and running with no clothes round our garden on the mine where my dad worked, my dad looked at me and said, "Just like a little Zulu." The name's stuck ever since.'

Down in the lands two combine harvesters proceed relentlessly through the fields, consuming the tall maize. The operator sits in an air-conditioned cabin ten feet above the earth, an eye on the controls where computer numbers flicker and lights flash. At his back the golden maize kernels pour down into the container whose contents are offloaded from time to time into a vast bin on the border of the field. Du Toit checks it with satisfaction. Last year's harvest from this and his other farm was 27,000 tons; this crop will be as good. Three men, seated on their haunches, are eating. Other workers are engaged in co-ordinating the operations. Perfunctorily they acknowledge the farmer's presence. He is the only white man about.

The Du Toit family descends from the French Huguenots who came to the Cape 300 years ago. Zulu's great-great-great-grandfather, Andries François du Toit, trekked from Beaufort West in the Cape to the Transvaal to farm in the Middelburg area. His son, Gerrit Johan Wilhelm du Toit, was its Member of Parliament in the first Union Parliament in 1910. His son, Zulu's grandfather, also Gerrit Johan, as a boy of seventeen had fought in the prestigious Captain Danie Theron Scout Corps in the South African War at the turn of the century; later he rose to the rank of commandant. Zulu continues, 'We've still got a photo of him, behind the rocks, with the English troops below. When I was a youngster he took me to Ladysmith where Dick Cunningham won the Victoria Cross in the battle of Spitzkop. I can remember it very well. Then he went with Smuts on the East African campaign in World War I and was awarded the Military

Cross. The old man was very proud of his military prestige. Then, when World War II broke out he was quite old, fifty-seven, and he insisted – he actually went to *see* General Smuts – that he must enlist. They said, "You're an old man; nobody wants you." But he said, "Well look, I've been through all these wars and I'm going with you again." And they eventually gave him a job at the transit camp at the Union Grounds in Johannesburg. I remember well, as a kid, going to fetch the old man and he'd slip through the fences and come home and spend the weekend with us and then go back and issue uniforms and so on.

'I sort of grew up pro-English. I grew up standing to attention when they played "God save the King". My grandfather's home, when you walked in there, Jan Smuts' picture hung on the wall in the lounge; he was in the dining-room, he was everywhere. They were good friends.' Zulu explains that his family were Sappe, a name deriving from the acronym of the old South African Party, led by General Louis Botha and General Jan Smuts. 'My family were big Jan Smuts people. I never grew up in a home where there was antagonism towards an Englishman. I remember, when I was a youngster, my grandfather told me that Louis Botha said to them (referring to the war in which the Boers had fought the English), "Look, the war's finished: we must bury the hatchet."'

When World War II broke out in September 1939 South Africa was a divided country and it was only by a narrow parliamentary margin that it joined the Allies. Many Afrikaners objected to fighting on the side of their erstwhile enemies, the English, and felt themselves to be much closer to the Germans. There were, however, large numbers of Afrikaners who, like Zulu's four uncles, his father's brothers, enlisted. One became a captain in the Air Force. His father had a key job in the mining industry and was not allowed to go. Some of his uncles on his mother's side had different loyalites. They belonged to the Ossewa-Brandwag, a secret, semi-military organization, aimed at the establishment of a South Africa under exclusive Afrikaner rule. Its members also carried out acts of sabotage. 'In fact, for years they didn't come near my dad and his brothers because they just wanted to climb into each other.'

Zulu's grandfather had inherited his father's farms, but having mortgaged them in order to finance some venture (the nature of which has been forgotten) and lost them, he found work on the diamond mines at Cullinan, near Pretoria. Zulu's father, the eldest son in a family of eight, once more named Gerrit Johan, was born in 1908. Times were hard and he was put to work in the diamond mine at an early age. From there he moved to the gold mines which seemed to offer better prospects and became a shift boss in the New State Areas mine near Springs, on the eastern Witwatersrand. There he met and married Sylvia de Wet whose forebears had been sheep farmers, but whose family had fallen on hard times after the death of her father. Sylvia qualified first as a nurse, and later as a shorthand typist in the government mining training school at Crown Mines, south of Johannesburg.

Zulu grew up in the house on the mines property. His earliest memories are of roaming among the mine dumps and playing in the mine compounds close to the house and of the hundreds of black workers from different parts of southern Africa who were housed there. It was from them that he learnt *fanakalo*, the language used by mine management to bridge the communication gap between the many different linguistic groups. 'I just grew up speaking it; I never knew what language I was speaking.

'I've been hunting a lot in Botswana and up in Angola and in Mozambique and wherever you go and you meet a black man, he understands you. It's quite incredible how many of them have been to the mines and learnt *fanakalo*: it's a short cut to an international black language. You know, today it's dying; I think they have forgotten *fanakalo*, but in my youth . . . I went up hunting one year, in the bush, between Nata and Panda Matenga, on the Botswana side of the Wankie Game Reserve. We got hold of . . . well he wasn't a yellow Bushman, he was a cross between a Tswana and a Bushman – Bushman features, but black. This little chap, an old fellow, spoke perfect *fanakalo*; I don't know where he learnt it. He could converse beautifully.

'His name was Isidondo. We had a licence to hunt buffalo and on the Botswana side there'd been a lot of hunting, so the game moves over to the Wankie National Park. But the game also becomes clever; they come through at night and graze, because the grass on the Botswana side is good, and in the day they go back again. Isidondo was our tracker and he picked up the spoor of a herd of buffalo; we followed their spoor and just about four o'clock in the afternoon we saw them, just on the edge of the Wankie. So we'd been walking for, it must have been twenty-three miles that day; we were very tired and it was hot. Isidondo said, "There are the buffalo." And I came close to look at them and I said, "But they're on the Wankie side." So he said, "Doesn't matter. Shoot the buffalo." So I shot the buffalo with a .458 soft-nose and it went through the lungs, but the buffalo ran for, must have been 150 yards, before it dropped. And it dropped in the Wankie Reserve. So we waited until the sun went down and went in and cut up the buffalo and brought the meat back. We got back to camp at about ten o'clock that night and we were really tired. But to celebrate the buffalo we took out a bottle of brandy and we gave old Isidondo about half a bottle in a cup, and he downed it. Straight, neat brandy. We were having a wonderful conversation about the hunting; but he was beautifully shot, this guy. He was sitting on his knees and he wanted to get up, but he just couldn't move. Isidondo was drunk.

'And he was telling us a story about how he visits his brother in the Wankie and he says it takes him three days to get there. I asked him, "Isidondo, aren't you scared to walk through the Wankie for three days when there's lion there?" And he said to me, in *fanakalo*, "*Zonke*" [that's all of us] "*hena lo flowers kalo Jesus*," [We are all flowers of Jesus] and "There's a place for every flower of Jesus in this world." If the lion's in his way, he'll watch the wind and he'll go downwind of it and the lion won't bother him. He says, "They all drink from the same fountain and that's the fountain of Jesus." Now wasn't that a wonderful philosophy? That should be our philosophy in South Africa. We're gonna go through bad times . . . but we all drink from the same fountain. He had us open-mouthed, listening to him.

'Nowadays the ANC [African National Congress] burns

— 11 —

homes and the AWB [Afrikaner Weerstandsbeweging] wants to hammer everybody, but that's not the answer. We have to find each other somewhere and I think we will. It's a great country. We're a multinational country. There's so many Afrikaners today that even hate the blacks, but *still* every morning they have a Bible reading with them. Now how can a person have a Bible reading and eventually not live with them? But of course there are those who say they begrudge the blacks nothing, but that they're like the birds in the trees who can all live in the one garden, but at night they must all go back to their own tree. They do believe that, even today, and that's why the NG Kerk has a Sendingkerk.' The *sendingkerk* is the missionary arm of the Dutch Reformed Church and is involved in providing and funding churches for the black and coloured people.

Zulu's early schooling was at the Maraisburg school, a dual-medium establishment where the pupils were taught in both English and Afrikaans. From there he was sent on to Potchefstroom Boys High, 'because my parents felt I must learn English and be a dual type of South African. You must speak both languages. So', and he chuckles, 'I'm an anglicized Dutchman. We're certainly not from the Afrikaner side who hated the English. After I passed my matric my dad felt that all they could afford was to get me a mining bursary and let me do mining. So just after school I worked as a skipman on the mine. Then they put me as a sampler. I was sampling down at Rand Leases and that was about 4,000 feet down on leader reef. It dipped at 80 degrees and was as hot as Hades. I came back one day and I said to my dad, "When they pay me on Friday, that's the last time I go down the mine." He asked me what I was going to do and I told him that I was going to farm. He said, "You must be mad! There's no way you can farm. How can you farm? We can never afford to buy you a farm." But he agreed that if I wanted to farm he'd phone his cousin, T. C. Robertson, who was then the editor of *Veld Trust*. Uncle T.C. said, "You want to farm? Do you want to go to varsity, or be a practical farmer, research, or what?" I said, "I want to be a practical farmer. I want to plant mealies and have cattle."'

His uncle advised that he should first gain some practical experience of farming and then go to an agricultural college. T. C. Robertson sent him first to a Mrs McDougall who grew seed potatoes and ran a dairy at Scorfell in the Underberg, an area of rich, rolling grasslands leading to the great Drakensberg Mountains. 'I spent three months there, milking cows. It was beautiful, absolutely beautiful! I went up one weekend on horseback with a pack-horse, right up and over the *berg*, to the eye of the Orange River in Lesotho. I was there for two days, on my own. At night I'd make a fire and then roll up in my sleeping-bag under the rocks. There's not a soul around. On the first day I was climbing a ledge – I'd left the two horses down below – to see where I could find a cutting to get over the top. Now I'm climbing up the grass, it was very steep, right up in the mountains, and you're looking down on Natal. And I looked down and just opposite my knee there was a puff-adder! And the puff-adder was looking at me and his tongue was darting in and out. He was, I would say, about four inches from my knee and I had shorts on. Now I'm right up the mountain. I had no snakebite serum with me and here I am and this guy's waiting for me. So I froze. Fortunately there was a loose rock, and I took it in my hand. It was now or never, because if I move he's going to get me. I threw the rock and I hit him. As I threw the rock I *jumped*. Whew! I nearly broke my neck, but the puff-adder didn't get me. It was terrifying!'

After three months Zulu moved to Viljoenskroon in the north-western Orange Free State, a rich maize-growing district. Here he worked for a Mr Bruce Evans who, in addition to growing maize, had a stud of Sussex cattle. 'It was a marvellous experience to work for Bruce Evans. In fact, a lot of the things that I do on my farm today I learnt from Evans. I remember getting forty bulls ready for the show and the old man would say, "How many bags of mealie-meal have you got in the store? How many bags of peanut oil cake?" And so on. I'd tell him thirty or twenty, or whatever, and he'd say, "That's not good enough for me, young man. Get your notebook and show me in your notebook when you fed and how many you have left."

Everything in a notebook. Anything you had to report to him had to be written down – all little things. He was a fantastic farmer!'

At the beginning of 1956 Zulu left the farm to study agriculture at the Cedara Agricultural College near Pietermaritzburg in Natal, working at the mine during his holidays. After two years he gained his Agricultural Diploma.

He graduated at the end of 1957 and set off for Rhodesia where he'd heard that 'the tobacco chaps' were making money. However, no one wanted to employ him. Ideas of joining the British South African Police and being stationed in some area rich in game were knocked on the head when he discovered that he would first have to spend two years as a traffic cop in Salisbury. So, prompted by his mother, Zulu sold his motor bike which he had bought with his holiday earnings and boarded the *Caernarvon Castle* for England.

'I arrived in Southampton and I had four pounds in my pocket. I knew that I must head for London where there was an Overseas Visitors Club in a place called Earls Court. I eventually found a chap, Max Wilson, who ran the Overseas Visitors Club and told him I wanted a job. He said, "Go and start washing dishes *immediately!* There's a bed in the attic." So I washed dishes for a month. It didn't bother me. I quite enjoyed it, really. I had food and a room while I found my feet. It was the middle of winter and there were no agricultural jobs, but I saw that Laing's Construction were looking for labourers to build the London to Yorkshire motorway.'

Zulu applied, was hired and given a train ticket to Newport Pagnell in Buckinghamshire where he dug trenches. 'I was in a compound with Irish navvies. Man! They were tough sods! They used to stink like hell. They speak about some of our dirty coons, but those guys, with their dirty gumboots – when they took them off at night you just about die of the pong! And cold showers in the middle of winter! All there was was cold water.' He progressed to engineer's chainman. 'In fact I chopped those trees for the theodolite to look through, at the Duke of Bedford's Woburn Abbey. I worked there for about five months. It was tough, but when you're young you can take it. Anything any other fellow could do, I thought I could do it better. If he chopped with an axe, I could give him a go. If an Irishman or a Welshman could pull the chain, so could I. From there I went on to construction and got jobs on those big Euclid machines and started earning money. I worked there for four or five months, every day including Sundays, and I stuck my money away. Not a break.'

In the summer of 1958 Zulu took his savings and toured Europe, sleeping in youth hostels or in the little tent he carried with him. Upon his return to England he did a course on artificial insemination with the Milk Marketing Board, but the pay was poor. Winter set in and he wrote to his father asking him to send money for his return fare. The reply, conveyed in a telegram, was crisp: 'If you want to come home, swim.' 'Hell, that nearly broke me!' The solution appeared to lie in joining a ship's crew and working his passage back. Meeting with no success in England, he and a cousin heard that there were jobs going in the Norwegian Merchant Navy. They had no money, so they decided to stow away on a ship going to Norway. After hitching up to Newcastle upon Tyne they got onto a ship but were discovered and arrested. 'The cops caught us and when they were taking us out of the harbour there was a coloured fellow working at the gate. My cousin and I spoke Afrikaans and he turned round and said, "*Waar kom julle vandaan?*" And we said, "*Man, ons kom van Suid Afrika.*" ["Where do you come from?" "Man, we come from South Africa."] 'He told us he was in the Cape Corps in the war and he'd married an English girl. And this guy, he knew the police, and he squashed the whole thing and they released us. Then he helped us, through a friend of his, to get up on deck and sit there for the crossing to Norway. He was a good Cape South African.'

Back in South Africa, Zulu got a job with the subtropical fruit estates of H. L. Hall and Son, outside Nelspruit. It was here that he met Marie Nefdt, his future wife. Her mother was from the illustrious Pretorius family, the great-granddaughter of Andries Marthinus Wessels Pretorius, president of the old Transvaal

Republic. Marie and Zulu resolved the problem of his being a Methodist and her being a member of the Nederduitse Gereformeerde Kerk (Dutch Reformed Church) by marrying in November 1959 in her church with a Methodist minister officiating. After their marriage Zulu became a member of her church which was the one to which his parents had originally belonged. They had left it during World War II when the dominee of the NG Kerk had refused to perform the marriage ceremony of one of the Du Toit brothers because he was in military uniform.

For a short while Zulu became a partner in a dairy at Greytown, rising at three in the morning to do the door-to-door milk deliveries – 'a dreadful job' – before he and Marie returned to Johannesburg. His father, who remembered the bitter plight of the workless in the 1933 depression, advised his son to find a job where there was a pension and security. His mother approached Val Bolitho, the chief sewage engineer for Johannesburg and an old friend of the family's. There were no vacancies, but he could create a tractor driver's job. 'In those days there were no blacks on tractors. I told Mr Bolitho, "I just want to have a foot in. I'll drive a tractor and then we'll see where we go."' This was to be the begining of a memorable relationship. 'Val Bolitho is one of the most wonderful people God ever made.'

At that time, 1962, sewage farms were simply places for effluent purification. After he had been working there for almost a year, Zulu devised a plan for the development of the farm on scientific lines. He presented it to Bolitho who, after considering the idea, agreed that he should be allowed to experiment with a portion of the farm below a dam and that 100 cows be placed in his care. Zulu drew up further plans, contoured the land, laid pipelines for irrigation and brought in electric fences. A year later, when the manager retired, Zulu was promoted to his position. He recounts with delight, 'We went to town on that northern farm and within three years we had our own AI [artificial insemination] station and eventually we had 4,000 cows inseminated. Today Johannesburg has one of the most marvellous farms and organizations in the country. And they've developed their own breed, called the Boervelder.'

His recreation was horse-coping, buying horses, often off the race-track which he trained as show-jumpers. As a little boy he had galloped round the mine property, often bareback, on the Basotho pony which his father had bought him. Years later, while showing cattle at the Rand Show, he had watched the show-jumping in the main arena and been seized by the challenge of it. He built jumps on the sewage farm and began training the horses already there. He took lessons from the experts and school-ed his horses in the covered manège he built; it was fitted with electricity so that he could work his horses at night. His nest egg grew as he made a thousand here and a thousand there on the show-jumpers he sold.

Holidays were ruled out. Each year his leave money was put away for his farm. 'We had to look after the pennies. I'd started off with the Council at twelve pounds a week and over the years I'd accumulated a few thousand and had thought that the way to get on my own was to get a loan from the Land Bank. I'd worked out a thousand schemes – a cotton crop, a tobacco crop – Marie's still got the book here where I reckoned it all out.'

One weekend, while hunting at the bushveld farm of his friend Albert Janowski, he spoke of his plans. 'I said that I'd consider anything as long as I could get a foot into something of my own. I was obsessed with the idea of owning a bit of ground.' Janowski suggested that they go into partnership and offered to invest a sum of 40,000 rand. That, together with the 15,000 rand that Zulu could muster, would make 55,000 rand, enough for the deposit on a farm. In high excitement, Zulu searched. They bought Kwaggafontein, a farm of 300 morgen (nearly 700 acres) on which he could plant potatoes, a quick cash crop. Tractors and farm implements were taken over from the previous owner and a loan negotiated with the Land Bank.

Over the seven years during which he had been working for the Johannesburg City Council he had become the general mana-ger of both the southern and northern sewage farms. Mr Bolitho was shocked to hear of Zulu's plan to leave. 'I loved old Bolitho and I think he felt the same for me. And he said to me, "You've got a typical trek-boer mentality. You're just like the *Voortrekkers*. Since the day you came to this farm, as soon as one thing's done, then you want to do something else." And my father nearly had a fit! My dad came to see me not once, but ten times. He said, "You're absolutely bloody mad! You've got a damn good job here. You've done well. You've got a pension, security, everything. How can you ever think of leaving this job!"

'Marie was quite happy. Marie's always stood by me. She packed the kids and we brought our stuff down in truckloads in the car. The first year I planted seven morgen of potatoes; that's all we could afford because we had to get the seed on tick; everything on tick. Seven morgen is nothing. But we hit the jackpot that year! The spuds were beautiful. The price was good. Then I hired a bit of land and I hired another with an option to purchase and so I eventually bought up five farms here within a period of ten years. Janowski's capital grew. I eventually bought him out after ten years and he didn't do too badly. I don't like to talk about it because it feels as if I'm bragging. Some portions of our farms went through where they've now got opencast mining and so Anglo American bought us out for a million rand for portions of these farms.'

With this capital Zulu bought Dirkiesdorp, a farm not very far away in the *middleveld* between Piet Retief and Wakkerstroom. The land was still cheap for it had been used only for grazing sheep, and it was a considerable distance from the silos, a disadvantage for a maize farmer. Ever systematic, Zulu had soil profiles taken and pedalogical surveys done in order to establish the soil potential. Then he started ploughing. 'I remember one farmer came to me and said, "You're going to regret this, my boy. No one's ever ploughed here. One night you're going to trek from here like a *sleg kaffer in die nag* [a bad *kaffir* in the night] because you can't plant mealies here." The good soil was there, the rainfall was there, but no one had ever grown mealies. I thought, well if everything's there, why not take a chance?'

It took ten years to overcome the problems at Dirkiesdorp. Cutworms were a formidable problem. 'The first year we were there – I think we planted something like 600 hectares that first year – my manager and I were sitting drinking whisky one night and I said, "You know, here we are drinking whisky and those cutworms are cleaning us up."' Within three days the cutworms had put paid to the crop. He learnt to put down cutworm bait as he planted and to use systemicides. Aluminium toxicities had to be countered, ideal cultivars found. 'So every area you have to learn. Today I think that's probably one of the most beautiful mealie farms in the country. We've got 3,500 hectares and the turnover this year should be four million rand. It's quite a big turnover if you think we started with nothing, just scratching around.'

There is a permanent labour force of 145 men on the two farms, a figure that is doubled when casual workers are brought in for lifting potatoes or other seasonal tasks. 'Experiments have shown that in this area October is the best month in which to plant mealies. It's very critical, when the rains come, to get your crop in. We plant within fourteen days – that's the kind of stipulation we've got – because the quicker we get it in the better our yields will be. We start at three in the morning and we finish at eight or nine o'clock at night. There's never a day in the planting time that I have to get up and get my boys to work. And I've never had one guy come to me and say, "I want overtime," because he knows that if it's a good crop I'll pay him at the end of the crop. I give him a planting bonus – that's normally a double cheque, sometimes a bit more – but at the end of the year we pay him another bonus.

'You know, my boys come to me not once in the season, but five or six times and say, "We should pray for rain." And the Zulus go up on the mountain and pray for rain. I haven't been up on the mountain with them, but I often give them the day off so that they can pray. Now why are they praying for rain? They are praying for us, for everybody. They know that their bellies are full if it rains. And they know they'll get a good bonus if there's a good crop.'

Farmers tend to complain about the carelessness of their workers in handling machinery and equipment. Not Zulu, who maintains that the farmer should set the standards. Believing that it is speeding which damages tractors, he has introduced a rule that they may not be driven in top gear. Drivers infringing the rule are demoted to less well-paid jobs. 'You do find some farms here where the tractors run around like lunatics, but that's the boss, the management. If you don't allow a thing and it's the law, then *it's the law*, *klaar* [finished]. And if he doesn't comply, he's out.' There is an incentive scheme in which the driver of the cleanest tractor each month is paid a bonus.

Up-to-date houses, complete with electricity, are provided nowadays for labourers on many farms. Not on Kwaggafontein or Dirkiesdorp where each permanent labourer is instead allowed to run five of his own cattle, a total of five hundred or so. Zulu has offered them the alternative of relinquishing their cattle, so that he may put the land on which they graze to profitable use; the proceeds could finance the building of modern housing. All have turned it down. The Ndebeles on the top farm have each built a small homestead of houses, colourfully decorated in geometric designs. The Zulus on the lower farm have their own groupings of huts to accommodate, in some cases, two wives. Dung floors and thatched roofs are warmer in winter and cooler in summer and the women like their traditional cooking arrangements. Two schools for the considerable number of children have, however, been built. One of the boss boys has installed a small generator from which he runs his TV and charges an entrance fee. Football matches on the box assure him of a full house. It is a stable labour force and Zulu will tell you, 'I must say that in the 145 permanent workers I haven't found one bit of hate or nastiness in the eighteen years that I've been here. Never has a chap come to me – one who does his work and we get on well – and said, "Look, here's my notice. I'm leaving."' Dismissals are rare.

The boss boys are paid 660 rand a month and the lowest paid labourers, young men who are just starting, get 280 rand a month. All receive food rations of a bag of maize meal a month, beans and tinned pilchards as well as grain to feed their free-running chickens. Each family has milk from its cows and eggs in the laying season. 'They're supposed to have five cows per boy, but some of them have ten and we kind of close an eye to that. As long as they don't overgraze too much.' Each man's cows should yield five calves a year which he can sell for 600 rand each. This, together with the planting bonus, the end-of-year bonus based on the value of the crop of the preceding year, and a double cheque at Christmas, constitutes his income. He lives rent free and has free schooling and medical care. During the potato season labourers may have as many potatoes as they can eat and *morogo*, the green herb rather like spinach, much relished with their staple food, mealie-pap, grows wild on the farm. Football is the chief recreation of the men and Gerrie buys them their football togs in their team colours. 'They're forever borrowing the truck on a Sunday to play other teams. The great occasion of the year is when the teams from the two farms compete.'

All the workers at Kwaggafontein are Ndebele, while those on the lower farm of Dirkiesdorp are Zulu, a situation that stems from the composition of the labour force when Zulu bought them. The Ndebele take pride in their children being able to speak Afrikaans at an early age. The Zulus believe that the farmer must learn their language. When it is time for harvesting and reaping, the two huge combine harvesters, costing 300,000 rand each, are taken by their Ndebele drivers to the lower farm where there are another two machines, driven by the Zulus who work there. There is also a young boss boy who has been trained in Johannesburg on the management of the combine harvesters. The Ndebele workers stay at Dirkiesdorp while the combining is in progress, sleeping in single quarters especially built for them. At the weekend they go back to their families, returning for work on the Monday. Because the Ndebele in this instance are the more sophisticated workers, Zulu has offered two of the boss boys all kinds of inducements, including trebling their salaries, in an effort to persuade them to remain on the lower farm, but to no avail. They will stay for the two months of harvesting, but no longer. He is aware that blacks going to the cities intermarry and mix, 'but I don't know if you'll just eliminate tribalism overnight. I think the African National Congress would love to eliminate tribalism, because then the people haven't any roots. But as long as there's tribalism . . . '

Wherever possible men are matched to jobs. 'I think the main thing with labour is to try and see what the man's good at. If a man's mechanically minded then he must be moved into the correct position. If you can place the fellow in the right job then he's going to be successful because he enjoys doing that.' Hans, in charge of the sixty horses, is a case in point; a small, slight man, he has the shrewd eye, slightly hunched shoulders and bandy-legged walk of the classic stableman. He leads Wagman, the Hanoverian stallion imported from Germany, out of his box and releases him into the paddock. The great horse snorts, then breaks into a trot, and such is the power of his propulsion that at each stride he is, for a moment, magically suspended. Visiting experts from Germany have marvelled at how Zulu managed to extract such a valuable horse, whose progeny is already winning international show-jumping contests, from their country. Hans's bonuses come from ensuring that a mare is in foal and that the foals are born alive and well.

The eldest of Marie and Zulu's four sons is the fifth Gerrit Johan in the Du Toit line. After graduating in agronomy at Bloemfontein University and doing his military training, he joined his father on the farm. Zulu, himself a straight-back-and-sides man, was irked by Gerrie's long hair. 'I said to Marie "When this guy comes to the farm I'm going to knock his head off within the first week."' But Gerrie cut his hair and bought himself khaki shirts and trousers. The boss boys, who have watched him grow up, call him by his name; the younger ones say *baas*. Zulu told them all, 'Gerrie's got the book knowledge, but he doesn't understand how the farm works. You blokes must teach him. He's an *appie* [apprentice].' Gerrie, asked what he'd do when he began to earn money, smiled shyly and said, 'I'd buy land.'

Zulu relates how one day he had remonstrated angrily with one of the boss boys in charge of women picking up potatoes in the fields because the work was being done slowly and inefficiently. Gerrie stood by. 'Coming back in the *bakkie*, [a small farm truck] Gerrie says he thinks I'm wrong – well, my bad habit is that I shout – because I'm making an idiot of the boss boy by shouting at him in front of the girls. He told me I should call the boss boy and tell him and let *him* go and perform. So he's right and I'm wrong and I stay away from there now.'

The second son, Peter Nefdt, is also at university studying pasturage, sheep and wool. Zulu sent him and Gerrie to the United States in 1986 for three weeks to study one of the latest agricultural developments, intensive farming under a centre-pivot irrigation development; it is linked to a system which provides infra-red satellite photos which show up deficiencies in the soil and in the crops. Of the two younger boys who are still at the Middelburg High School, one will probably farm. 'I've never said to them they should farm, but the farms have got to the stage where I need them. One of my life ambitions is that I'd like my kids to inherit ground. I've got an absolute mania for buying ground.'

Jeanne, the only daughter, is twenty-five and trained in personnel management. She married in July 1986 and her husband, a teacher by profession but a farmer by inclination, has joined the family at Kwaggafontein. 'My children are very progressive in their thinking and they feel that there's a place for us all, that this country's big enough to accommodate us all. And that we'll find each other.'

Zulu looks upon farming as a way of life as well as a way of making money; 'You know, when you put a plough in and you smell the soil, there's nothing like it!' But he has had his reverses. 'I bought a sheep farm in the mountains at Wakkerstroom, then three years ago we had a drought and down on the bottom farm we got half a bag of maize a hectare. I had a loss of, I think, 900,000 rand. I had to sell that farm. I feel very sorry about it because there was my second youngster doing sheep, wool and pastures at university and it would have been the ideal set-up. But we'll buy another one. We'll just have to carry on and try to plan our way and see how it goes.'

Where should we go? How can we get our money out? For South Africans such questions have been in the air. Zulu and

Marie travelled to Brazil a few years ago. 'We didn't really think of emigrating. It wasn't a question that we thought we'd pack up and go. One just wanted to have a look at other parts of the world. Brazil is a marvellous country, blessed with everything that God could give the earth. Marvellous soil, marvellous climate, but I wasn't there long before I realized I'm a man of Africa. I've been born and bred in Africa. In my heart I don't think I could ever leave. This is our home and what will be will be. It's in the hands of the Almighty. And my children, too, have just never thought of leaving Africa.'

Many members of the Nederduitse Gereformeerde Kerk, in which racial segregation had previously been practised, were appalled at its recent decision to open its doors to people of all colours. Not Zulu. 'I've no objection to someone of another colour coming to the church. It wouldn't bother me at all. I'm quite convinced it'll take a long time. The black man's attitude to church, the way he sings, it's all so different from the whites. It's like the American Negroes, their spiritual churches, they do things in a different way. Perhaps twenty thousand people will leave the Church, but that's a drop in the ocean relative to the membership of the NG Kerk which is millions. Splits have come before over whether you sing a hymn or a psalm. Ninety per cent of the people won't leave the Church.' In Middelburg there has been no noticeable drop in attendance at its NG Kerk. No black has sought admittance. Large numbers of coloured people attend their own NG Sending (Mission) Church in their segregated township.

Over the past two years there have been rebellions in black townships throughout South Africa. 'Violence builds hate on both sides and that's something we must try to eliminate. I don't know how. The whites have treated the blacks unfairly and as some of the blacks are gaining education their frustration is increasing. They have many frustrations. But, at the same time, I don't think they can wish the white man away in South Africa. Whether it's the Afrikaner or the English 1820 settler, they're part of Africa. Surely we must have a common ground? I'm very positive. I really am. I think that we'll remain farming. We might go to a socialistic type of farming. We might eventually have to give the black guy shares in our business to make him understand that the more you can produce the more you can earn. They've never really had that, these guys.'

He sees communism as hardly a serious threat. 'If ever there was a capitalist, in my opinion, it is the black. They say a Jew can rip you off, but no one can rip you off like a black to a black. They buy potatoes from us at 50 cents a pocket and sell them at 3 rand in the black townships. I tell them, "You're mad! You're robbing them!" And they say, "*Nee, nee, nee, hulle moet betaal!*" ["No, no, no, they must pay!"] So he's not basically a communist.'

The Middelburg constituency was one of many that in the May 1987 general election registered the general swing to the right. In a contest between candidates of the ruling National Party and the right-wing Conservative Party, the CP won the seat by 600 votes. Zulu is distressed at the attitude of most of the English-speaking community in the area, some of whom he had striven to persuade to vote for the National Party, pointing out that in withholding their vote they were, in fact, helping the CP to victory. 'There are a thousand English voters here,' Zulu says 'and most of them refused to cast their votes. What upsets me so much is that people sit down and scream the odds instead of doing something constructive like keeping out the right wing that is doing us so much damage. And the NP fellow we had here was absolutely as *verlig* [enlightened] as they come.' He points to how little difference there is between the policies of the Progressive Federal Party and someone like Wynand Malan who quit the National Party to stand as an Independent in the last election. (He won his seat with the support of the PFP.) 'We must stop throwing stones and somehow work together and I'm sure that the middle-of-the-road people are going to do that. Hate on each side, cursing and swearing at each other, that's not the way to solve South Africa's problems. And I've got no time for these guys who are just Afrikaner or just an Englishman. We're South Africans.' He sees the radicals of the left and of the right as equally dangerous. 'The plans of the right-wing

Afrikaner Weerstandsbeweging to reclaim the territory of the older Boer republics and to reinstate their regime are ridiculous. It can't be done.' But he is not unduly concerned. 'You have them all over the world, that type of person, like the Ku Klux Klan.'

Zulu maintains that the same kind of moderate approach is needed in order to solve the black–white dilemma: 'The majority of moderate blacks and moderate whites will eventually come to an agreement to run this country.' He refers to what would seem to be a tendency in certain quarters, and particularly overseas, to accept without questioning any statement by a black. 'I think that we must accept that there are wrongs among the whites, but there are just as many wrongs among the blacks. I really and truly think that the person who works with the black man every day has a hundred times better chance of eventually living in harmony with him than the guy who sits in England or Germany and doesn't know the black at all. They try to tell you what to do. How the hell! . . . they don't know how this bloke thinks.

'We're all sitting with the problem of solving the political situation in South Africa. I don't think that anybody has the answers. There's no simple solution to South Africa's problem. People have to become accustomed to change. We have to meet the aspirations of the different peoples. If it was so simple, you wouldn't have a Europe with Belgians and Hollanders – they'd all be one big Europe. Certainly, in the long term, I feel we need the type of federation where there is a guarantee for every people: a guarantee for the Pedi, for instance. If we had an open society surely the Zulu would take over and suppress the Pedi, so we must have a guarantee for all the lesser people. The white man wants a guarantee, but I'm sure the white man would be prepared to share with the black man in a type of federation. We'd have to sit around a table.'

CARLOS GARÇAÕ

THE CHURCH OF St Francis Xavier stands in what was once So-
phiatown, a suburb a few miles west of the city of Johannesburg
where until thirty years ago houses were owned by people of all
races, some of them black. Legends have sprung up about So-
phiatown – robust, overcrowded and lively, not all of its inhabitants always within the law – and people are proud to be able to
claim some link with it. The Nationalist government proclaimed
it to be 'a black spot' in white Johannesburg. Despite protests, its
people were removed to Meadowlands in Soweto during the
1950s. The township was razed and a middle-class white township, Triomf (Triumph) rose in its place.

The church was built inexpensively, but of generous proportions, with a lofty ceiling. On Sunday morning it is crowded with
worshippers from the nearby coloured residential areas of West-
bury and Newclare, a few Indians and Chinese, twenty or so
blacks, Afrikaans-speaking and English-speaking whites as well as
Greeks, Hollanders, Poles and at least one Jew. Carlos Garçaõ, as
eucharistic minister, accompanies the priest in the procession to
the altar. His sixteen-year-old son, Pedro, plays the organ and has
trained the young choir. The priest, Father Vic Kotze, refers to
the church and its community (which *is* the church) as 'some kind
of miracle'. Carlos says, 'What we mean by "church" is the
people. I visit parishioners in hospitals or in their homes, talk to
them and give communion to those who cannot come to church.'

He returns with his wife, his younger son Sergio, and Pedro to his modest house in a quiet street in Crosby not far away. 'Come and see my little farm,' he jokes, leading through the kitchen into the back yard with its neatly shaped fig trees and two vegetable patches, fenced off to keep out his wife's maltese poodles. He shuts the little gate and bends to pick up a handful of soil, dark and loamy. He crumbles it gently. 'It wasn't always like this; I had to put in a lot of stuff.' Lettuces in a row unfold their outer leaves; there is spinach, and seedlings to be planted out the next day. 'I am so happy working here,' he says. 'It is like fishing, I can just be here and talk to the plants and the trees.'

Carlos Garçaõ was born in Lisbon on 5 November 1939. His paternal grandfather, Francisco Luis Garçaõ, had been a judge in Portugal, Mozambique and Angola. His father, Carlos Cesar Garçaõ, aspired to the same career but, marrying while still at university, found himself unable to support a wife and the expected baby. Without qualifications it was difficult to find a position in Portugal, so he availed himself of the opportunity to accompany his brother, who had been studying engineering, to northern Mozambique where they were to supervise the building of the railway line between Nakala and Beira. It was a government job. In 1942 he was living with his family, now consisting of his wife, two-year-old Carlos, and the baby, Paul, in makeshift huts in the bush, moving from site to site as the building of the line proceeded. Carlos remembers the stories his parents told him: 'We whites and the black people were living together in very bad conditions. The men kept their guns by them at night as lions sometimes came into the camp and took away someone.'

At that time Francisco Garçaõ, his grandfather, was the judge in Tete. His son gained the position there of town clerk and with his young family moved into the large parental bungalow, built on generous old colonial lines. Tete was then a small town, having been established some five hundred years before by Portuguese in search of gold and minerals in the area. Its position on the bank of the Zambezi river had been particularly important at a time when the river was the only means of transport. It lies between Malawi and what was then Southern Rhodesia, and when Carlos was a child the white population was five or six hundred.

'My grandfather's house was very old and with very big rooms, but no bathroom. When you wanted to bath they would heat water in those big, four-gallon paraffin tins and empty them into the bath tub. Later, I remember, they had a kind of shower, with a can suspended on a pole. A servant would go down to the river several times a day to draw water. He took two twenty-litre containers, carrying them each at one end of a long pole, suspended on his shoulders. Later, in 1948, water pipes leading from a large tank on the hill were laid. The toilet, off the back veranda, was a large bucket inside a box, emptied twice a day.' Fridges were paraffin powered, for electrical power was available only from five in the afternoon till ten at night. There was a punkah piccanin who pulled the pole of the huge, sail-like punkah suspended from the ceiling, whose motion provided some little relief from the intense heat. Motor cars were a rarity; rides in the rickshaws, the main form of transport, were a great treat for the children. A municipal water cart constantly traversed the streets, temporarily laying the dust. 'If you look at American films, showing scenes of the 1880s, with all that sand and dust around, that's exactly Tete. It was the hottest place in Mozambique and really a cowboy town, but a beautiful town.'

The children were allowed to play only in the very shallow, sandy parts of the river under strict parental supervision, for the crocodiles which abounded in the river were dangerous. 'They sweep their victim off his feet with their powerful tails and take him to the bottom of the river to drown. Most of the bodies were recovered, some without an arm or a leg.' There were pythons, some almost ten metres in length, which had been known to devour small sheep. The river banks were lined with large maçanica trees which bore amidst the tiny thorns a fruit like a small apple, rich in vitamins and relished by animals and humans. Water from the river irrigated crops, chiefly sweet potatoes, staple food of the poorer people, and ground-nuts.

'I remember playing with neighbouring children who were coloured, also with the son of our black cook. I learnt to speak the local language, Nhungue, exactly like a black. I had few white friends. Tete was a small town with only two or three hundred white couples.' Soccer was the main game for boys and girls, but soccer balls were hard to come by. 'We made a ball by filling an old sock with rags and wool. Tennis was popular and sometimes we got old tennis balls, but they had to be really old before we got them.'

When he was five Carlos was enrolled at the local government primary school. It was coeducational, and three-quarters of his class consisted of Indians, coloureds and a few blacks, most of whom would first have been at the special government school which taught them Portuguese. Nearly all the Indians had come from India, 'very low-class, dirty people'. After four years Carlos graduated to a Catholic college, San José de Cluny, established by French nuns about 150 years previously, and run by sisters. Pupils of all race groups were admitted, but only a small number who were not white could afford the fees.

Aged fifteen, Carlos was sent to Beira, a city about 600 kilometres from Tete, to complete his education at a state-run high school. In 1958, after three years there, he applied for and got a government position in the Department of Interior Administration where black people, moving from one place to another, had to register their jobs. It controlled the influx of black people to the towns and tried to facilitate their finding jobs. There were two parallel justice departments, one for whites and the other for blacks which was operated from the Department of Interior Administration. Blacks apprehended for a criminal offence such as robbery, or who had been found drunk, were brought before a special court where they were judged by Carlos's superiors who had Portuguese university degrees. 'They were punished by being hit on their feet and on their hands with a piece of wood. This was really a shock to me because I had never seen it before. In 1959 they stopped this kind of punishment and substituted a fine or a prison term of not more than six months. The penal colony was not really bad. They were living there, working on the farm and eating its produce, also making baskets. Skilled people could work in government departments without pay.'

Beira was a lively city, its night-clubs patronized by passengers on the succession of ships that called at its port, and by tourists, many of whom came from Rhodesia. The locals enjoyed family parties in private houses. 'I never drank much, normally a few beers, just enjoying the party and the girls.' He and his brother Paul lived as boarders in a private house, playing soccer in their free time. Initially they played for an Indian club – very good soccer players, the Indians – into which they had been invited by the club coach, an old friend of the family's. After three years the two young Garçaõs followed their coach to a 'white' club which was, in fact, multiracial and later they responded to the request of some coloured friends to play in their club.

Over weekends they would join a few friends to camp on the beach and fish all night, cooking some of their catch immediately and taking the rest back to town to share at a party. Prawns were plentiful and good, but the greatest delicacy was the large and aggressive crabs which could be caught on a line. He also hunted. 'I was fourteen years old when I killed my first leopard with a .303 gun, the old gun of the Portuguese army. In a place like Tete there was not much to do, only hunting, fishing in the river and playing soccer in the three months before it got too hot.' He took out a hunting licence which entitled him to kill three buffalo, two elephants, fifteen springbok, three rabbits and three guinea-fowl a year. It was buffalo the hunters were after and they used expert trackers who could judge, from their droppings, how close the animals were. 'Usually we would walk for two or three hours. I killed buffalo and was not really afraid of them, but one day we encountered elephants. They were so big I was really frightened of them. You should have special guns, good, powerful ones, to shoot them. The *size* of the elephants is the thing that kept me away from them.' After a buffalo was killed local blacks would carry the carcass to their village where it would be cut up. The hunters kept the fillets, 'very good eating', for themselves, also the head and horns as trophies. The rest of the animal was given to the helpers.

It was while he was in Beira that Carlos met his future wife, Elena Alves, who worked for a shipping company.

Army service was compulsory in Mozambique and in June 1961 Carlos enlisted. 'Everybody was trying not to go into the Army, but I enjoyed my Army time. There were whites, blacks, coloureds in the Army with the only thing separating them being qualifications, education. The companionship was beautiful. I didn't find it too hard, though the first three months were very tough, but I became really physically fit.' His close friends were whites he had known in Beira and a 'Chinese chap, Chong,' whose father was a businessman outside Beira. 'The second three months consisted of skill training in some particular field. At the end of the six months there is always a big exercise with the company having a simulated war. I just started to think of walking so many kilometres a day with guns and a full, heavy pack and that heavy helmet! In that heat! Now what can I do?' The sergeant he consulted advised him, 'Look, Garção, the only job that's really good is in the kitchen and everybody's looking for that job.' At about that time the sergeant of his unit was having difficulty producing his report. Carlos, who had learnt to type while working for the Administration, offered his assistance and was later called upon by officers in the unit to type documents for them. So when the call went out for special helpers, including cooks, Carlos's application was accepted. He had always enjoyed cooking, and became one of four cooks. 'So I was living in luxury, eating well, but not from that big pot that I was cooking, rice cooked to a kind of pap, and stew with meat and cabbage and potatoes.' At the end of six months the recruits were allowed a choice of three places where they would like to serve; Carlos returned to Tete, his first choice, in December 1961. He was in an infantry regiment, but there was no fighting at the time, so he became an arithmetic and mathematics teacher at primary level. 'Some I taught were black, some coloured and some were whites from Portugal who had only three or four years' school. It was easy because they *wanted* to learn. At a higher level they had night classes taught by professional teachers. Some civilians were teaching free of charge. The Army really educated a lot of people.'

In April 1962, while doing his military service, Carlos married Elena Alves in Beira Cathedral. They returned to Tete to live in Carlos's father's house. 'At that time I was playing soccer in the Army, just enjoying myself.' During the previous year the first contingent of four companies had arrived from Portugal to support the Mozambican company in Tete in dealing with the threat, increasing in strength since the uprising in Angola in 1961, of insurgent guerrilla forces. In February 1964 Carlos was discharged from the Army. The influence of a relative in Portugal enabled him to find a position in the Tete branch of the Reserve Bank of Mozambique.

As a junior employee, Carlos was able to rent one of the bank's subsidized houses. The first child born to him and Elena, in 1963, was Carlos Antonio. Then came Claudio in 1966, Pedro in 1970 and Sergio in 1973. The family had servants, a man who did the cooking and laundry, another who cleaned the house and a piccanin who worked in the garden. In between having babies, Elena worked for a government department. They played cards with friends, went dancing. Carlos hunted, played soccer and developed his 'farm', the patches on his property where he grew lettuces and cabbages. 'And at that time I was very keen on chickens. I had 250. Just a hobby, though I did sell some eggs to pay for the chicken feed. I *loved* it. I also bred rabbits at my mother's house.' He became a director and later the president of the Sporting Club de Tete.

The church had always been important to him and he joined a small group of members of various races who went out into the poorer areas, sometimes 20 or 30 kilometres outside Tete, and tried to help people with their problems. His facility in the language spoken by black people increased his usefulness. 'We tried to negotiate with their employers to get more money and better accommodation for these black workers. Then we explained why it was important to boil the drinking water and to have their children vaccinated. The infant death rate was very high and mothers were afraid of the hospital. They said that children always died there, but that was chiefly because they left it too late before taking them. We told them how the hospital and doctors could help them and encouraged them to go. My mother', Carlos continues, 'was "godmother" to a lot of blacks; she knew all their names and they came to stay with her, usually bringing a chicken with them as a present. They brought their sick babies and she would give them medicine for diarrhoea and explain that was what the hospital could do for them.'

Over the years Carlos had become increasingly aware of the way Mozambique was being exploited by Portugal. 'It was not well governed. Lisbon took advantage of Mozambique. You could mine only with permission from Lisbon and they took the profits from the diamonds and the gold. We started to realize that we were only a pawn and that the people in Portugal were getting richer and richer. It wasn't just the black people, white people were also unhappy with the way Portugal was treating us. There were huge cotton farms near Tete, run by government departments. Cotton pickers and farm workers, mostly black, worked just for the food, cigarettes and the equivalent of 20 cents a day. They were oppressed. FRELIMO [Front for the Liberation of Mozambique] was justified because the blacks could not go on living that way.' He pauses. 'Of course, today it's not better. It's worse, but that's another story.

'By 1972 FRELIMO was very active. The bank paid us a bonus because we were working in a war area. All the conversation in Tete was about a train being blown up, people being killed by a mine in the road, that kind of thing.' Trains were armour-plated, and carried armed military personnel. Aeroplanes flew between Beira and Tete although Tete airport had been attacked by a heavy gun from 15 kilometres away. Road travel other than in a military convoy was inadvisable. 'We started to have some problems with our children; they were beginning to dream about the war and the landmines. We were living under pressure. Then I told my wife, "It's time to move." It was really a very bad time.'

Carlos and Elena, with their young son Pedro, and Juan, a black boy who had been working for them, left their house in Tete at six o'clock on a March morning in 1973. They drove to the military camp on the outskirts of the town where a convoy was assembling: trucks with heavy machine-guns, others with mortars, armoured cars and civilian cars. 'Two or three military trucks led, then about five civilian cars, then an armoured car and more civilian cars. We travelled cautiously. There was a lot of bush lining the road.' Thirty kilometres from Tete they were attacked, by members of FRELIMO they supposed. Nothing could be seen in the bush into which the Portuguese soldiers fired. 'I can remember the soldiers – they were a special conting-ent of whites from Portugal – laughing and talking to the civi-lians whenever we stopped, creating a good spirit. They were without shirts and brown like Indians.' The convoy arrived at Shangara for lunch, having taken six hours to cover 100 kilo-metres. 'We left at about one o'clock with heavier support because the bush in this part was thicker. We were attacked and the soldiers started firing the mortars into the bush; again I saw nothing, just heard the shooting from the bush. The convoy stopped and the soldiers surrounded us to keep us safe. Later some of them collected water-melons and cucumbers that were growing near the road and gave them to us to keep us happy and we set off again. In the 70 or so kilometres between Shangara and Guru they seemed to be shooting into the bush all the time. A mortar to the left, a mortar to the right. A machine-gun to the left and then to the right. It was very frightening.' After Guru the military convoy turned back and the civilians continued unaccompanied. 'We thought the area must be less dangerous, but soon we heard some shooting. The fellow behind me started on his hooter and I realized he was saying, "Now we are alone". So I put my foot down on the accelerator and drove at 150 kilometres an hour straight to Gondola and we arrived at six in the evening to be met by my brother who was working in the bank there.' The men sat at the bar while Carlos related their experiences. 'After ten minutes I found I couldn't move my neck. The right side was sore, the left side sore, the back sore. I had been looking right and left, right and left – 350 kilometres of looking for terrorists.'

The next day the Garçaõ family arrived in what was then Lourenço Marques and Carlos found a job in a bank. Disquiet

within the country escalated and in early 1974 Portugal was said
to have 70,000 troops in Mozambique. The coup in Portugal in
April that year introduced a more democratic form of government and by September Mozambique was promised independence for June 1975. Throughout the period there were outbreaks
of violence and rioting in Lourenço Marques, precipitated by
both the right and the left, during which many people were
killed.

Carlos could see no future for himself and his family in Mozambique. 'The courts are not courts any more. There are no lawyers;
people with four years, or sometimes only two years of primary
school become judges.' Relatives of his, a couple educated at the
Sorbonne, had wanted to stay in Mozambique to help develop
the country, but had left 'because it was impossible for a lawyer
to accept that kind of law, the law of the bush'. The air was
charged with fear. Thousands of whites left, reducing their numbers from some half a million to perhaps 50,000. Carlos was not
aware at the time that some whites were sabotaging machinery
at their workplaces before departing. Others poured cement
down drainage pipes in buildings. 'In Johannesburg I met people
who told me how they had broken the machines where they
worked and removed crucial parts. But there were also new
machines that were left there, still in boxes, and they have never
been used because no one had the expertise.'

Carlos and Elena came to South Africa in January 1975, bringing three-year-old Pedro and Sergio, still a baby, with them. Juan
had been killed in a motor accident in Lourenço Marques. To
relieve them of some of their responsibility, Carlos's parents had
taken the two older children to Portugal. Carlos declared to the
South African authorities that the purpose of their visit was to
see a doctor, but he immediately set about looking for a job, any
job. Not being able to speak either of the official languages he
could not work in a bank, but was prepared to paint walls, lay
bricks, anything. Eventually, through a cousin who knew someone who worked there, he found a job in a steel factory in Roode-
poort, west of Johannesburg, where some 120 Portuguese from
Mozambique, a third of the workforce, were employed. The

family of four eked out Carlos's salary of 70 rand a week in two rooms (probably once servants' rooms) at the back of a house. He made continuous applications to remain in South Africa, even going to the expense of hiring a lawyer to represent him. The authorities, besieged by thousands of Mozambican refugees seeking work permits, called him to bring his family for inspection (in order to determine that they were not coloured), and pointed out that his only skill, in banking, was of no use in a country whose languages he could not speak. Other Portuguese in a similar plight were deported. Carlos, however, continued to work at the factory until, through the intervention of the Portuguese vice-consul in Pretoria, he was able to see the Secretary for the Interior who granted him a work permit and, six months later, a residence permit. In the ensuing years Carlos bettered his position by moving from factory to factory until the downturn of the economy in 1982. His was one of the many factories that closed. The only job he could find was as a barman in the Wanderers Club.

Meanwhile, Albert Nelson, a Belgian and one of the overseas directors of the Premier International group (an international marketing organization dealing principally in foodstuffs), had been involved in organizing feeding schemes in Lesotho. He had for several years been concerned about the food shortages and the hunger, sometimes starvation, that he had witnessed on visits to Mozambique. Plans to alleviate this situation were formulating in his mind, but he needed the right man to carry them out. Early in 1985 he discussed the idea in Mozambique with Luis da Costa Campos, who had worked in the same bank as Carlos. Campos told him, 'I have just the man for you!' In Johannesburg Nelson met Carlos Garçaõ, outlined his plans and offered him the job of organizing a scheme which would enable Mozambican workers in South Africa to send food to their families at home. Carlos accepted. 'Mr Nelson told me that he was not doing this only for the business, but for the *service*.'

Carlos began to organize the Mozambican Workers' Feeding Scheme in May 1985. 'It was very small at the beginning. A lot of people didn't believe that it would work, but I knew the problems the people from Mozambique had in sending food to their families and from the beginning I thought it was a good scheme and that it would work if we did it in a professional way. I had been living in Mozambique for thirty years and I knew the people, but I didn't know the Mozambicans living and working in South Africa. It was a surprise. They live in very close clubs; they don't mix with the Zulus or the people from Lesotho. They don't want to get into fights. They say, "We come here to work, to make some money to feed our people, to try to get money to build a house when we return." We didn't try to tell them what to buy; we asked what they needed. They buy peanuts, unshelled, in packets of 5 or 10 kilos, to mix in a kind of curry stew with vegetables or fish. Also rice, milk powder, condensed milk, salt, blue soap. Some time later we started sending cement and corrugated iron.

'There are over 60,000 Mozambican miners in South Africa and the plan was that a man would place an order, pay for it, and be given a receipt. The parcel would be delivered to his family from a warehouse which Premier International opened in Mozambique.' It was, Mr Nelson emphasized, to be a business venture, run on fair profits. The Chamber of Mines agreed to co-operate. The Mozambican government, recognizing the value of the scheme, has welcomed it. 'It's a big success. We cover all the mines in South Africa.' He and his young black Mozambican colleague, Zacharias Mabunda, visit the mines. 'They are a very closed society and it is difficult to get to understand the miners and the mine managers.' The men, many of whom had been defrauded in earlier and apparently similar enterprises, were suspicious, but some placed orders. 'In January 1986 we had taken 15,000 rand in orders. It was exciting! It was good, but for the company it was a big loss as they were employing Zacharias and myself, running our car, paying for the trips to Maputo and so on. But they saw the potential of the thing. Now we are doing hundreds of thousands of rand and it is still increasing.'

The Mariava restaurant in central Johannesburg has become a kind of club where Portuguese and Mozambicans of any colour gather to exchange news over coffee or a meal. Miners know that they can find Carlos and perhaps Zacharias there on most days round about noon. 'There were always Mozambicans waiting for us with orders, but it was too much, we didn't have time to eat our lunch and we told them they must go to our offices in town.'

The problem that Mozambicans had faced before the introduction of the Premier scheme was in conveying the goods they had bought to their homes. Numerous truck owners had come to the mines, offering their services. 'The miners were buying sheets of corrugated iron, cement, bags of maize meal, boxes of blue soap and so on. The trucks collected the goods and they charged exorbitant prices. They would charge 20 rand to transport a 25 kg bag of maize meal and the same for transporting a 25 kg box of blue soap. Something unbelievable! And the families in Mozambique never received the goods, or sometimes, if two bags were sent they received one.' Some hostel managers, according to Carlos, looked askance upon the new venture. 'I think that a few of them had been involved with those trucking schemes and some of the white miners had too, but now they have really lost.

'When I started to do the first orders I asked men who were buying a box of blue soap how they were going to use it and they told me, "There are twenty-five bars in the box: five bars are for my wife, five bars for my parents, five bars for my parents-in-law, five bars for my divorced sister." And it is the same with the food they send, so one man is feeding between fifteen and twenty people in Mozambique every month. Five to seven thousand miners are placing orders every month, which means that there are a quarter of a million people in Mozambique benefiting from the scheme. It is a business, but at the same time we feel really glad when we consider these things. What is important is that some of the miners now consider us as friends and come with letters from their families, saying, "Look, Carlos, you see this letter, my wife says those beans are very good and the rice and the soap very good, too."' After an early morning start, it is generally seven o'clock by the time Carlos reaches his home, but the satisfaction of doing a good job compensates for the long hours and the hundreds of kilometres he often travels in a day.

There are now eighteen people, based in Johannesburg, working for the feeding scheme. 'Four whites, three coloureds and the rest blacks who must be able to speak English, Portuguese and Shangaan, the language of most of the Mozambicans in South Africa. We are really a team.' It is necessary to have one white worker in each area as few of the (white) officials with whom they have to deal on the mines react entirely favourably to blacks. 'In Mozambique there are about thirty Mozambicans controlling the stocks and seeing to the thousands of tons of food to be delivered.' Although agents have been appointed on some of the smaller mines this is a step they try to avoid, the handling of money being such a sensitive matter. 'We don't really have any effective control. Yesterday somebody ran away with three orders and 400 rand in cash, nevertheless we deliver the goods for the sake of our name. We are always tightening, tightening, tightening our controls.'

Considerable numbers of Mozambicans, ineligible for South African work permits, are in the country illegally. 'They buy South African nationality and identity documents for about 400 rand. They change their names. If he was José Antonio he is now Anthony Gideon, or something like that; he keeps the Anthony so as to be in touch with what he was before. These people also send food home through us.'

Members of the team are dispersed over some of the main mining areas such as Welkom and Stilfontein. Carlos is the manager and visits mines in the same way as his colleagues, taking orders and money. Some mining groups refer to their miners' residences as compounds, the more enlightened generally call them hostels, the term Carlos prefers. 'I saw lots of really *poor* hostels where the rooms and facilities are very, very old. Some were so bad that *we didn't believe!* So bad! Some had not been painted for dozens of years. Then the dining-room, not really a dining-room, with tables with a piece of sheet metal on top and they place the food on this with a lot of flies around. And the kind of food they are giving the miners in some of the hostels is so bad, so bad, that one day I was with a black chap and he said, "Sorry, Carlos, I cannot take it. I must go out. I was breakfasting an hour ago and I must go out." Other mines have clean hostels, nice beds, nice food and nice, beautiful kitchens, *beautiful* kitchens. I cannot forget a hostel here at Western Deep Levels, an Anglo American mine, the kitchen was *shining*, really shining. The pots were shining, and clean black and white cooks were cooking beautiful cabbage and carrots. In Rustenburg there are also good mines and at Impala Platinum Mines inside Bophuthatswana I saw good hostels with halls where they were watching TV and enjoying it.

'But on some of the mines, really, I'm telling you, when I hear of the strikes and that they don't receive enough money and they're not treated well, I can really see that they are right. They are living under very difficult ... something that we couldn't believe until we visited it.' He is shocked at the overcrowding on a lot of the mines. 'Three, four, five thousand men in some of the big hostels. When a good-looking boy comes and starts work there's always an old one who'll say, 'This is my boy. No one must touch him.' Between men, they marry, they have weddings at the hostels. Saturday afternoons and Sundays they have weddings there ... it's a terrible thing. I never saw one of the weddings. I was never invited. But I know that every week there are weddings with someone who performs the ceremony. And big parties.

'A lot of the Mozambican miners here went to Standard 8, some to matric and some even went to university in Mozambique. They are educated people. One of the men who works for us now was in the mines and he was at the university in Mozambique and also in Bulgaria or Romania and did three or four years' engineering. And there are more miners like him, with matrics and university degrees. How do they feel, living on the mines in that way? If a hostel cannot give the men nice homes, a nice hall to watch TV and a nice place where they can eat a plate of good food they really go mad. It is really a very difficult life. We can see, at the end of the year, that there are millions of rand, *millions* of rand profit on the mines. *Millions* of rand! But what are they giving, in return, to the miners?' Carlos's English vocabulary cannot match his indignation. His voice rises to a high note of incredulity. '*We don't believe what we see! We don't believe!* Some mine officials say, "We give food, we give TV and a nice place to eat; they don't really need more." It's not true! If I work hard I want to keep some money for myself.'

Mozambican miners have told him, 'Look, Carlos, I have been working here for four years. I send food home. I haven't a cent. At the end I look and say, this was a waste of time. We are not keeping money because we are not receiving it. I am going back sick.' Carlos corroborates this, adding that many of the men, when they leave the mines, suffer from some sort of lung complaint because of the air underground. 'They have no money to build a house. When they finish on the mines they receive a kind of pension in cash, a lump sum. So small, so small, a few thousand. Last year I saw an old man, so happy. He had been working for thirty years and after thirty years he was receiving 8,000 rand. Immediately he spent 1,500 rand on food and cement from us, trying to make a house. And already he was a sick man. The mines try to give a good image, but they are not really giving a good life to the miners. I do not know about the white miners. They need somebody to push for the black miners.'

The black National Union of Mineworkers (NUM) organized a three-week strike in August 1987. 'I think the union is a good thing. It can press the employers when they start to exploit the people.' It seems to him to be 'very politically oriented', but he has only a limited knowledge of its workings. 'The union is doing good things, but also bad things – at some mines they try to influence the miners to revolt against the mine management; some Mozambicans told me this – it varies from person to person and from mine to mine. They don't know yet how to negotiate.'

Carlos's views do not seem to conform with those generally believed to be held by the Portuguese community in South Africa. Most of them, he explained, had originally lived in the Portugal of Salazar. 'He was a fascist, a friend of Hitler's. During the revolution in Portugal we found some gas chambers which Hitler had given to Salazar. Now they are in a museum.' The security police, over the years of the Salazar regime in Portugal, assumed increasing power and authority. There was freedom neither of speech nor of the press, and elections became a farce. 'Many of the Portuguese people here in South Africa have had only four or five years' schooling; some no schooling at all. They learnt from the government-controlled radio. Then they came from that country to another country with exactly the same way of thinking. In Portugal everyone who didn't think exactly like the government were called communists. In South Africa it is exactly the same. If I don't think like the government, if I say we must help the blacks, then they call me a communist. The Portuguese community think like that. They think the blacks want to take over our houses, our schools, our salaries, our cars, our jobs.

'Portugal is now a free country, governed by a social de-mocratic party of the centre, but the Portuguese newspaper on sale in South Africa is still the newspaper of twenty-five years ago, keeping alive the Salazar image. That is why the Portuguese community here in South Africa is really a right, right, *right* party. I am not a leftist, but I like to give the others the same rights that I am enjoying. I am not for apartheid.'

Carlos will stay in South Africa. 'I'm not scared of bombs, because in Portugal, Paris, Madrid and London there are also bombs. I think that there are thousands of people trying to work out a just society for South Africa. My fear is not of a black government, but that the rightists or the leftists will go out of control. South Africa is not a lost cause. Around South Africa are a lot of puppets from Russia like Zimbabwe, and that is dangerous. Mozambique is a dictatorship; it makes no difference if it is a right one or a left one, it's all the same. There are no free people in Mozambique, no free radio, no free papers. We cannot talk. It is worse than here. There are no political parties in Mozambique; there are no elections. Here in South Africa people can swear at the President, but not in Mozambique. The educated people of Mozambique, those who can really work for democracy, are not in Mozambique; they are living in France, Portugal or the USA. The educated people still living in Mozambique are helping FRELIMO, so they are not working for democracy.' He dismisses RENAMO (The Mozambican National Resistance Movement) as 'mercenaries in the pay of somebody'.

He is troubled by the rise of the white Afrikaner Weerstandsbeweging, and finds it illogical that the government can outlaw the African National Congress and yet permit the rise of the AWB, in his view a right-wing terrorist organization. 'I think it is a very difficult situation here in South Africa. We must do something, but we must take care how we do it. We must take *care*.'

KIDGER HARTLEY

FROM THE SUMMIT of the Outeniqua Mountains the road, blasted and hewn into the mountainside, winds downward towards the sea. At intervals there is a recess where travellers may leave their cars and pause at the edge of the precipice to wonder at the spectacle of the mountains rolling, fold upon fold, intersected by gorges and deeply wooded ravines and *kloofs* where hidden arum lilies bloom. The further chasms and summits are bathed in bluish light. If you drive down through the loops and bends where, on the grassy slopes, spring flowers bloom, you soon enter the little old town of George, named after George III of England in whose reign it was established. Some of the oaks planted by the earliest settlers still spread their shade across the streets. From George the way is along the fertile plain that lies between the mountains and the sea. The indigenous forests in which the prized stink-wood and yellow-wood may still be found, nestle on the lower slopes. At the edge of the Swartvlei lagoon the road to Sedgefield turns off towards the Indian Ocean from whose sometimes sharp winds high sand dunes protect the settlement. Flowering gum trees line the tranquil sandy streets. Many of the residents are retired couples, living in quiet bungalows where hydrangeas mass against the walls.

The wooden gate in Flamingo Avenue opens into the garden where Kidger Hartley, for nine years general manager of De Beers' Kimberley division, emerges from his extensive aviary at a purposeful lope. He is a large, craggy man, wearing baggy shorts, ankle socks and *tackies* (plimsolls). His wife, Eleanor, is a neat, gentle woman, who undertakes tasks such as concrete-mixing that daunt her husband. 'She's stronger than I am,' he says.

Not wanting to stay on until 'the decay set in' as he had seen happen with others approaching the end of their careers, Kidger took early retirement in March 1985 when he was fifty-seven. 'I never wanted to get to the stage where people would say, "that doddering old so-and-so". Because, in mining, ours is an active life; we've got to be on our toes all the time. And I enjoyed it and I thought, "While I'm enjoying it, let me get out."

'I had this place and I prepared it and I'm extremely happy here. One of these days I want to write a book about my experiences, a satirical one, because I have quite a good sense of humour and I've had lots of fun. I do carpentry, plumbing, a bit of welding, that sort of thing, and I love it. And of course I have my birds to keep me quiet. I've had all the holidays I need. I've got this place now and I've bought a nice boat for the kids, so this brings them here for their holidays.'

He sits on the *stoep*, a glass in his hand, and stretches his legs. Kidger is a practical joker, a humorist, tendencies not all the directors of De Beers appreciated. A gifted mimic, he emulates the tones and turn of phrase of eminent men, adding the illumination of a gesture or mannerism. 'I'm a rough diamond,' he tells you, the merest suggestion of a twinkle in his eye. A Knysna loerie alights in the saffron tree a yard or two away from him and the talk is about birds, those from India, Australia and Africa in his aviary, and the proteas he has planted to attract the malachite sunbirds.

Some 400 kilometres eastward up the coast from Sedgefield, in the Albany area, is the rustic village of Bathhurst, established by English settlers in 1820. Its Pig and Whistle, one of the most celebrated hostelries of the eastern Cape, was built in 1821 and was originally attached to the blacksmith's shop of Thomas Hartley, Kidger's great-great-grandfather, a steelwright, who brought from England a ton of steel for making wagon wheels.

He and his nineteen-year-old son, William, also farmed the land, but it was not long before they ventured northwards, hunting elephants, up into what was to be Rhodesia and where a town, Hartley, would be named after a cousin, Henry Hartley, one of the few explorers and big game hunters permitted into Mashonaland by King Lobengula. William Hartley was, years later, to form friendships with some of the Afrikaners who had loaded their wagons and begun their trek away from the vexatious British authorities in the Cape. He was able to guide more than one of these *Voortrekker* leaders into what was to them unknown territory.

Hartley descendants moved into the Orange Free State where they farmed, and it was in Bloemfontein, in this province, that William Kidger Hartley was born on 16 December 1927. His father, also William Kidger, had been orphaned at the age of five and sent to live with foster parents. At the age of twelve he became a messenger with Frank Hill, a firm of attorneys in Bloemfontein. The deficiencies in his education were more than compensated for in the succeeding years when he attended night school, studying a range of subjects that included shorthand and typing; these skills proved particularly useful when, during the depression of the early thirties, he went into journalism and became sub-editor of *The Friend*, the Free State's only English language newspaper. He then entered into civic employment and eventually became town clerk of Bloemfontein. 'He had a very tough early childhood,' Kidger relates, 'but he used to say to me, "To battle builds character".

'My mother came from farming stock, in the Kroonstad district. Her name was Anna du Plessis – that's a Huguenot name.' She was one of fifteen children; her parents had been impoverished during the South African War when their farm buildings were burnt by the British and all the livestock commandeered. After the war, avid for education, Anna sold her horse in order to be able to continue to board at Mrs Campbell's farm school. At the age of eighteen she married Kidger's father. 'She only went as far as Standard 4, but she was the driving force in our house. I think it was she who drove my father to study.' Kidger, born in 1927 when his elder brother was already at university, was a *laatlammetjie*, a 'late lamb', the child of his parents' more mature years. There were also three girls in the family. His parents had agreed that English, in which his Afrikaner mother became fluent, should be the language spoken in the house, but it was interwoven with Afrikaans. Anna Hartley not only consigned her language to second place, but left the Nederduitse Gereformeerde Kerk to join her husband's Methodist Church and to become, in later years, chairman of its Women's Auxiliary Association. Kidger's father was a circuit steward of the church and his brother became a Methodist minister and eventually president of the South African Methodist Church. His mother made concessions, 'but she never lost her identity as an Afrikaner and went on to become president of the *Vroue Vereeniging* [Women's Society] of the Orange Free State,' an organization founded chiefly for rural women.

Kidger's childhood in a suburb of Bloemfontein was quite a lonely one, enlivened by visits to farms of relations. There were holidays spent touring in his father's old Ford and camping at the sea or in hired cottages. His early schooling was at St Andrew's, an Anglican school in Bloemfontein; at thirteen he moved to Grey College, a government school, superior at the time from both an academic and a sporting viewpoint. It may well have been chosen because it was run on a parallel-medium system, a style of education encouraged by the United Party in power at the time, but that was to be discarded by the Nationalist Government. Each standard had its English and its Afrikaans class and it was possible, if you wished, to take some subjects in English and others in Afrikaans. The languages were used on alternate weeks at assembly, in debates, on the sports fields and at cadets. Kidger's particular friends were Afrikaners and he was not aware, at any stage of his schooling, of anti-English or anti-Afrikaans feeling. 'And, of course, we had a wonderful principal, Mr Meiring. It was during the war and he was very loyal to the war effort. He lost his elder son, a pilot in the air force. No politics were allowed. In fact, a pupil was expelled from the school for expressing anti-Jewish feelings.' There were a good many Jewish boys at the school; the majority of their parents probably ran general dealer's stores in the little country *dorps* where Afrikaans was the predominant language.

Kidger became a prefect, played in the rugby and cricket first teams in his final year and matriculated in 1945 with a university pass. As a child he had sung in eisteddfods and at high school was drum major and trumpeter in the school band. During the war, as part of the Imperial Training Scheme, one of the several Royal Air Force training schools was situated outside Bloemfontein and it was Kidger who would be called to play the 'Last Post' at the funerals of men killed in air crashes. 'The principal would call me and say, "You've got to do your duty this afternoon," and I would say, "But sir, I'm playing rugby!" "Your country comes first," and off I would go to yet another military funeral.' He looks back fondly upon the early years. 'I had a very close relationship with my father. He was a very good sportsman, still playing hockey at the age of forty-five. He was a very fine man. I had a very happy home life.'

The University of the Witwatersrand erected prefabricated lecture rooms on its lawns to accommodate returning servicemen, who were also given priority in enrolment. Kidger was one of those adversely affected by their influx in 1946. He had always wanted to be a doctor, but there were at the time only two medical schools in South Africa, at the Universities of Johannesburg and Cape Town and he could not get into either. He was accepted at the University of the Orange Free State at Bloemfontein where only the first year of medicine was offered in Afrikaans. Kidger passed, but again failed to find a place for his second year. His father's attempts to place him at a university in England failed for the same reason. Determined to continue his academic education, he settled for an engineering degree at the University of the Witwatersrand. 'They sent me a list of all the different categories of engineering and asked me to indicate my order of preference. I put mining plumb last and that's what I was accepted for. I'd never really seen a mine.'

Only seven in Kidger's class of forty-five graduated at the end of 1950. The path for mining graduates was relatively clear-cut.

'You had to go and start as a miner, do the practical, then become a shift boss, become a mine captain, and you hoped to become a general manager one day. I was very keen to work on the gold mines and in my final year already had a job lined up at Venterspost. Very few graduates wanted to go and work for Anglo American mines in those days because it was felt that they had no use for graduates. It's a stigma they carried for many years – all their top men were non-graduates.' On many mines, where the bosses were non-graduates, it was difficult for those who were to make any headway.

Although many people speak about Anglo American and De Beers as though they were interchangeable, the two companies are in fact independent. What these two large mining groups, the Anglo American Corporation and De Beers Consolidated Mines, have in common is that the largest single shareholder in each company is the Oppenheimer family. Anglo American is primarily concerned with coal and gold mining, but has a wide range of industrial interests. A third company, Minorco, based in Luxemburg, represents the international interests of Anglo American and De Beers.

The first time Kidger went down a gold mine was in his second year of study in 1948, during an organized university visit to the Simmer and Jack South Deep shaft which was 6,000 feet in a single drop. 'I loved it! I could never have sat in an office. It was constructive. You had a job to do, to finish. I still love that – I love a goal. I love accomplishing things. This has developed in me a sense of urgency. Mining men develop a sense of urgency because, for example, you've got to drill holes in a tunnel and blast by the end of the shift. It's no good making excuses if the water breaks down, or anything like that – you've just got to fix things. In mining you've got to blast at the end of every shift and you can't say to your mine captain, "Sorry, I didn't blast today."'

Then, days before he was due to start at Venterspost in the Randfontein area of the west Witwatersrand in 1951, Kidger's mother phoned with news that his father was ill. 'So I went down to Bloemfontein. They were living on a little farm and I could see that they were going to battle. So I sat there and thought, why not try Kimberley? At least it's near. I'd never, strangely enough, been to Kimberley. So I phoned De Beers and they put me through to the assistant general manager.' Kidger told him his story and an appointment was arranged for the following day. 'So I drove over, saw him and I got the job. I think that he liked the fact that I was a graduate.' He was sufficiently near to be able to visit his parents, both of whom died six months later in 1951, within five days of one another.

The move to Kimberley proved fortunate. He began with the most menial job (for a white man), working with and supervising a gang of blacks laying underground pipes to bring water and compressed air to the working places. Communication between them was in *fanakalo*, the industrial and sometimes domestic vernacular of south and central Africa. After two years, he became a shift boss, supervising white miners, and was then appointed technical assistant to the assistant general manager. 'My colleagues at university were still slogging it out as shift bosses on gold mines, while I was doing technical work, the kind of work for which I was really qualified. Most interesting and rewarding.' Another two years and he was promoted, at the age of twenty-six, to underground manager. For the next three years he worked in various mines within the Kimberley division: Wesselton, De Beers, Bultfontein and Dutoitspan, as well as Jagersfontein, about 100 kilometres to the south-east.

One evening in 1953, driving back from the mine, Kidger was astonished to see, silhouetted against the sunset sky, a young woman, painting a roof. 'I'd met so many of these fancy girls in Kimberley; this was something different. I knew the chap who lived next door and so I asked him, "Who's this girl next door to you, painting the roof?"' It was Eleanor Bryant, a secretary at De Beers, and his future wife. Her father was an engineering foreman at De Beers. Kidger and Eleanor were married in her church, the Presbyterian Church, on 12 October 1953.

The more experience he gained in the mines, the more his respect for the black workers grew. 'It was tremendous! Tremendous! Those guys taught me a hang of a lot. They are courageous people, ideally suited to mining work. They are physically strong, they work well as a team and I've never seen one show fear.'

Were they, in turn, aware of the fear that occasionally almost overwhelmed him? 'You had bad ground. You had rock falls. You had accidents. You saw people killed. You had to apply first aid and try to get them out of some gruesome accidents and there's no question of going home and saying "Hang! That's a dangerous place to work! I'm not going to work tomorrow." It became part of you – I think men like adventure. It's an adventurer's job. You don't take unnecessary risks, but you can't always predict that the rock pressure is going to build up and a piece is going to fall in on you, or the rope's going to break in a shaft, that sort of thing.' A great deal is done, he explains, to prevent accidents, but some are unavoidable. The worst experience that used to assail miners in the Kimberley area was the mud rushes. 'It's difficult to explain, but a diamond pipe is a volcanic pipe and when you mine the ground from the bottom, you create a void above as you get a certain amount of material falling in from the sides. When water gets into that it gets very moist and then you get what you call adiabatic compression – that's the compression you get when you push a bicycle pump and you feel the heat. There is this pressure and the heat can't be dissipated and the mud gets boiling hot. And it can burst out and fill thousands of feet of tunnel in minutes. It's boiling and so most people who are trapped are virtually cooked. We had a lot of that in the early days of mining, but we've removed the threat by putting ring tunnels around the pipe to drain the water. When you were working on a level where you expected mud to be coming at you, you had candles all over the place and you had guards watching and as soon as the candles went out, indicating a rush of air, everybody used to run to the next level. We also had compressed air whistles that were pulled to sound the warning. We lost quite a lot of people and I would say that working under those sorts of conditions was quite scary.'

Kidger, whose career has been mostly in diamond mining, with short spells on gold and copper mines, also esteems the white miners, many of them Afrikaners, who spend so much of their lives underground in the dark and dust and heat. Leadership qualities are essential in a good miner who may be supervising, with the aid of black team leaders, up to 300 black workers. Particularly since the immediate post-war period, during which 'you signed up almost anybody', he has noted a marked improvement in the overall quality of miners; this, he believes, is due to improved working conditions, drastically reduced accident rates and better selection and training techniques. 'In the early days the nucleus of miners was outstanding, but the balance were drifters and drunks who came to the mines as a last resort. Assaults by white miners on blacks were common; this I attribute to poor working conditions, poor calibre of white miners, unsophisticated and poorly trained black workers and of course, absence of union representation of blacks. You will find that the bad miner doesn't organize properly, things go wrong and he gets all worked up and takes a swing at the first chap. There's nothing malicious about it. And it's a funny thing, you had very little of that reported – assaults. I'm talking now about the early days. But a lot of those chaps accepted it, if they'd made a mistake and they got a clout. This has changed and today assaults are most infrequent. In my last nine years with De Beers I can only recall about two incidents of reported assault.'

Under the Mines and Works Act, repealed midway through 1987, only a 'scheduled person' might blast: blacks could not be 'scheduled persons' though, in some instances, coloureds could. This prohibition blocked any possibility of blacks attaining higher positions, of rising, for a start, from labourer to miner. At one point it seemed that the government was considering amending the Act to allow blacks to become certificated miners, but it was under pressure from the white Mineworkers' Union not to do so. Arrie Paulus, who heads the MWU and who is now the Conservative Party Member of Parliament for Carletonville, is a powerful man; he and his union command votes. Kidger's attempts to persuade Paulus and his union to agree to a relaxation of the law were to no avail. 'I don't agree with his philosophy, but he was always prepared to see you. He really was a straight shooter; you always knew where you stood with him. He was a man I trusted.' Kidger's faith in the competence of the black miner is based on his experience in Zambia where he supervised the first licensed blasting by black miners. 'The blacks make good mining men and it is just a matter of time before this happens in South Africa.'

In recent years, he points out, blacks have been allowed to charge up: to drill in the appropriate places and insert the dynamite cartridge into the drill holes. The white miner sets light to the charge. 'They can do anything now, really, under the supervision of a scheduled person. And that scheduled person may only supervise a certain number of tunnels. It's all to protect the white miner whose fear is that once black miners are allowed to blast they could then be paid less and so replace them.'

During his move to the Rhokana copper mine in Kitwe, Zambia, in 1963, Kidger was offended by the debasement to which the blacks were often subjected. 'Being a diamond mining man I will probably be accused of being biased when I say that our black/white relationships at De Beers, as early as the 1950s, were way ahead of the gold mines and also of the Zambian copper mines. In Zambia, as late as 1963, that horrible word *kaffir* that I hadn't heard in De Beers for years was still commonly used. There were assaults and much cursing and swearing at the blacks. Blacks were made to sit on their haunches when they travelled in the cage with whites. That hurt me very much because it was in conflict with my upbringing and with my experience and training in De Beers. I had worked in Zambia ten years previously and I was amazed that things had changed so little.'

In the Zambian mines strikes seemed to occur with increasing frequency; the issues were wages and shift times. 'There was a terrible feeling. Every day there was a strike by either the whites or the blacks – this was in 1963, just prior to independence. There were so many strikes that I can't really sum it up. The whites were trying to protect their position and the blacks trying to gain more.' On several occasions he was called out at night. 'Something would have happened underground and the whole afternoon shift, due to surface at midnight, probably about a thousand men, would refuse to come up. And I used to go underground and get out on the station and walk along and say, "I want five men, five spokesmen," and I used to walk way into the middle of them, past the crowd and ask, "What's your problem?" I'd discuss it with them. I used to say, "I'll fix it up tomorrow," and they would come out. And it was something that wasn't done very frequently, you know, communication with these people. It was their way of bringing to the attention of management their dissatisfaction of some occurrence underground. It has always been my belief that people listen more readily to their boss than to an industrial relations officer. Too many managers avoid the issue and pass the buck.'

Black mineworkers in Zambia lived in townships near the mines with their families. One evening, having gone back to his office to work, 'thousands of chanting and screaming men and women' made their way towards his window. 'They said they wanted to talk to me about a problem – the police were there with Sten guns. So I thought, it's not my section, I'd better phone my superior. I phoned him and said, "All these people want to talk to me. I'm quite happy to talk to them. I don't know what the problem is." "You do not talk to them!" So I sat in my office half the night and the cops kept coming, saying, "Man, these guys want to talk to you," and I'd say, "Look, it's not my section." But it was a funny attitude, the whole attitude of management in Zambia, I should say.' The head of the section put in an appearance only on the following morning and was found up in the headgear, surveying the scene through his binoculars, 'damn scared' in Kidger's view. 'He probably left the problem to be dealt with through industrial relations departments whose job it was to negotiate with the unions.'

Upon leaving Zambia in 1964 Kidger was appointed head of planning at the Anglo American Corporation head office in Johannesburg. He became part of the team that planned the execution of large engineering projects such as the Orange River tunnel, almost 50 miles in length, which carried water for irrigation southwards into the dry, but fertile Karroo regions bordering the Fish River. He also worked on Johannesburg's immense Carlton Centre and the vast Cahora Bassa power scheme on the Zambezi River, as well as a number of major shaft-sinking projects. But although they enjoyed the theatres and cinemas, Johannesburg did not suit the Hartleys, 'I was inclined to be a small town guy and what put me off – I actually asked to go back to the mines – was that beastly traffic. Life is too short to spend about two hours a day sitting in your motor car.'

Consolidated Diamond Mines, or CDM as it is generally known, is at the mouth of the Orange River, on the Namibian coast. There was a time when diamonds were found simply lying on the beach and an anthropologist, Dr M. W. D. Jeffreys, believed this to have been the coast referred to in the tale in *A Thousand and One Nights* which tells of a beach strewn with jewels. The Germans, in the last century, when they invaded and colonized the territory, had white men supervising hundreds of blacks crawling on their hands and knees, picking up the diamonds. De Beers, in this century, has created its own town at the mouth of the river for the ten thousand or so Ovambos (the black people of that area) and thousand whites employed there. The Hartleys had two stints of duty at CDM, the first a relatively short one in 1959 and a later one in 1970 when Kidger was assistant general manager. 'It was like heaven there. You were spoilt. All the food was subsidized and there was free housing, water and light. Free schools, too. It's very isolated and so they had to attract people to go and live in the wilderness.' In 1974 they moved south across the Orange River to Kleinzee in Namaqualand where Kidger served for a year as general manager.

Then in 1976 came promotion to the prestigious position of general manager of De Beers' Kimberley division. The Hartleys moved into one of the most spacious of the many fine Victorian mansions in Kimberley. There were four well-trained servants, and Ezekiel, the cook who produced the lavish dinners. 'It was a big job, with lots of entertaining. You had to be on your toes all the time. You're almost a second mayor of the town. You're on every committee – perhaps to see what they can get out of De Beers. He had the foresight, when he was in Johannesburg, to enrol in a Dale Carnegie course, with a view to improving his public speaking. 'They teach you not to be unhappy about making a fool of yourself in public. My position required me to do a lot of public speaking and my Dale Carnegie training stood me in good stead.' A woman who had grown up in Kimberley and observed a succession of general managers of De Beers, commented, 'Kimberley was virtually owned by De Beers and there was so much social crap, with senior people in the company carrying on as if they were royalty, and Kidger just cut right across it. He was very popular.'

Koffiefontein is the mine in the Kimberley district that produces the most beautiful diamonds, but the biggest one, 600 carats, bigger than a golf ball, was found at Dutoitspan. 'Those big ones are called Capes, they're yellow and aren't always the best quality. I was always phoned if a big stone was found and I used to shoot down to see it. We often got big stones, beautiful stones, but as you go deeper in the diamond mines, the size of the diamonds diminishes and also the number of diamonds. I never picked up a diamond personally underground, but you used to have forty to fifty men working for you and they used to find them and hand them to you; you'd give them a receipt and then when you got to the surface you'd hand it in and that man would go along and collect his bonus.'

Theft of diamonds and illicit diamond buying (IDB) will probably never be entirely eliminated, but it had greatly diminished since the early days when De Beers had 8,000 people working underground, many of them with shovels, loading the blue ground into trucks. Each shovelful turned over might reveal a diamond. Under the Diamond Trade Act passed by the Cape Parliament in 1882 people accused of IDB were presumed guilty until they could prove their innocence. At that time punishment of those found guilty was severe, involving high fines and possible banishment from the territory; for blacks it included flogging. An independent detective branch, which made considerable use of 'trapping', was formed to concentrate on IDB. In order to restrict the possibility of black workers selling diamonds which they might find underground, they were confined in compounds (based on the system that had been used for the convicts working at De Beers in the years after its founding by Cecil Rhodes in 1880) and allowed no access to the outside world for periods of months. Body searches were instituted for all men as they came out of the mine; those for white workers were less degrading than for blacks who were required to strip and whose body searches were particularly humiliating. However, during the present century considerable changes have been made. Furthermore, mechanization of the mines has reduced the chances of people finding diamonds and now, from the time the diamondiferous ground arrives in the treatment plants, the gem is never touched by hand. In the final sorting the gems are in closed glass containers into which are inserted a pair of long, flexible gloves; the sorter fits his or her hands into the gloves and so is able to handle the stones, though never to remove one. 'But there are always ways of getting the things out,' Kidger admits. 'People always beat a system, so you've always got to be improving it.' The penalties for illicit diamond buying are very heavy, but nailing the culprit is not always easy as he has to be apprehended with the diamonds in his possession.

De Beers owns three farms in the Kimberley district where, in the grasslands, broken at intervals by low trees, herds of springbok graze. Of a number of shoots which were organized during the year, the general manager's shoot, held in midwinter, was the most important. Kidger had shot as a child, 'but I became too fond of wildlife to go there and slaughter these animals. So I used to go up for the party, arriving at noon, in time for a couple of drinks.' It was he who, as he put it, introduced the 'fun and games' into these occasions during the late 1970s. 'We started off with rugby with beer cans until I broke a rib and there were a few other injuries. And I'm sure there were quite a few broken homes because the chaps only left when the liquor was finished – they enjoyed the singing and joking. We used to get home at about eight o'clock at night.'

Kidger discovered on a trip to North America in 1980 that racism is not confined to South Africa. 'In America we were often patted on the back for being South Africans and for the way we were ill-treating our blacks. And it was downright embarrassing to hear this because we were doing so much for our blacks – I'm talking about the mines generally. I would say I'd rather be a black man living in this country than a black man living in Harlem. One fairly senior man said, "We like the way you shoot those black bastards." My reaction, of course, was one of horror.' Kidger believes that the blame lies with the press and the politicians, 'I think the politicians in America try and make capital out of this sort of thing to encourage their blacks to vote for them.' In Germany he was to encounter businessmen who displayed the same kind of prejudice against the blacks. 'The problem in South Africa', Kidger pointed out, 'is that racial division and prejudice has been legalized. However, attitudes are changing.' The racial situation on the mines owned by Anglo American and De Beers has, he maintains, improved progressively over the years. Early in the 1950s the general manager of De Beers abolished the system whereby the black worker was known only by a number; he was to be recognized as an individual with a name. At the same time the first black personnel officer was appointed. Simultaneously, there was a series of lectures, given by people with expert knowledge of black people, directed towards the education of whites in relation to blacks. 'OK, we didn't get perfection, but we taught our whites to greet the blacks underground, for instance, and to call them by name, and to drop the word "boy". We were many years ahead of the mining industry. We changed the word "compound" to "hostel" and senior officials used to be seen going to have a meal in the canteen in a hostel. We opened personal files for individuals. And the response from our blacks was tremendous, much more friendly.' Many of the underground workers were from Lesotho, one of the world's poorest countries. The system whereby the Basotho had to travel all the way to Kimberley to queue for jobs was replaced by one where the more skilled workers, when they went on leave, were given a card guaranteeing them a job and stating the date on which they should return. Leave rosters were drawn up, assuring miners continuity of employment. De Beers, unlike the gold mines, has never had to resort to recruiting offices. 'They'd all come under their own steam to look for work. We're very proud of that record.

'We trained our own white miners, recruiting very few qualified men from outside. Assault cases were virtually unknown. But we still had a long way to go. If you can get this situation right in the workplace, then I think it will develop in the wider environment.' Kidger, when he was general manager, made strenuous efforts to improve communication and inter-racial understanding. In one of the techniques that was introduced, white supervisors from the treatment plant and the blacks who worked for them were placed in parallel groups. Blacks were asked about aspects of the behaviour of whites that irritated them and their responses were conveyed to the whites for discussion. The procedure was then reversed, with blacks being invited to consider factors in their own behaviour that whites found annoying. There was also a control group. All discussions were facilitated by personnel experts. 'I was terribly keen on this. It took quite a battle to get the powers-that-be to agree to it. They don't like anything that isn't their idea – I say that jokingly, but it took many trips to Johannesburg to convince them.'

Kidger initiated a custom of weekly talks to groups of his white and coloured employees, twenty of them at a time, 'and I used to say to them, you know, by the turn of the century there'll be forty million in this country, and guess who's going to be in the majority? I see this country hopefully, so let's find a solution. I stressed the similarity in the history of the blacks and the Afrikaners. Under British rule the Afrikaners had to be educated through the English medium. It was only after World War II that Afrikaners became officials on the mines. They were oppressed, but this made them more determined. The blacks are in much the same position and history has shown that you cannot keep a people down. We have got to live and work together harmoniously. That was the kind of message I gave them, and having an Afrikaner mother I could talk like that. We never had a negative response from those courses. The Afrikaner is a lot more flexible than is generally believed.' He questions the strength of support for 'terrorists' and deplores the fact that the government doesn't get down to discussing things with the real black representatives who, it seems to him, are either terrified to come forward, or in gaol.

Attitudes can be changed, Kidger believes, by changing behaviour. 'For instance, a black man comes in and his wife's been rushed off to hospital and he's late for work. Now the white guy often won't listen to that story because he gets a thousand of these stories – but this is a genuine one. Now we have the machinery for the supervisor to check, to send somebody to go and verify this. This is important.' It takes energy and enthusiasm to develop such systems. 'I used to spend hours trying to let the people feel that that's what this guy at the top wants. And I used to open each course and close each course. You generate enthusiasm by being enthusiastic yourself.'

During Kidger's time as general manager, 1976 to 1985, all the Kimberley mines received the five star award of NOSA, the National Occupational Safety Association, and he himself gave trophies for the best safety record within their own mines. 'You only have to look at the improvement in the accident rate to see how, over the last twenty years, it's become a lot safer, a lot less fatalities. Your accident frequency rate in Kimberley, for instance, was reduced by 400 per cent over approximately twenty years. I'd say that what contributed largely to it was a safety drive programme, but also more mechanization of the mines, improved methods, less labour working underground, more sophisticated labour.'

The Urban Foundation, funded by various large mining, financial and business firms, was established after the 1976 Soweto rebellion with a view to enabling blacks in the urban townships to improve the quality of their lives. Kidger was chairman of its Kimberley committee, a difficult position as most of the expenditure on development was in the Johannesburg area which provided the largest donations. He had deliberately chosen his committee members, all black, from among what he terms 'the more outspoken types'. 'I felt that one of the big problems in this country is that the majority of blacks who serve on community councils do not enjoy the respect of their people. And by having a couple of difficult customers on the committee I was able to get a better feel about what was needed in the community.' The effectiveness of the committee was hampered by inadequate funding, so that it succeeded in little more than improving the old people's home for blacks in the township of Galeshewe. 'It was rather frustrating. I've always liked to think that I'm a person with ideas. You know, we're rather spoilt in Anglo and De Beers because we were always able to get things done, especially as Mr Oppenheimer was so keen on the social side of things.'

In 1982 Kidger was approached by numerous black members of staff, concerned at the school boycotts that had been organized within the black community. They asked him to try to get their children back to school. He therefore called together the men who had been members of the Urban Foundation committee, although this was to be an independent undertaking. One man, about thirty-five years of age, a Galeshewe resident of some achievement, was outstanding. (He names the man but feels that if the name were to appear in print it might be prejudicial to him, particularly in his own community.) As the meetings of the committee shed little light on what was behind the boycotts this man offered to form a committee of school children. 'But he warned me,' Kidger relates, '"Mr Hartley, I'm going to get into trouble, because people are becoming jealous of me."' Many black pupils, owing to diverse educational problems, are in their twenties by the time they reach matric, so this committee of matric students was not composed of children. 'I never asked him for information about who they were, what they told him, or anything that I could convey to anybody else. I knew that they were quite assertive. He handled that situation.'

This student committee devised a plan for improving black education: the standard of each class would be upgraded progressively, on a carefully planned system, starting with the lowest class, Sub A. At an arranged meeting, the scheme was put by Kidger and the man to the responsible cabinet minister. To their dismay he brushed it aside. Two days later in the early hours of the morning Kidger was awakened by a call from his friend's wife, telling him that the security police had arrested her husband and five of his committee members. 'I had to fly to Johannesburg on business the next day and I thought, blow this! It may be five in the morning, but I'm phoning the Attorney General, whom I knew. And he said to me, "Look, the security force is a law unto themselves. I have no control over them." I phoned the chief of police and he said exactly the same thing. Well, I didn't sleep that night, thinking about this bloke; we'd got so friendly.' All Kidger's efforts were to no avail and the next afternoon he aroused the colonel of the security police to extreme ire by offering to put down 1,000 rand as assurance of his friend's probity. Ten days later, after intensive interrogation, all the men were released and Kidger invited them and their wives round to his house. 'They weren't bitter and twisted at all. One could weep. They all said, "We told you. It is our own people who informed on us. *Ja*, our own people. We were becoming too important and they were jealous."'

In the 1980s De Beers began a policy of phasing out migrant labour. Previously the majority of workers had come from Lesotho or Transkei. It had been an unwritten law that when a miner reached the age of about fifty and thought it was time for him to retire, he would bring his son to take his place. It was with considerable distress that men learned that their retirement at the age of fifty-five would bring to an end the association with De Beers. It would be difficult for their sons to find work elsewhere. Future labourers would be recruited from the townships around Kimberley; this policy would alleviate the considerable unemployment in the area. The whites, who tended to see the location youth as *tsotsis*, irresponsible and possibly lawless lads, were apprehensive. It took five years for the labour turnover to stabilize. 'The location chaps had the advantage that we were mechanizing our mines and most of them can drive motor cars and they've grown used to fixing things and they've seen machinery and so they're more amenable than the rural men to mechanization.

'We built 500 lovely homes in Galeshewe for them, beautiful homes, and today many of the black employees have bought their houses under the De Beers home ownership scheme.' There were lengthy and exasperating negotiations with government bureaucrats from whom permission had to be obtained before construction could begin. 'I used to fly up and see the Minister in Pretoria. They changed so fast. People don't realize how *verlig* some of these chaps really are. When you speak to them on their own, of course, they speak a different language to what they speak on the platform.'

In 1983, almost a century after the establishment of Cecil Rhodes's De Beers Mining Company in 1888, the first black foreman was appointed. 'It was quite an achievement! One finds that one is inclined to be a bit timid about this sort of thing, but I just decided that we were going to start appointing black foremen. So I went down and I called all the white foremen together and I told them that this was going to happen. I just explained to them that these people also had aspirations in life and it was terribly unfair not to allow them to advance as they were competent chaps. And then I sat back and waited for the reaction. And there wasn't any.' The foreman was to be appointed in the treatment plant, a section of the mine which does not fall under the white mineworkers' union. The whites were invited to appraise black workers and to suggest suitable candidates, who would be given tests and put on six months probation. 'And now', he adds, with no little satisfaction, 'we have them throughout De Beers.'

De Beers, under Kidger Hartley, were the first mines in South Africa to establish a union for their black workers. He negotiated on behalf of all blacks in De Beers with the multiracial and conservative Boilermakers' Union, who operate on the principle of the rate for the job. The black National Union of Mineworkers came into existence after Kidger's time. He negotiated with the white engineering unions for the employment of black and coloured artisans who would be trained in De Beers apprentice school. This, he maintains, was an achievement which gave him great satisfaction; it was a difficult negotiation, but one which drew less resistance from his own white employees than from the national unions (other than the Boilermakers' Union). 'It was quite a tough one; it took me about eighteen months to negotiate.'

There were about 400 coloured men working at De Beers in Kimberley. Many were clerks and drivers and some were artisans. 'Really, in De Beers, we had outstanding coloured people. One of my best friends in Kimberley is a coloured chap, a painter, who also has birds. He drove all the way down to see me the other day – a tremendous chap. They are very superior people. I'd have him and his family stay with me any time.' Coloured men, however, were found to be poor supervisors. 'They would not discipline or reprimand and when it comes to the yearly appraisal, all their men are "outstanding". I got to the bottom of this; it is that they all live in the small community and if it gets round that somebody has lost his job, or somebody has been demoted, the supervisor is virtually ostracized by the community. Now, strangely enough, you won't find that with blacks. Blacks make tremendous supervisors and company men – they are very loyal to the company. Some of them go to extremes and become ruthless.' He quotes the case of an outstanding coloured man, 'We promoted him. He had many coloureds and a couple of whites working under him, and we tried our best for years, and then we had to demote him because he couldn't exercise any discipline.

'A coloured man has a big problem; they suffer from this terrible complex – you know, a Zulu is a Zulu, he's a proud man, he's got something to hang on to. But a coloured doesn't belong anywhere. The blacks despise them: they despise the blacks.'

De Beers had established the Diamond Sports Club, with cricket pitches and a bowling green, for the coloured people. The white bowling clubs had no objection to competing against the coloured club, but SACOS, the South African Council of Sport, decrees that there can be no mixed, or normal sport in the abnormal society and endeavours to stamp out such mingling. 'SACOS is mainly controlled by the school teachers; they are the difficult ones. So that when a man whose children go to a coloured school plays league cricket in Kimberley – we've got quite a lot of coloureds playing with the whites in the League – his children suffer at school because they won't allow them to take part in sport at school. Oh, it's a nasty business. They're very much connected with SANROC, the S.A. Non-Racial

Olympic Council. *Ag*, it upset me so much that one day I sent out a letter saying I want every coloured employee in the Community Hall at eight o'clock on such and such a day. I went there and addressed them. I gave them stick – without much success, because they live in fear of intimidation by a few agitators.'

Kidger does not align himself with either the Conservative and Herstigte Nasionale Parties of the right, or the Progressive Federal Party to the left of the National Party government. 'I do a lot of thinking. If the Progressive Party gained power, then I'd emigrate. Straight away. You can say what you like, the black revolutionaries want to take over *completely*, as they've done in Zimbabwe. There's no sharing. They just want to take over. And that is the ultimate . . . I would say that I feel darn sorry for blacks in this country if it was taken over by the blacks. From what I've seen in Zimbabwe and Zambia . . . if they offered Zambia to me for one rand, I wouldn't buy it. They're in an absolute mess because they can't handle the situation. Things happen too fast for them. Now just look through Africa – even the World Bank's just about bankrupt, helping these people out.' He considers the PFP to be out of touch with reality, 'They live in these mansions. They are mainly the wealthy people. Their security is not as threatened as the other part of the population. They're always moralizing. You can't only moralize, you've got to be practical in life. And the other crowd – the HNP and CP – they're a lot of lunatics and I wish they'd disappear off the scene because they have a negative function. I think, under the Nats, we have a longer and safer passage in South Africa, but I had to fight them like anything to get houses for my blacks in Kimberley, even though Anglo American was prepared to pay for them. What puts the brakes on them is that they're too concerned about a blooming by-election result. The Nats are regularly creating crises to justify their position to the right wing; they seem to enjoy creating unnecessary crises, but they are not expert at solving them.

'Over the years I have had contact with people like Pik Botha and Piet Koornhof and I know they are *verlig* as anything, but they and their like in the party are too concerned about the right wing. Nobody can deny that reform is taking place in South Africa under the Nat government; the question is, is it fast enough? We should have started at least thirty years ago and it could have been done in an orderly and controlled fashion. The fact is that we didn't start thirty years ago and now we must be careful that we don't jump overboard and try to do too much too quickly. The majority of Nats are aware of this dilemma, but this is a new ball-game to them. Their attitudes *are* changing fast and I'm sure that in the next few years we will see far-reaching changes. Thank goodness they will be in a controlled society. I see a great future for this country.'

EMILY KOK

Bᴇᴛʜʟᴇʜᴇᴍ, ᴀ ɴᴇᴀᴛ little town in the Eastern Orange Free State, is white by night. The black workers who service the white businesses, clean the white houses, tend the white babies, disappear at nightfall into the black township a mile or so beyond the environs of the town, hidden from all but the most prying eyes. On the gates leading to the precise little gardens there are no signs, such as one finds on most houses in Johannesburg, proclaiming the name of the company that has installed the security system. The Army camp located at the entrance to the town makes such precautions unnecessary.

Set on a hill in a select quarter is Sederhof, a home for the aged. A group of grey-haired men sit in the pale August sunshine in desultory conversation. A Mosotho woman waits all day behind the folding iron gate at the entrance to the building, a precaution against unwelcome intruders; she is surprised to be greeted, smiles and unlocks it to let you enter. White residents greet white visitors courteously; the language, as it is everywhere in Bethlehem, is Afrikaans. Emily Kok's room, which overlooks the town, is number 305 along the bare, white-tiled passage of the third floor. At eighty-seven years of age she is still trim and has an air of reserve and quiet distinction. Her forebears were English and she tells you of the leather-bound library which her grandfather once had and of her father's insistence upon his children reading regularly, a practice which stands her in good stead.

She was born in Villiers, a village set on the southern bank of the Vaal River which then separated the Republic of the Orange Free State from that of the South African Republic, now the Transvaal. 'So I am a republican,' Emily remarks, forgetting that she is once more a member of a different Republic. Her maternal grandfather, John Atwick Hipkin, farmed in the district. 'He was from rather a good family near Chichester, in the south of England. We had a couple of titles amongst our relatives there. I don't know them, of course, but when my brother went over and met some of them he told me, "They're a class above us."'

Atwick Hipkin had been among those who, in the 1870s, were drawn by the discovery of diamonds to Kimberley. 'I always told my children', relates Emily, who enjoys her own, often ironic, little asides on history, 'that there were two great treks in South Africa, the one in 1838 and then the other one in the 1870s when diamonds were discovered in Kimberley. All those people, they found it wasn't so wonderful down in Natal, so they just packed their wagons and yoked up their oxen and they went to Kimberley. And my grandmother, Johanna van den Bergh, she was a beautiful woman, much admired, and my grandfather was one of those who fell in love with her, even though he couldn't speak Afrikaans and she didn't know much English. Her family, Afrikaners, came from Greytown. They were very proud of that "h" at the end of their name.'

It was not long before the van den Bergh family, disillusioned with Kimberley, returned to farm in Greytown, followed by Atwick Hipkin who had likewise failed to realize his dreams of wealth amid the dust of the diamond diggings. He and Johanna were married and journeyed northwards, halting south of the Vaal. Here he acquired the farm which he named Uitsoek, meaning that it had been carefully selected for its superiority. Emily recounts her version of the manner of its acquisition according to a commonly repeated settler myth. 'It was the old way of buying a farm. They could go and decide more or less where they'd like it and then they'd go on horseback, from sunrise to sunset, to set the beacons of their farm, all four beacons on the same day. It had to be the same horse, you see, and as fast as the horse could trot. Of course there were no roads, no fences, nothing.' Sophia, the couple's first child and Emily's mother, was born at Uitsoek in 1874.

Charles William Hodsdon, Emily's paternal grandfather, had left Sussex in the 1860s, intending to settle in Australia. Instead, he was shipwrecked on the Wild Coast which lies between the Cape and Natal. Thankful for their survival, he and several of the other passengers made their way to Natal where he settled in Durban and engaged in trading. He married an Englishwoman, Harriet, and their son, named Charles William after his father, was born in Durban in 1870.

Drawn by the gold fever emanating from the Reef, Charles Hodsdon travelled northwards in one of the wagons experimentally powered by sails. At Villiers, on the banks of the murky Vaal, he established a general dealer's store. Emily recalls, 'In my grandfather's shop you could buy anything from a needle to an anchor, practically.' The nearest railway station was Harrismith, about a hundred miles to the south, so Villiers was almost halfway from there to the Witwatersrand goldfields. It became a convenient stopping place and a trading centre. A pont, operated by cables, conveyed goods and passengers over the river. On the return journey to Harrismith wagons would be loaded with wool for export.

The younger Charles, upon completing his education in Durban, joined his father in Villiers and in 1895 married Sophia Hipkin. 'She used to hate that name. All South African people who are named Sophia, they hate the name, because coloured kitchen girls are called Sophie. It's like my name: every second black woman you come across is Emily.' The couple's first child, named Atwick after his grandfather, was born in 1897 and Emily on 20 March 1899, closely followed by Edith. There were to be two more children of the marriage, born some fourteen years later.

The Anglo-Boer War broke out in October of that year, when Emily was six months old. Charles Hodsdon joined the ambulance corps on the Boer side. 'His people never forgave him.

They said he should have got out of the Republic when all the British subjects were told to do so. But my father asked me, how could he leave his wife and small children? Just leave them and clear out? He told me that they thought, most of them there, that it was just another skirmish, because there were lots of skirmishes and false alarms.

'And then the columns came – they used to call these regiments columns – and they collected all the women and children from the farms and the *dorps*, those little towns, because the men had gone to war. So they collected us, too, and took us down to Merebank in Durban.' Emily's earliest memories of Merebank were of the games played under the floorboards of the houses in which they lived, to the consternation of their parents who feared the Natal snakes. She recalls no shortage of food. 'It was only in the concentration camps in the Free State that the women and children suffered so much. General De Wet was to blame for this because he *enjoyed* the life he was leading, you know, the British never being able to capture him. They called him *Vlug Generaal*,' the Elusive General.

The ambulance corps to which Charles Hodsdon belonged had been attached to the commando of General Cronje who surrendered to the British in February 1900. Being composed of Englishmen and having a non-combatant status, the corps was despatched to Merebank concentration camp where Hodsdon's family had been sent a year before. They were urgently needed to minister to the people there, most of whom were living in tents and where typhoid fever, or enteric as it was then known, was rife. These English ambulance men who had served on the side of the Boers were nevertheless regarded with a degree of suspicion by the occupants of the camp.

Three years later, when the war was over, the Hodsdon family returned to Villiers. Farmhouses and farm buildings, as well as houses in the *dorps*, had been destroyed by the British, but the walls of their own house were still standing and the roof intact. Much had been stolen, by both blacks and whites, according to Emily, 'though, as a child, you know, you're really not interested.'

'People were poor after the Boer War, very, very poor. Men went away to work as farm labourers, or on the mines, or even on the roads. We were all right because, you see, my father was better educated in general and he could provide and make a living for us.' Emily could speak only English and Zulu which she had learned in Natal, but she soon picked up Afrikaans from the children with whom she played. 'And now I think about it, they used to say nasty things about us and to us and swear at us in Afrikaans. And of course we didn't know any better. Perhaps they had reason to; there was very bad feeling at the time. Children were, naturally, allowed to play with one another, but later on, when they grew up, most decidedly they wouldn't have an English suitor visit their daughters. And I suppose the other way round, too. There were quite a number of English families in these little villages.'

Life for the English in the Orange Free State was changing. Simmering animosity surfaced when upon the outbreak of World War I, the South African government declared itself to be on the side of the English against whom the Boers had, at the turn of the century, fought so bitterly. An attack was mounted on German South-West Africa. There was a rebellion, led by Generals De Wet and Beyers, both renowned Boer leaders. The Prime Minister, General Louis Botha, called out the Afrikaner citizen force to subdue the rebellion which was quickly and effectively quelled. One of the young rebels, Jopie Fourie, refused to surrender and was shot by a firing squad on the orders of General Smuts. Hence the uprising added a final martyr to Afrikaner sacred history, one whose name is recalled at almost every religious/political gathering of Afrikaners. Afrikaner attitudes hardened, many of them transferring their allegiance to the National Party. Emily, referring to her sister and brother, Johanna and Charles, born in 1913 and 1915, says, 'They're Afrikaans. Afterwards, here in the Free State, you never heard anything but Afrikaans.'

In Emily's schooldays history had been learnt from Whiteside, the history book published in England, but the history her younger siblings learnt was about the larger-than-life Afrikaner leaders all of whom, it was stressed, were heroes and devout men.

School holidays were always spent at grandfather Hipkin's farm: 'We couldn't wait for the schools to close!' He was known as 'the Englishman who reads books' and it is to the knowledge he thus acquired that Emily attributes his success in farming. He had been appointed Justice of the Peace for the area. Many of the English soldiers had volunteered for the constabulary after the war and in the farmhouse there was a special room kept for the white constables who stayed overnight in the course of their duties. 'I remember my father telling me that they were all men from very good families. Of course, being a policeman in those days, I often think about it, heavens! If I see what they wear now, safari suits and so on! The uniforms they used to wear buttoned up to the neck, a jacket and a pair of riding breeches and leggings or puttees for the blacks. They had to ride, all of them, and on patrol it was usually a white man who couldn't speak Afrikaans and a black man who couldn't speak either English or Afrikaans. I don't know how they got on.' *Platteland* (rural) Afrikaners, in whose hearts memories of the Boer War rankled, would not permit them into their houses; interviews had to be conducted on the *stoep*.

Even quite poor people had servants, for they paid them very little. White settlers in other parts of the country had been employing blacks as domestic servants for more than a century, but Emily relates that in earlier times the whites in the Free State had believed that the skins with which the black women clothed themselves were verminous and so would not allow them into their houses. She continues, 'Blacks were very,very . . . well they were nearly barbarians still. They didn't know anything about washing-up, they knew nothing about chores as such. Each white woman had to do her own cleaning and washing.' Eventually some of the black women were taught to do the washing, but they weren't allowed to hang it up lest it be infested by the 'vermin'.

People gathered for musical evenings at houses where there were pianos and someone would generally recite poetry. There were parties where Emily wore the dresses her mother made on her sewing-machine, a rare luxury in those days. 'I remember The Lancers was a favourite dance at that time,' she says, her eyes alight, 'and I loved the waltzes. We danced on board floors in the bigger houses, or on the earth floors of the barns to the music of concertinas and violins; there were also some little pedal organs.' The first motor car bumped along the roads in about 1915: 'a Ford, black, with a canvas hood and brass headlamps; we thought it was wonderful. You'd run your legs off if you heard a motor car. And uncomfortable to travel in, but we thought it was just the cat's whiskers!'

Travellers were welcomed for the news they brought of neighbouring farmers or of events in the wider world. Emily speaks with delight of the *smouse* or travelling merchants. 'It was *most* exciting when I used to visit my grandmother, to see the *smouse* when they came, to the *back* door, of course. Most of them were Jews. It's wonderful how they progressed. They would start on foot with a bundle on their backs – they called them *bondeldraers* [carriers of bundles] – and soon they'd have a little cart with one horse and afterwards they'd have a bigger thing they could sit on and go from farm to farm and they were the newspapers of those days; they brought the news and the gossip. Besides, it was very convenient, you didn't have to go to the *dorp* for whatever you ran out of.'

As the country settled into an uneasy peace, spinster schoolteachers came from England. Emily remembers some by name, Miss Lies, Miss Rose, Miss Coverdale: 'They were old maids, you know; perhaps they thought they might meet husbands. I often think about it now; they must have been very unhappy.' Her own mother had been educated, as were numerous children at that time, by governesses brought out from England to live on the farm. She had been eager to pursue her education further, but this had not been considered suitable. Emily sighs, perhaps not for her mother alone, 'If she had had a better education I wonder what she wouldn't have accomplished. Even when I was young one had to sit at home and wait for a husband; there was nothing for you to do.'

Emily did not wait long. At eighteen she married Mr Isaac Jacobus Marais, principal of the Villiers school. He was an Afrikaner, born in Ladybrand near the Basutoland border in 1885, and so fourteen years Emily's senior. She refers to him as 'my husband', saying that she lacked the *vrymoedigheid* (candour) to call him by his name; it is evident that she held him in considerable awe. Generally she called him 'hubby'. He had learned his English, so he told her, from the Black Watch. 'They were Scotch really. They were stationed at Ladybrand and the Boer boys used to go into the camps – of course the parents were furious. One of these men gave my husband a lot of very well-bound English classics.'

She glosses over questions regarding the reactions of her upper-class English parents to this marriage to an impecunious Afrikaner. Schoolteachers were respected but poorly paid, and life was a struggle. 'We were always hard up; you had to live absolutely so thriftily, but I just took it in my stride. Fortunately I'm made that way. I can face life as it comes to me: not moan about it.'

Emily and her family escaped the flu that swept through the country in 1918. The school was closed in order to accommodate the sick. There were insufficient beds, so some lay on mattresses in the classrooms. 'We were all kept busy, cooking soup and looking after them. There were cases where the whole family, black or white, would die.'

In 1919, after the birth of their son, Leon, the Marais family moved to Paul Roux, a newly established village in the Eastern Free State, the Canaan of the province. Mr Marais was appointed head of the school, a position he was to occupy for twenty-one years. Children came to school in donkey carts or on ponies and a paddock was set aside for the animals. Those who lived too far away to make the daily journey were sometimes left to fend for themselves all week in the little *kerkhuis* (church house) which their parents used for overnight stays when they came to town for *nagmaal*, the communion services held in country districts at three-monthly intervals. As the school grew, the accommodation became inadequate and classes were held in the church vestry or in large rooms of nearby houses.

The Marais family house, like most of those in the *dorp*, was built of dun-coloured sandstone blocks, quarried from behind the nearby hill. The inner walls consisted of what Emily terms 'children-of-Israel bricks' made from topsoil, *kraal* manure and straw, mixed with water, trodden into the right consistency by donkeys or mules and finally baked. The corrugated iron roof was painted red. A *stoep*, or veranda, ran along the front of the house and Emily was to remark upon how much she would have enjoyed relaxing there if only it had afforded more privacy. But as in nearly all South African villages in those days, the houses were built close to the street, despite the large size of the plots on which they stood. People kept a cow or two, chickens, and perhaps a few sheep, and towards the back of the plot there would generally be a *waenhuis* for housing a carriage or cart and sometimes stables.

Mr Marais was a stickler for convention. 'We used to call, in the olden days, very formally. We had to walk on the dusty street, but never mind, my husband used to insist, if I was going out that afternoon, on gloves and a handbag; everything had to be just right. I had to stand for his approval.' And because he would not allow his children to be cared for by a black woman Emily always had what she referred to as the 'tail' of her children behind her. 'Leon, the little blighter, wouldn't walk, so I had to *abba* him,' carry him on her back, just as the black women did.

The Free State tends to aridity and farms were generally established where a *fontein*, or spring was to be found, hence the common suffix in so many of their names. Paul Roux was sited close to the Zand River where, as with so many South African rivers, there was nothing but sand for much of the year. However, it was generally possible, by digging into the sand, to find water. There were three village pumps which were unlocked only in the morning and the evening. 'It was a wonderful time at the village pump! We would go down every afternoon and talk there, a time for all the women to meet.'

'The houses had no bathrooms. Water was a scarce commodity. What did you want a bathroom for when there was no water? A tin bath had to be brought into the kitchen every night and the water carted along and put on the stove . . . and I must tell you I used to bath more frequently than I do today. I used to bath my children and then myself and that wasn't the end of it. My husband, of course, refused to bath in our bath water; he had to have his own. Then the children's clothes – they didn't have so many garments so you had to wash them every day. And after that the water was put onto your plants.'

Emily always had a servant, a 'kitchen-girl' who was paid the usual salary of a pound a month – 'people imagined they were paying them a fortune!' The servants, *kaffirs* as they were called in those days, lived in the location which, in order not to offend the sensibilities of the white residents, was situated more than a mile from the town, on the far side of the Zand River. On the small stands allocated to them, black people built their houses, but the space and facilities available to them were minimal. 'Their latrines, in order to facilitate night soil removals, were on the street frontage. Imagine the state, especially during summer, of these badly constructed conveniences, mostly with an old bag for a door and with a full or running over bucket, right next to one's front door. As can have been expected, enteric fever, dysentery and other stomach ailments were the order of the day and infants and smaller children died by the dozen.

'From such an environment came the servants whom we expected to be clean personally and tidy in the way they executed their duties in our homes. People had very little consideration for them then; they were expected to come early, before sunrise, and they left late at night, after supper.' There were, however, occasions when no servants came to serve the traditional early morning coffee. For when the river came down in flood, neither servants nor cows could cross, thus upsetting the housewives who needed milk for their babies and, more important, someone to fetch the early morning water from the village pump.

In the twenties and thirties there were no cinemas in Paul Roux and the bad state of the roads did not encourage even the few who had motor cars to leave the *dorp*. People had to provide their own entertainment. There was chess and bridge. Younger men packed satchels and over weekends journeyed on foot to farms, either to visit or to court. The women had work meetings on one evening a week to which they brought sewing or mending, discussed events or exchanged recipes. For the men a target-shooting club was combined with a debating society, the surprising combination being apparently a legacy from the experiences of many of them as prisoners during the Anglo-Boer War. Small travelling groups of actors came occasionally from Johannesburg or Bloemfontein and would perform in the schoolroom or the hotel dining-room. Concerts and church bazaars were held on the town square in structures of poles covered by bucksails; seating was a wobbly affair, for members of the audience had to find a relatively level piece of ground on which to place the chairs they had brought.

The Great Trek is an important part not only of Afrikaner history, but of a treasured folk lore. In 1938, to mark the centenary of the departure of the original trekkers from the Cape, a symbolic *Ossewatrek* (ox-wagon trek) was organized. Plans had been laid over several years and a network of advance publicity had generated considerable enthusiasm, particularly in the smaller and predominantly Afrikaans-speaking towns where the event would provide welcome excitement. In fact, so great was the response that it was found necessary to have not one, but nine wagons, each of which would take a different route so as to include even the smallest *dorp* that wished to participate. For those who devised the plan there was a deeper purpose, that of eliminating divisions both of class and of rival political parties. The intention was to weld the Afrikaner people into *volkseenheid*, Afrikaner unity.

The wagons, each named after one of the legendary heroes of the trek and drawn by teams of oxen provided by the communities through which they passed, wound their way through the countryside, to be greeted joyously by Afrikaners who wished to affirm their nationhood. The poverty in which many Afrikaners had lived, particularly since the South African War, had been exacerbated by the depression and prolonged drought, both occurring in the same decade of the late twenties and early thirties. Here was an opportunity for Afrikaners to celebrate and assert themselves. Each local group of 'Voortrekkers', Afrikaner equivalents of Boy Scouts, had built in whitewashed stones on the hillside behind their town a large '1938', to remain as a reminder of the great event. Most of the wagons had departed from the Cape in August and some were to arrive at the Blood River Monument on 16 December, the anniversary of the day on which the Boer forces overcame the Zulu *impis* after making a covenant with the Lord that if he afforded them victory they would ever after commemorate the day and keep it holy. Other wagons would proceed to Pretoria where they would encamp on a hill behind the city and on the Day of the Covenant a huge gathering would attend the laying of the cornerstone of what was to be the Voortrekker Monument.

This travelling pageant, infused with religion and politics, was calculated to heighten within Afrikaners the legendary and idealized sense of their history and hence of their place among nations. At each *dorp* the ox-wagon would stop for about twenty-four hours. There would be prayers, considerable oratory, as well as celebrations and *braaivleis* where lamb chops and *boerewors*, the locally made sausage would be cooked over open fires. Isaac Marais, Emily's husband, in common with all loyal Afrikaners, had grown a beard and wore *voortrekker* clothes. 'I remember making him the authentic looking brown corduroy suit. My, how I struggled! I'd get one trouser leg right and the other one looked like a concertina! I spent hours, especially over that *klap* [flap] that they had, before the fly – they called those trousers *klapbroeke*. And then I had to make him a flowered brocade waistcoat, buttoning right up to the neck. It was a very successful suit.' The women wore long-skirted, full-sleeved dresses with matching bonnets, but Emily did not dress up for the occasion. 'These things cost money and money for teachers in those days was "rather few".' She was known not to be a Nationalist, but a sympathiser of the old South African Party and agrees that this may also have affected her decision. 'Mr Marais's tendencies were Afrikaans, but he was a broad-minded man and to him this was a historical event.' Certainly it was difficult to escape the fervour; babies were baptized and given *voortrekker* names; couples were married in *trekker* dress. Men dipped their handkerchiefs in the grease of the wagon wheels to keep as a memento. The main street of the town, De Kok Street, was renamed Voortrekker Street and another was named after one of the trekker leaders and became Piet Retief Street.

Mr Marais died in 1940. Emily, at forty-one, was neat and slim, as she is today. She found work in the Post Office to supplement the very small sum left to her. She now drove a Chevrolet, bought with a small legacy left her by her father, and took it to the garage one Wednesday afternoon. 'All shops and businesses had Wednesday afternoon off and we worked on Saturday afternoons. At the garage a man I knew started teasing me, saying, "You're too young to spend your life alone; it's time you got married." I said, "Do you think I'll ever get married again? Now I'm my own boss and I do what I like and I buy what I like and go where I like." And I remember Mr Kok, who owned the garage, looking up from the car he was working on and saying, "It's a damn selfish life you're leading!" '

Hermanus Jacobus Kok put an end to such selfishness by marrying her on Armistice Day, 1945. They were almost the same age and had known one another over the years; their children had played together and Emily's father, while in the ambulance corps during the Anglo-Boer War, had helped to bury Mr Kok's father after the battle of Spion Kop. There is deep affection in the timbre of her voice whenever Emily pronounces the name she used for him, Manie. 'We were very good companions. We were very happy together. My first husband, he was very intelligent; he was my mentor. Manie I fell in love with.'

As a boy of seventeen, Hermanus Kok had been involved in the Rebellion led by General De Wet against the decision taken by Generals Smuts and Botha to enter World War I on the side of England. He was living in Frankfort at the time and a contingent of rebel troops were *laagered* in the vicinity. 'These boys from town took food out to their people and enjoyed themselves immensely being big patriots. One night the government troops descended and surprised them and they arrested the lot. Hermanus was one of them. He spent three months – he never used to tire of telling me that – in the Fort at Johannesburg. They were locked up in cells that there had been natives in, full of vermin and bugs. It must have been terrible for these boys. They used to have to wash their own clothes and all that rigmarole of prisoners of war. The younger ones were released first.'

In September 1939 the South African Parliament decided by 80 votes to 67 to declare war against Germany, thus throwing in their lot with the Allies. Large numbers of Afrikaners, particularly those who belonged to Smuts's United Party, joined the armed forces and fought in the war on many fronts. Other Afrikaners were opposed to the cause. Hermanus Kok was one of those who joined the Ossewa-Brandwag (literally, the ox-wagon sentinel), a semi-military organization devoted to the perpetuation of the *Voortrekker* spirit and the pursuance of the struggle for an Afrikaner republic. They held secret camps and military parades in the countryside. They also manufactured explosives in order to sabotage government buildings and vital installations. It was a movement in which rich and poor could participate and which engendered a resurgence of the unity of purpose of the Boer commandos during the war. 'He was nearly in gaol on account of that, too. He used to carry messages for the O.B. The police were just over the road from where Mr Kok and his first wife used to live at the time. The wife of one of the constables was pro O.B. and she used to eavesdrop. When messages came for her husband she'd quickly run over to Mr Kok, even in the middle of the night to warn him.'

Emily had always been a member of the South African Party, the acronym of which led to its adherents being referred to as Saps, or the Afrikaans plural equivalent, *Sappe*. Even after the fusion of the Sappe and General J. B. M. Hertzog's National Party to form the United Party in 1933 the Sap label stuck. 'I was always known as a *bloedsap*; it was in my blood.' Her first husband, although a Nationalist, had not been keenly involved in politics, but Hermanus Kok was what she terms 'a red-hot Nat'. 'People said we'll never get on a minute. But we just agreed to differ on politics. Latterly, I remember how my husband started getting unhappy with the National Party. He reckoned they were going all awry; they had been in power too long, since 1948.'

The garage was a good business and the couple made a fair living. Hermanus Kok had learnt something about mechanics as a young boy when he had worked for the town engineer in Frankfort. He had begun by tinkering with motor cycles, then progressed to motor cars. Emily saw to it that the garage workers were well fed; their midday meal was cooked in her kitchen and the ingredients charged to the garage expenses. It was carried over to the garage to be eaten in the lunch hour, from one to two o'clock. Everything closed during this hour, and if a motorist drew up for petrol, which was pumped laboriously by hand, he would be expected to wait. Petrol pumps were filled from the fifty-gallon drums brought from the nearest railway station, Kaallaagte, by what were known as donkey trains, wagons pulled by donkeys. Forty years later Emily still has all the garage accounts which she kept meticulously.

Running a business challenged Emily's intellectual resources and provided her with the confidence to launch into a new business venture, brick making. She had been driving her own Chev for some time and she needed a garage for it. 'The building boom was on at the time (more or less '46 or '47) and I went to Bethlehem especially to order bricks and they told me that if I was prepared to wait for six months they could let me have some. So I went back to Paul Roux and I said to my husband, "You know, I think we must start a brick-making business." And so we started. I supplied the capital from the sale of a piece of land my father had left me and Manie did the work. There were lots of people who used to make bricks on their farms, just from topsoil, but we started going round the bigger brickworks. In Afrikaans they say, *Jy steel met jou oë*, ["You steal with your eyes."] People were very nice and helpful.

'We were fortunate to get John – his name was really Fieta Mabula – he had worked at Brickor, the biggest brickworks in the country, at Vereeniging. He knew how to build kilns. Our brickworks were very remunerative indeed and I'm still grateful to John; that's why I still pay his house rent at Paul Roux.'

The main road which ran through Paul Roux, linking Beth-lehem and Senekal, was untarred and generally corrugated and rutted. Cars seemed to break down quite frequently, bringing business to Kok's Garage. When the drivers were black students or black clergymen Mr Kok would charge only for the parts used and not for the labour. Emily relates, 'One day, just after I lost my second husband, my girl came to me and told me that there were two – I forget what she called them, their native name for men – to see me. I had been doing something in the bedroom and then I walked into my dining-room and there, lo and behold, were two black men sitting on my chairs! I was a bit shocked; you know it wasn't done in those days.' She had often enjoyed a cup of tea and a slice of bread with native women, but they had always sat on the floor and she on a kitchen chair, while they conversed in Afrikaans; that was the way she believed they preferred it. Adjusting herself to the present situation, she shook hands with the black visitors. One man was a professor at Roma University in Basutoland and the other a minister in the Dutch Reformed Church. 'He told me that when he was an *umfaan* [little boy] he used to work in Mr Kok's garden and it was with Mr Kok's help that he had been able to pursue his education at Roma. He was assisting with the translation of the Bible into Sesotho. He had come to thank Mr Kok.'

Her youngest daughter, Adré, had married and was living on what she terms a 'plot' of 10 acres at Pienaar's River, just north of Pretoria. Although Emily was critical of the urge of so many young Afrikaners to own a piece of land – 'All these young people think they must have a plot, or the sky will fall' – she boarded the train northwards to be with her daughter for the birth of her first baby. She found the plot to be particularly unsuitable: isolated, no telephone, no white dwelling within sight. She took charge and moved mother and child to a flat in Pretoria. The problem was what to do with James, one of the two young black waifs whom her son-in-law, Louis, had found one evening wandering about the streets of Pretoria and had taken home.

'James and his brother, they were ten or twelve years old and they were Rhodesians. They crossed the Limpopo and used to talk about the crocodiles. They were starving and they'd heard about the golden city and had wanted to come to Jo'burg and find something to do. I suppose they thought they'd pick up gold on the streets.' These children had been dubbed, as is commonly done in South Africa, with white names. Emily, whose relationship with the boy would appear to be kindly, though proprietary, seems to remember that James's real name was Nyama.

'Well Louis kept James for himself and found a job for the brother.' However, when the family moved from the plot into town, it was decided that James should return to Paul Roux with Emily. 'He couldn't speak English or Afrikaans, but he seemed to like my face, so he came along. I'll never forget that night on the train. I was so afraid they might bundle him off and so I got up every now and then – and of course tipped the conductor.'

James proved to be a 'wonderful kitchen-boy', but it was not long before Mr Kok and his son perceived his potential and 'just simply took him off to be a "garage-boy". He was *very* well liked in Paul Roux. Everybody used to talk to James. He was a *very* nice boy, a nice "petrol-boy."' Shortly before his marriage James came to Mrs Kok with a catalogue from John Orr's, a department store in Johannesburg, and asked her to order certain items for his bride's trousseau: a handbag, shoes, as well as undergarments, including a bra. She is particularly amused at his insistence upon this last item as African women had not, at that time, generally taken to wearing brassières.

James and his bride were married in the Dutch Reformed Church. When asked if this was the white church, Emily laughed as she replied, with ironic emphasis, 'Of *course* not! How can you mention such a thing!' Blacks, like slaves, were encouraged to assume the religion of their masters, but there was a separate church and an appropriately separate building for them, the Sending or Missionary Church. Prior to the reception which was held on the farm where the bride's parents lived, Emily drove the couple slowly through the town in her car, festooned with ribbons and balloons, making detours so that everyone might greet them. Returning from the first stage of the reception, Emily insisted that her husband accompany her to the second stage where the bride would wear her 'change clothes'. Asked if Mr Kok, particularly in view of his political persuasion, had not been reluctant to take a step so unusual for those times, she laughed and replied, 'Well, I think he'd given me up already. But he enjoyed himself, though he wouldn't admit it.'

'We were always having trouble with the police because we didn't do as they wanted us to do. If they said *this* then you had to do it, whether it was reasonable or not. I must tell you about this friend of ours. He had a little rheumatics; he was on a pension and complained about these pains and so one day someone said to him, "Go to the police station, let them shock you." (One of my brick boys, he was continually in trouble with the police and he told me about the electric shocks the police give them, on the most sensitive parts, you can imagine.) So this friend goes, and he says, would they do him a favour and give him some shocks for his rheumatics – and of course those policemen were as innocent as babes unborn; they knew nothing about such a thing!

'My husband used to read up the law a bit and know when the police were right and when they were wrong. One day the sergeant arrests all my "brick boys" and puts them in a little cell as big as this room. Fourteen of them, in November, when it's so hot. Locks them up for the night.' It is morning before this comes to Emily's ears. 'So I walk down to the police station and I say to him, "Look, the law says that every human being must have so much cubic space of air." I ask him how many cubic spaces of air there are in that cell. So he says to me, "I don't come into your kitchen and look into your pots. You've got no business to interfere here."' The affair ended with the men being released on bail and Mrs Kok having to pay 50 rand in fines. 'I don't know, to this day, why they were arrested. The police and I were continuously having little tiffs. But I needed the work to go on and so I paid the fines.'

Johannes, one of the brickmakers, was continually being

arrested. He had previously worked in a hotel and so could make beds expertly, lay tables and cook. 'The police liked him a lot. A policeman told me one day that they liked to arrest Johannes because they used him in their houses when he was a prisoner and waiting to be charged and sentenced.'

In the early 1940s government-sponsored school feeding schemes for both black and white children had been introduced. There were numerous poor white children, most of whom came from large families 'There were too many to start off with and they were all badly nourished. Those children used to come to school ill-clad and hungry and cold.' Emily was already involved in running a clinic in the black township and became secretary and treasurer of the black children's feeding scheme. In summer the children were given wholesome biscuits and milk, and in the winter soup and two slices of bread and butter. In the early 1950s the Nationalist government which was then in power decided that the black children were coming to school only to get the food: school feeding for black children was terminated, that for white children was continued.

'At the time they stopped this feeding scheme in the 1950s I said to them: stop the feeding scheme and they'll still come to school. And my words were true. At the time I used to take my stepson to school in Bethlehem and you'd find these little black children coming into school from the farms in the winter; then summer heat and all that and you'd find them coming to school. The blacks were keen on their children learning. Of course they couldn't afford very much. I used to buy my black servants' children's school books.'

Racism simmered below the surface and sometimes burst forth. 'I used to see the youngsters on the streets and you know, they just, for no reason at all, would molest the black children. And that's how they grow up: because you're black therefore you've got no right to breathe the fresh air in this country. I had neighbours just over the street and I often used to sit and watch them. Some black children would pass there and they'd set their dogs on them. And of course the black children would retaliate by throwing stones at the dogs and then these white children used to attack the black ones. Not once, but frequently! That's the attitude. It's some antagonism in the homes.' Questioned as to why she did not intervene on such occasions, Emily replied that she would remonstrate with the children if they came past her house, but she said nothing to the parents. 'They weren't my type. I didn't associate with them. The mother used to work in a shop in Bethlehem; the husband was a technician on the telephones. She was a grade above him.'

The few shops were mostly general stores owned by Jews. 'Afrikaners have no business sense. I remember my late father saying that an Afrikaans businessman seemed to think that he must be able to *verneuk* [cheat] another person to be successful in business. I think he described it in a nutshell.' A certain amount of the business was done by bartering produce such as wool, skins, mealies, or butter and eggs, for which the farmer or his wife was issued with what was known as a 'good-for' a cardboard facsimile of a coin of a certain value, stamped with the name of the business. The best-known family was the Kristals; he had progressed from being a *bondeldraer* to running what was considered quite an emporium. Even fresh fish could be bought on a Friday morning. In addition, he had a Shell petrol bowser (petrol pump) on the pavement and as he and his family lived behind the shop, motorists could call him up in the middle of the night to supply petrol. Mr Kristal was mayor for two terms.

'Some Jews', according to Emily, 'are not to be trusted, but as Jews go he was fairly honest.' She attributes any anti-Semitism to religious differences, denying that there might be other factors at work. Perhaps it was such feelings, stated as a resolve to cut out foreign traders, that prompted a group of farmers, soon after the 1914 rebellion, to launch a general store to be financed and run entirely by Afrikaners. It was not a success and, ironically, the premises were taken over by Jewish immigrants, the Koseffs. They soon mastered some Afrikaans, a little English and a smattering of Sesotho. The family progressed to owning one of the foremost furriers in Johannesburg.

Moving nearer to the present time, she spoke of the State President, P. W. Botha, whom she has known since he was a little boy. 'He grew up in our area. He never omits to tell me when he sees me that my late husband taught him English.' Emily sees this as a tribute to Mr Marais's ability. She reflects upon the political changes she has seen; the rise of the Herstigte Nasionale Party, and some years later, the Conservative Party, but distances herself from the resulting friction. Although she has been at the old people's home in Bethlehem since 1984 she is still entitled to vote in Paul Roux and travelled there in order to cast her vote in the recent elections. 'I never thought I'd ever vote for the National Party, but I did so, to keep the CP out. But they got in, the CP, by two votes.'

Vida, Emily's elder daughter, has several degrees and is now a librarian at the Afrikaans-speaking University at Potchefstroom. Adré, the younger daughter who became a nurse, died a few years ago, leaving two daughters. Leon, Emily's son, is a prosperous accountant in Bethlehem. He visits his mother each day and brings her English daily newspapers, the *Citizen* and the less conservative *Star*, as well as a local Afrikaans paper. She follows events keenly and comments upon a recent incident in the area, involving a young woman from nearby QwaQwa, the black homeland for Sesotho-speaking people. 'Look at this nasty thing that happened here. A black girl and her companion were waiting for a bus to go to QwaQwa and four white boys – I call them boys, they are still boys, though they're all married; the youngest was eighteen (a shotgun marriage) – these four boys pretend to be policemen and ask for these servants' pass books. Now this young girl, she's from QwaQwa and doesn't need a pass here, so she couldn't produce one. So they pretend they're arresting her and taking her to the police station. But they take her right out there to the dam and they rape her and kill her; stick a knife in her. And then they ride over her and reverse over the body a couple of times and leave her. The blacks here, they are . . . they said, if those men aren't hanged, *they* will see that such treatment is meted out to white girls. Can you blame them? Now those youngsters must have been brought up with an antagonistic feeling towards blacks. A lot of Afrikaans people, many of these elderly people here, refer to blacks as "*die goed*", "these *things*". I say to them, do you thank God sufficiently that your skin is white? That you're a privileged person, eh? But your spirit, your soul, I say, is just the same as theirs. Six feet of earth make us all of one kind.'

On many farms in South Africa white children play with the black children. This was a practice opposed by Emily's father and by her first husband, both of whom believed that the blacks would teach their own children to lie and steal. For similar reasons Mr Marais would never permit their children to be in the care of a black nanny. To illustrate a point she wishes to make, Emily gives to a black woman the common name of Fytjie, explaining how Fytjie feeds the child when he wakes, cares for him and puts him to sleep. 'So when he wakes up whose is the first face he looks into? The last face he looks into before he goes to sleep? It is a black woman's. I say, can you blame a white boy if he is fond of a black skin afterwards?'

Residents of Sederhof, in the manner of old people, spend many hours reminiscing, recalling in particular accounts handed down to them of experiences in the Anglo-Boer war, heroic exploits performed not only by the men engaged in the fighting, but by the women they left behind. They are nearly all Afrikaans-speaking and resent Emily and an English-speaking woman conversing in English. Despite this, Emily believes that tensions between the two language groups are diminishing.

Emily is conscious of some of the injustices of the past and once made what would be considered by most white South Africans to be a quite heretical statement, 'Of course, we *stole* the land from the blacks.' It is not a point of view that she elaborates. Concerning the future, she maintains that steps should be taken to improve the quality and standard of black schooling. She is not in favour of one-person-one-vote: 'There are too many blacks and we'll have a black Prime Minister in no time. I suppose it'll come, but I don't like it. And I don't know if that is going to work . . . I think it was our first Prime Minister, Dr Malan, who said, "Let *time* solve these problems," and I think he was right. The whites are getting scared and there are too few of us against the blacks. There are *so* many blacks, really.' There may be violence in the black townships which adjoin the cities, but Emily believes that in the country people live together quite amicably: 'I'm not concerned one bit. We're just going to rub shoulders and carry on.' Her belief in the contentment of the blacks is not uncommon among whites. She sees no reason to abandon the Group Areas Act which limits in particular the areas in which those other than whites may live. 'When I was small the blacks on the farms lived in their area and we lived in ours and we got on beautifully. And with the townships it's the same thing as on the farms.' While admitting that 'it's just prejudice', she wouldn't like to find black people living next door to her son.

DALENE MOORE

DALENE MOORE IS dark-eyed, tall and big-boned, with fine, competent hands. She works two mornings a week as a senior operating-theatre nurse at a large private hospital which stands high on Durban's Berea, looking out upon the Indian Ocean. She has not been nursing for the past four years and it is ten years since she last nursed in Durban. She notes the changes: 'I was amazed to come back to this hospital where I did my theatre training to find that there are lots of senior black nurses: Indian, coloured and African, on the staff, and that they all get on so well together. In the operating-theatre, too, there are black staff nurses who do a two-year course and they help the anaesthetist. They have been trained specifically for that and they're very, very good at their job. And they've got black doctors and black anaesthetists.'

Her morning's work done, Dalene walks home along the streets of the Berea, past some of the city's oldest and most gracious houses, many of them double-storeyed with upstairs balconies, decorated in intricate ironwork. The Moores' own front door is along a quiet lane, splodged with brilliant pink bougainvillaea. Jock, the boisterous Dobermann, bounds out at her, and Bryce, her year-old son, gurgles his delight from his cosy perch on the back of Thandi, his Zulu nanny, as she prepares his lunch.

Dalene was born in 1954 in a very different part of South Africa, the Orange Free State. She is Emily Kok's granddaughter, the child of her youngest daughter, Adré Louw. It snowed that year, a rare occurrence, and the Basotho, each of whom receives during his or her life a succession of names, marking each rite of passage, gave her the name Mmaserame, meaning 'mother of the cold'. The grandmother who dominated Dalene's early years and after whom she was named, was her father's mother, Hester Magdalene Louw, for it was upon her farm, bordering what was then Basutoland, that Dalene spent the significant hours of her childhood. Her parents lived in Bethlehem where both worked; their marriage was fraught with dissension, and so Dalene lived with her grandparents for long periods. Her earliest memories are of Rita, the Mosotho woman on the farm who had bathed and fed her from the time she was a baby; thus Sesotho, which both her grandparents also spoke fluently, was her first language. Dalene relates the story told to her by her *ouma* (grandmother) of how, when she was two and her mother came to visit her, and spoke to her in Afrikaans, she turned to Rita, 'What does this woman want? What is she saying?' Her father, who understood Sesotho, laughed and translated for his wife. Dalene resisted vociferously being taken with them back to town, spurning the nanny they had brought. 'I remember scratching and hitting her and saying, "I don't want this horrid *meid*! I want my Rita!" I didn't want anything to do with her. She was actually very nice.' (The Afrikaans word *meid* may be translated as 'maid', but the two words have very different connotations. 'Maid' has a distinctive English class connotation, whereas *meid*, always used for a black servant-girl, conveys a sense of racial inferiority and is generally resented by black women.)

The thousand-hectare farm, Opstal (which means homestead), is situated on the fertile plain stretching between massive flat-topped sandstone mountains, the eroded vertical slopes revealing layers of ancient desert sands, oxidized into shades of yellow, orange and red ochre. From the main road bisecting the valley a rough track winds over the veld, past nondescript sheds and a huge barn, to the farmhouse. It is all quite bleak; the splendour of the setting appears to have evoked no response in whoever planned the homestead and its surrounds. Two black women sit on the grass outside the back door, legs stretched out straight in front of them, burnishing a pile of metal saucepans and dishes that glint sharply in the midday sunlight. They do not expect to be greeted by white visitors and continue their rubbing and their lilting conversation. The kitchen is huge with a large coal stove; the remainder of the rambling house is a succession of box-like rooms. An extensive *stoep*, a sort of common room and constantly in use, overlooks a terraced garden, and is enclosed with bulging wire mosquito netting.

Ouma Louw ran the domestic affairs with martial efficiency. Her practice of standing at the back door and yelling for a particular servant had caused her to be given the name of Mmahweletsa, 'the one who shouts from a long distance'. The summons was imperative; wherever she might be, at her house, or in the fields, the required woman would come running in answer to the call. 'She ran that farm like a factory.' There was a cook and a cook's helper, three *meide* whose duties were to do the delicate washing, the rough washing and the dry cleaning and valeting of Grandpa Louw's clothes. There was an inside *meid* and a chicken *meid* and a turkey *meid* who also helped the chicken *meid* sort the eggs. All these women lived on the farm and were the wives or daughters of tenant labourers. At six-monthly intervals this team would be changed for another one, apparently almost identical; thus all women were free for six months of the year to work in their own homes. On Friday there was a general turnout of the house when every window was cleaned, all the carpets were carried outside to be beaten and brushed, and every object that might respond to elbow grease was burnished. All the women living on the farm were obliged to participate; for those other than the regular servants this was unpaid work exacted for the right to live there. Some of their husbands would be the sons of resident labourers, young men who had gone to the cities or to the mines to work and who are debarred by law from bringing their wives with them to the towns. Farmers resented these 'idle' women staying on their farms, 'breeding like flies' (a phrase often used by white farmers and their wives) while their husbands were not even working for them.

Together with her three cousins who often came to visit, Dalene played with the black children on the farm. Sometimes, in emulation of the little black girls, they would bare their bodies and wear only a *thethana*, a tiny skirt composed of dozens of strands of twisted grass stems, each encased in dung and ochre mud and suspended from a beaded belt. A necklace with two little flat, beaded pieces, twice the size of postage stamps, lying just below the hollow of the throat, completed the outfit. To add to the incongruity of these strangely pale skins clad in so little, the girls had to wear their *laphoede*, soft khaki hats, for Ouma, who prized her own beauty, intended that they should do the same. But they had other priorities. 'The best thing was to go and eat when the black servants were eating. You had to go and wash your hands and only use your right hand and eat out of this big pot with them. It was always so tasty and delicious! They were so amazingly tolerant. If I think of it now, these little brats running around and poking their noses in everywhere – whenever anything happened, we wanted to be part of it. They were so tolerant, never scolded us unless we really got out of hand.'

Ouma Louw, whose maiden name had been Botha, inherited the farm from her parents who, when she married Jacobus Wynand Karel Louw, moved into Bethlehem. It was a dairy farm and the couple had built it up into a prosperous concern. 'In those days', commented Dalene, speaking of her childhood, 'it wasn't like now, you didn't have to work so hard, just have enough winter feed. It wasn't as efficient as it is now, didn't yield as much milk, but it was good enough for them to get rich on.' It would seem that Ouma enjoyed the exercise of her competence. She had, according to Dalene, a room for everything and a team for everything. She exported goose down to England or Europe and the plucking of the geese was a delight to the children. 'I can still recall the smell of feathers burning. There was this huge shed and the women would come and whenever any black women came to the house for any job they used to have a big feast and they were so excited and used to chatter away all day. It was very exciting for us and we used to be in the way, getting into the feathers, being shooed away.' Geese and turkeys were marketed at Christmas and there was the fruit from another of their farms that had to be laid out in the sun and dried before being sold.

'Slaughtering cow day, that was a big day. It had to be in winter, because they didn't have electricity and there was no refrigeration. Everybody, neighbours too, had to help. They'd make *biltong* [dried and salted pieces of meat] and *droëwors* [dried sausage]; as a rule they killed a pig at the same time and pork was added to the *wors* for flavour. There was hardly any farm work because the men had to come and help to turn the meat grinders and with the heavy work. And the women had to cut all the meat off the bone for mincemeat. Some of them had a huge black pot on an outside fire where they boiled all the intestines to be used for sausages. Everything was used. All the insides would be there, on a big stone slab, next to the pot of boiling water, all scrubbed with sharp stones and knives. The hoofs were boiled to make the jelly for brawn and silt, which is like curried brawn. The whole operation had to be done that day, with the best pieces of meat pickled or corned. All the fat from the pig and the cow was kept for Ouma to use for making soap the following week. The skin was hung on a tree to dry with a huge stone to hold it down and stretch it and it was turned and turned until it was ready to be cut into *rieme* [the strips of leather used to tie the cows' legs at milking, or to make yokes for the oxen].'

As the three girls and Kobus, the only boy, set forth each morning, Ouma would say, 'Put on your hats, you little girls,' adding, 'and you little girls must stay away from the *kaffertjies*,' the black children. 'Always this thing', Dalene recalls, 'about "stay away" ... I still don't know ... It fascinated me. She had this thing about "you little girls" and "the *kaffertjies*" – and of course that's exactly where we wanted to be. We didn't want to be anywhere else because that's where everything happened. And we got on very well with them. It was the black male children she didn't want us to be with. We couldn't wait to get away.' The children had observed the black children bringing the midday meal for the men, each in a tin container about the size of a large jam tin, held by a heavy wire handle and with a curved lid which could be turned upside-down and used like an old-fashioned soup plate. The men sat in the sun behind the dairy wall and ate. It seemed enviable and so they persuaded their grandmother to buy them such tins. Sometimes they would skip breakfast and pile the fragrant yellow *putu-pap*, or mealie-meal, into their tins, topping it with sour milk from the clay container that stood in a dark cool corner of the kitchen. 'We'd eat it in the poplar wood below the house and then cut walking sticks and go off, visiting at the huts behind the hill. We'd call formally at each hut, waiting outside and calling, "Ko! Ko!", the sound like knocking, and waiting to be invited in, when we would greet in the correct Basotho manner. We used to take sweets and oranges and whatever we could pinch as gifts.' The mothers would sometimes give the children *maheu*, a smooth drink made from ground mealies and mabela and kept cool in calabashes. They relished its sweet-sour taste. At other times they would go into the mountains where the young black boys herded cattle and where they would join in the war games that African herdboys played. 'It was great fun to go and find them and they'd hide and we'd have a big war, but all in fun. They knew that place so well and they'd hide behind rocks and in little caves and we'd attack. We'd have a war up there, in the mountains, with *kleilatte*, willow sticks with lumps of clay stuck on the ends; you bent the stick back and when you let go you hoped the clay-lump would hit the other fellow. We'd get together afterwards and swim in the stream and under the waterfall. We kept our panties on when the other children were around.'

The land behind the hill, fertile and deep, had been set aside for the use of the farm labourers, each of whom was entitled, as part of his wages, to cultivate his own small piece of land and to graze a limited number of cattle. On most farms the poorest land was allocated to labourers, but because it was difficult to reach and divided from the rest of the farm by a public road, these workers were given good land. They built their own thatched huts, each with a courtyard in front, screened with reeds.

The wives, when they weren't working for the farmer, cultivated their fields and the young boys herded the cattle. Daughters looked after babies, ground the mealies and helped in the fields. Soon after reaching puberty they went to initiation school held behind a *koppie* (a little hill) near their homesteads and overlooking a stream. They were generally married not very long afterwards. Dalene and her cousins found it strange that their black contemporaries became women and were married while still at high school.

December 24 was Grandfather's birthday, an occasion for the whole family to gather for Christmas dinner. 'I don't know why they ever did it because they would get together and fight most of the time. There they were, every year, shouting at each other.' Christmas Day was for the blacks, the only celebration throughout the year provided for the farm workers. 'My grandmother spent weeks beforehand sewing little pockets out of old mealie-meal bags; these were filled, one for each child, with biscuits which she baked and home-made toffees.' The birth of a baby had to be reported to her and she would bestow on it an English name, (in contradistinction to its Sesotho name which would almost always have a special meaning and significance). This would be recorded in a book which was taken out before Christmas to see how many children there were. The parents were driven to Fouriesberg, or perhaps Bethlehem, in the farm lorry in order to buy new clothes for their families. On Christmas Day the mothers, swinging their hips a little to show off their new dresses, would gather in the poultry room, specially cleaned for the occasion, to eat the home-baked cake and drink beer brewed by the cook. Excited children, dressed in their new clothes, would be on the back lawn with cool drinks and their little parcels. They sang songs and danced, joined, after a few mugs of beer, by their mothers. 'It was great fun! We loved it! To us, that was more Christmas than anything. Whenever I go to a farm at Christmas-time now I want *that* and it doesn't happen. Grandfather would slaughter a young ox for the men and join them over the cooked meat and beer.'

Mr and Mrs Louw went on a cruise in 1957 and Dalene's

father came to manage the farm while they were away. Upon her return Ouma told how, sitting on deck one day, wrapped in a blanket against the chill wind, she heard someone speaking Sesotho. Without turning round, she chipped in and chatted to the unseen woman. 'When they both got up out of their chairs my gran realized that the woman was black and the black woman realized that my gran was white. My gran had thought it was a white woman who knew Sesotho well and was, just for fun, speaking it to her friend. And the other woman had thought my gran was black. (My father later told me that it was King Moshoeshoe's mother, Queen Mantsebo Seiso, who acted as regent while her son was at Oxford.) So my gran used to get invited, for the rest of the cruise, officially invited by the ladies-in-waiting of the Queen, to have tea with her because she had no one to chat to. And they were, in fact, from the same area, just a mountain separating them.' Many South Africans, Afrikaners in particular, have a strong aversion to blacks drinking out of their cups and according to some blacks cups so sullied are smashed. Mrs Louw, enjoying tea with the Queen of Lesotho had no such problems for, as she said, 'It wasn't *my* house and I knew she wasn't drinking out of *my* cups.'

The children seldom missed the early-morning expeditions to take the milk in cans to Slabberts, the nearest station. The girls would have to put on their khaki hats. 'She thought that as long as we had a hat on we were fine. And as long as Kobus was there, because he was a boy, that was all right.' And Ouma would say, 'You little girls must sit in front.' This they would do, with Kobus in the back. Oupa, the children's grandfather, generally drove the lorry and at the farm gate they would all tumble out to open it, and swap places. 'Kobus liked talking to Grandpa about manly things and us girls would be on the back, together with the *kaffertjie* who had to offload the cans – and of course that's why she didn't want us to sit at the back. We got away with murder with Oupa; we could just twist him round our little fingers. When we got to Slabberts he used to buy us sweets from Oom Tom's shop. Sweets before breakfast! That was lovely! Our gran had this thing that you're only allowed sweets after lunch because they're bad for your teeth.' The farmers would admire the children and remark on the gaps from lost baby teeth or pigtails that had been grown. 'They'd drink tea or coffee at Oom Tom's and sit and chat about not having any rain – from their talk, it's never rained, as far as I can remember.'

Going to town was an important expedition for Oupa and Ouma. 'There would be a hot bath for Oupa in this huge bathroom with the massive bath (all five of us grandchildren used to get into it together). Water was heated by a maize-cob fire under the copper geyser in the same room. Andries Mofokeng would get this huge old motor car out of the garage and clean it. Ouma would get dressed either in pink or purple from head to toe, with a big hat and beads and gloves. There were dust roads, terrible roads, all the way to Bethlehem so they'd both wear dustcoats and off they'd go. Before they left we'd get special instructions and a special *meid* had to come from the huts to look after us all day. As soon as we saw the car disappear over the hill we were off on to the corrugated iron roof of the dairy where we weren't allowed to go.'

The real farmer at Opstal was Andries Mofokeng, the headman. He had two wives and fifteen children, factors which enhanced his prestige in the children's eyes. He would come each morning to the window of Mr Louw's bedroom where the children would have clambered into their grandparents' big bed. 'Andries would tell about cows that had calved and what else had happened in the night and my oupa would give him instructions. That's all that he did. And he would drive out in the afternoon with all his dogs just to check and see what they were doing. I never saw him doing any farming work. He either worked on his books in the office or in his workshop, welding. Those were the things he liked doing. He was the first farmer in the area to install a milking machine and because there was no electricity a room had to be built to house the large generator. But although the house was wired up no electricity was installed in his lifetime. We used paraffin lamps and candles.'

One year the children built themselves a hut out of earth sods just as they had seen, over and over again, the Basotho building. They felled poplars and cut them to size for the roof, topping it with an authentic straw roof. To the girls' indignation, Kobus inscribed on the wall when they had finished: 'Built by Kobus Louw and *ho dila* [smeared with cow dung] by the girls.' 'We were *furious* as we had done most of the work and he had just directed us! And that smearing with cow dung, it got under our nails and you just couldn't get that stink out for months.'

'We had tin mugs and plates, just like the black people, and swept outside with grass brooms. We would try to persuade Lucy, my ouma's chicken *meid*, to play with us because she was great at making a fire; we could never quite get it going. And she would come and test the *putu* we were cooking and we would gather *morogo*, the wild spinach, to go with it.' Lucy was also persuaded to ride with them on the cart which they constructed; a fifth person was essential to balance the thing and it was the fifth person who, in the course of the sharp turn that had to be made at the end of the hurtling downhill run, was thrown off into the stream of manure emanating from the cowsheds. 'We always had a great fight as to who was going to sit there and if we could we'd get Lucy to sit there because it didn't matter if she fell in the muck – isn't that terrible! We were such good friends with her and yet we also had this thing in the back of our minds: they're not 100 per cent humans like you are: they're black. They're human, but it doesn't really matter if bad things happen to them. Only when I grew up did I get out of that feeling.'

When she was five Dalene moved back to her parents' home in Bethlehem and started school. She hated it. In emulation of the Africans, she removed her shoes as soon as she could and walked home barefoot, with them tied together over her shoulder. The school was Afrikaans-medium but Dalene had been taught English by her ouma, who considered it an essential accomplishment for getting on in the world, and made friends with English-speaking girls. 'My cousins eventually went to English schools and so on holidays we used to speak English to each other and Afrikaans to my grandfather. I still speak English to

Ouma and she's my Afrikaans grandmother.' There was no English-medium school in Bethlehem and so there was a special class for them in each standard. 'I found the English easier to get on with. Afrikaans people are snobs, great snobs. My grandmother was one of them. You had either to be a dominee's son or a daughter of a doctor, a member of the town council or a professional man. If your father wasn't one of those then you were no good and kind of ostracized. We looked down on the few Portuguese children because they were not "pure". We had a teacher, a very masculine woman, and she was always drilling us about *pure* Afrikanerdom and telling us not to speak English: we should make everyone speak Afrikaans. I remember children telling what fun they had had, going to Durban and refusing to speak English. Afrikaner children who mixed with the English were looked down upon. Before every national holiday we would have a parade and salute the flag and remember the trek. They really indoctrinate you. The history they teach you is so warped and you believe it because the history book says so and so it must be right. It's a shock when you grow up and read other books and find it's not so.

'I was always a bit of a rebel and didn't fit into what a good little Afrikaner girl should be. So as I grew older I was friends with the English girls. Afrikaners have such a rigid way and the English have a freer kind of life. You could wear more modern clothes and have much more fun.' Dalene joined the Brownies pack when she was seven and became a Girl Guide four years later, whereas the girls in her class went to Voortrekkers, a sort of Afrikaner equivalent, infused with the mythology of the Great Trek. The threat of the *swart gevaar* (the black danger) was conveyed by one of the masters who would warn the children, when they did badly in their tests, 'Yes, *you* don't want to learn. And', menacingly, 'the *kaffertjies* are *running* to school.' During her schooldays she would look foward to the long weekends or the end of term when the large, navy blue Mercedes would be waiting outside the school gate to take her to the farm.

Her friends and cousins were going to the English-speaking University of Natal, but Dalene, alienated by her father's stormy behaviour, made a conscious decision that she would accept nothing from him and so could not go to university. She had made little effort at school, but passed matric. 'I was seventeen and I went nursing in Durban so as to be near some English-speaking school friends. I was independent.' The city seemed huge and alarming and she was glad of the safety of the nurses' home in which she stayed.

The first occasion on which she ventured out at night was during her first year when one of her colleagues, a nurse from East London, persuaded her to join a 'blind date' outing to the rugby club dance at the university. 'It was terrible because I was so naive and so out of the *plaas* [farm] and all these city boys. There were hardly any girls. It was just like varsity boys going to pick up a few nurses for a good time, and I'd decided not to wear my glasses so as to look nice and I couldn't see very well.' She describes how eventually she sat in a corner with her back to the room, took off her shoes, put her feet on the table and fell asleep. 'I woke up and my friend and just about everybody except some drunk rugby players had gone (my friends thought I'd gone home), and there was this fellow, sitting in front of me, also with his shoes off and tickling me with his toe. He took me home and I was terrified of him because I hadn't been out with men. Next day when he arrived I didn't know him because I had my glasses on. That was 1972. His name was Robert Brice Moore, but he was always called Rob. He lived with his family in Durban and was doing accountancy at university.' His grand-father, she was to discover, had been one of the Irishmen who came out to fight against the Boer forces during the South African War. Rob had been educated on English public school lines at his father's old school, St Andrew's College in Grahams-town, a boarding-school for boys. 'We went out together for a year, then broke up, then went out again.'

In her third year she was allowed to move out of the nurses' home and she and a nurse from New Zealand took a flat near the Point Road, a notoriously bad area near the docks but also handy to the hospital. 'Nursing is a hard life, but it teaches you self-confidence and to be self-reliant. It was good for me because

I was very withdrawn, shy and scared of people. But I wouldn't recommend it to anybody. I would never do it again if I had the choice. It's such a restricting world, such a narrow world, especially when you are a student nurse. You work so hard and have such long hours that there's no time for anything else.' She was determined to go overseas and saved all she could out of her salary of 100 rand a month. 'As soon as I qualified, at the end of 1975, I went overseas on my own. Just took off. My mother nearly had a heart attack and she insisted that I join a club which organized camping tours for young people. I remember being terribly nervous about it, not knowing what was going to happen to me when I got there.' Despite her luggage being lost for a week, she soon adjusted and found a South African friend. After an adventurous tour of Europe she returned to London where she joined seven girls, New Zealanders, Australians and a Canadian, living in a basement flat in South Kensington. She got a job at St Mary's Hospital, working in the renal unit, and did a course in haemodialysis with kidney machines. During her eleven months away from South Africa she and Rob wrote to one another and when she landed in Cape Town she telephoned him.

Returning to Durban in December 1975 she did a post–graduate course in operating-theatre techniques, in order to become an operating-theatre nurse. She lived in a commune in the suburb of Morningside with English-speaking friends, two of them from Bethlehem; one was a nurse, the others newly qualified accountants, teachers and a geologist. 'There were two maisonettes, twelve bedrooms (one for each of us) and six bathrooms. One night we gave a party for all the parents, who were somewhat shocked at the set-up. It was wonderful. I lived there for two years, seeing a good deal of Rob.'

In December 1978 she and Robert Brice Moore were married in her parents' house near the railway siding at Slabberts, the tiny village not far from her grandparents' farm. In November they set off for London where Rob had a job with a large accounting firm. Before he started work they visited his relations who lived in Northern Ireland, just outside Belfast. Dalene was shocked to find in this distant country antagonism that seemed even more virulent than that which she had known at home. 'Just ordinary people, like you and me, living there on their little farm and they *hate!* They don't admit it, yet it comes out all the time. They feel an antagonism that they haven't got a reason for. Strange. They grew up with Catholics like we grew up with blacks and I feel much better about the blacks than those people feel about the Catholics. Strange, the same origin, same language, same colour of skin and they hate each other so much.'

In London Dalene found various jobs, one of which was at an agency for temporary employment in Watford. 'There were seven other interviewers, all around my age and all white British. The others dealt with secretaries, clerks, accountants, catering staff and so on, while I interviewed nurses going out on daily or weekly jobs. I found that I was the only one in this whole agency who was tolerant and treated the blacks equally, who didn't think they had to be treated in any different way. It was all very new to me, as a South African, but I tried very hard and it worked very well and I found it was easy to do. My most loyal girls were black girls.' Had they been in South Africa she would have described her co-workers as pro-apartheid. She tried to explain to them how apartheid worked, that though the blacks have to live in separate areas, there are no fences. 'I told them that blacks walk in the streets, like you and I do, but they are not seen as *people*, that blacks are seen as maybe 80 per cent people and whites are 100 per cent people.' She tried to explain the hidden laws, like influx control. 'There was one girl in particular who said, "It doesn't matter . . . these bloody niggers!" They *hated* them.'

Rob and Dalene bought a London taxi, one of those high, square, black vehicles, and toured the Continent where tourists everywhere begged to be allowed to have their pictures taken next to it. They returned to South Africa in 1981 and after a year in Bethlehem Rob got a job with a large milling company in Randfontein on the West Rand, adjoining Krugersdorp. It is a small, undistinguished town and most of the residents are

Afrikaans-speaking, many of them members of parties and organizations to the right of the government. In 1987 the Krugersdorp town council, challenged on the issue by Ster Kinekor who own the cinema and distribute the films, voted to close its only cinema rather than let it become multiracial; this decision was subsequently retracted.

'Living in Krugersdorp was like living in a foreign country.' Dalene had grown up in the Free State, a less than liberal environment, but found herself angry and repelled by the hatred in the air: the unveiled hatred of racist whites reflected, in a different key, by some of the blacks at whom it was directed. 'A lot of these whites trekked off the farms to the mines round here, poor people making a pitiful living. They wanted to shake off the poor white image and so they just trod on everyone else to get away from being poor. I think that they were scared that they would go back into that same situation and that the blacks would take over. I don't think that they even fully realized it or admitted it to themselves, but I think that's what, deep down, motivates them to *hate* the blacks so much. To suppress them so much.'

She and Rob considered emigrating, but eventually abandoned the idea. Both have a deep attachment to South Africa and Rob pointed out that wherever they went they would be foreigners for the rest of their lives. Instead they moved to Durban, Rob's home town, where Dalene had spent many happy years. Rob found a position (not quite as well paid) in a large clothing manufacturing and retailing company. They bought a house on the Berea, the high ridge behind the town, running parallel to the beachline, where it is cooler in the summer when the temperature and humidity soars. Brice, their little boy, will soon be two and they hope to have other children. Dalene says, 'It may sound crazy, but I feel there's a bit of hope for this country in Natal. There's not the racial tension that we had in Krugersdorp.'

Friends of friends have been involved in opposition movements and she has wondered about this: 'The people who are involved and committed, so many of them, are in hiding, so what do you achieve by opposing? You get nowhere. You get shut up in every sense. This government is so efficient and successful in clamping down that people who have something to say and who do achieve something are either in hiding or doing it in secret, or continually in court, or banned, or something. So you end up thinking, "It's not worth it. I'll just keep quiet." At the moment I am just one of the masses in South Africa who are waiting and hoping for the best: that's why we're in the mess we're in.'

The Moores had followed the reports of the first inter-racial constitutional conference held in South Africa, the KwaZulu Natal Indaba, with great interest and had felt that its initiation of negotiations represented an effort to break the stalemate in South African politics. When its final report was delivered in February 1987 they contributed to and joined the Indaba Interest Group: 'They send us literature and they're still working on it, but I don't have any real hope that the government would allow anything like they propose.'

Dalene is enjoying her professional involvement at the hospital and watches with interest the developments across colour lines. One of the innovations at many hospitals throughout the country over the past few years has been that white staff look after black patients. 'I think it's very good for white staff to have to nurse blacks. You're really down to basics in nursing and to have that . . . to find out that these people they're nursing – it doesn't matter that they've got a black skin – they're a person like anybody else. Some of the nurses have never touched black people and it must be quite an adjustment for a lot of them. I think they're very brave,' she says with a smile, 'from the point of view that they've got this massive prejudice, but they're doing it and finding out that they're surviving, that nothing is going to happen to them because they're nursing black people.'

A white surgeon, practising open-heart surgery, has come with his team from the government hospital at Wentworth, Durban, to the one in which Dalene works. 'He brought these five trained African sisters and they are now teaching the white sisters and they are very, very good. I saw open-heart surgery done in

London; these ones are far better; they've got it down to a fine art. I was really very impressed to see them work. I'm delighted to see it. And there are a few white, ex-Zimbabwean women here who talk about *kaffirs* all the time and the matron in charge very diplomatically doesn't let them work with the black people. But on the whole everyone gets on very well, interacts like anybody else, jokes with each other and chats about their families. I'm amazed.' The hospital has just sent a black nurse who has been chiefly involved in ear, nose and throat surgery up to Johannesburg for a month to learn about implanting bionic ears.

'Most of the nurses here are English-speaking, there are some Afrikaans-speaking ones, but Durban is an English town. I'm Afrikaans and hardly any of them know that and they're surprised when they find out that I'm Afrikaans and that I'm also very broad-minded as far as race relations go. It seems to be working well; I've heard no one complain about it except these two Zimbabwean women. It makes me *mad* that they come here – what a cheek! – to bring their prejudices here! We've got enough of a problem and they just come and spread it. If I'm prejudiced about anybody I'd say I'm prejudiced about these white Zimbabweans – I suppose it would be more correct to say ex-Zimbabweans – because of the hate that they bring here.'

'Sometimes, now that I am a parent, I get depressed. Is there really any hope? You think of this circle of violence going on and on. The reason for the violence on the part of the blacks I can understand and don't condemn because I understand that there is all this injustice and oppression. Anybody who is fool enough to take it for so long deserves it. They should have done this long ago, I feel, not that I condone the violence, but I can understand the desperation that causes it. I used to wonder why they just take it, take it lying down. Now they're standing up and saying, "We're not taking it any more." It shouldn't be done to them, but what worries me is that there is this small bad element in the townships who jump on the bandwagon and use it for their own ends. And this circle of violence is going to become a way of life in the black community. It is too easy to take something by force. I think, "Will it ever end? Even when there is one-man-one-vote, which I firmly believe there should be, will the violence stop?" Because the children growing up now are learning that if you want political rights all you have to do is burn down a few houses. That's all they know.' Dalene believes that she and people who feel as she does have a duty to educate their fellow whites. 'Blacks are blacks: they're not just *kaffirs*. They are people, people with full human rights like you and me. But I don't want the rest of my life to be tied up with continual struggle. I don't feel that I had any hand in creating it.'

GABRIEL NOTHNAGEL

On 16 DECEMBER 1880 some 6,000 Afrikaners assembled at a farm called Paardekraal to renew the vow they had made in Natal forty-two years earlier, on the eve of the Battle of Blood River at which they defeated the Zulu army. It was an occasion of deep religious humility, coupled with an affirmation of re-publicanism. Those present stated their resolve to continue the struggle for independence and to protest against British attempts to annex their country. It is told that, at a certain point in the proceedings, each man spontaneously picked up one of the many large stones to be found in that part of the country, and that the stones were placed, almost ritually, to form a cairn. President Kruger himself was present.

In 1887 Paardekraal, which was to become one of the sacred shrines of what one writer describes as the Afrikaners' civil re-ligion, was incorporated into the newly proclaimed town of Krugersdorp. During the South African War the stones that formed the cairn disappeared; some said that a British Officer had ordered their removal. A sandstone monument, however, that had been built on the site and dedicated by President Kruger, remains to this day.

Krugersdorp is a somewhat featureless town, lying west of Johannesburg, on the gold-bearing Witwatersrand reef. During the early part of this century many impoverished rural Afrikaners were drawn there by the prospect of jobs on the mines in the area, chief of which is the West Rand Consolidated gold mine. The region has remained predominantly Afrikaans-speaking.

On the north-western border of Krugersdorp lies Munsieville, a black township. The official estimate of the number of people living there is 6,000, but some informed people have suggested a number almost double that. The dire shortage of accommodation for blacks here and throughout the Witwatersrand area is the result of a political system which held that blacks should be prevented from coming to the towns and which has restricted the provision of black urban housing. The Group Areas Act limits land areas for occupation by blacks and the situation is further exacerbated by the refusal of the authorities to lower minimum housing standards so as to enable people to build homes within their often limited means. Consequently many people, finding themselves homeless, constructed shacks in the back yards of existing houses. Shelters, erected on stretches of open land, are regularly demolished by the state officials, but those in the townships come under the black township authorities who have not always seen fit to act against the people who erected them.

Separated from Munsieville by some 300 yards of rough veld is Gordon Grey Street, in the white suburb of Dan Pienaarville, named after the Afrikaner General Dan Pienaar, loved and respected by the troops in the western desert of North Africa during World War II. It is there that Gabriel Nothnagel lives, with his wife and two children, in a neat little bungalow, set in a quarter acre of garden. He was born in 1953, the fourth of nine children, and grew up in Swellendam in the Western Cape. As is often the way among Afrikaans-speakers, he was soon known as Gawie, the shortened version of the name Gabriel, where the 'b' becomes the 'w' that sounds like the English 'v'.

His father, Michiel Adriaan Nothnagel, had been born in 1919 on an ostrich farm in the Ladismith district of the Cape and when those who dictated women's fashions no longer decreed that the ostrich feather was a natural extension of the female form, his father was one of the many ostrich farmers bankrupted. Like many others, the Nothnagel farm fell into the hands of one of the Jewish entrepreneurs who had bought the feathers and sold them on the international markets. 'It didn't give my father an anti-Jewish feeling in general, I never got that impression, it was just an isolated incident. Whenever you talked about Jews as businessmen he would say. "Yes, they are good businessmen, but be careful . . .' There were quite a number of Jews in Swellendam, such as the Singers who ran the hotel, quite popular people, and the Singer guys played in the cricket team."

The limitations that the loss of the family farm imposed upon Michiel Nothnagel's education accounted, in part, for his efforts to ensure that his own children should not be similarly disadvantaged. He was educated at a little farm school in the Ladismith district where there was one teacher for several standards and left in Standard 8 to work in the Provincial Administration on road building. At the same time he studied for and gained a technical diploma offered by the province. In 1952 he moved to Swellendam where he was appointed clerk of works to the municipality. Later he was to work for various civil engineering firms engaged in developments within the Cape Province, sometimes too far away for him to be able to return to his family at weekends.

Swellendam, renowned for its avenues of fine oaks, lies in the valley of the Cornlands River, almost enclosed by the Langeberg range of mountains. Founded in 1747, it is old by South African standards. What wealth there is within the town has been generated chiefly by the wool farmers of that region. Gawie relates, 'We didn't recognize how poor people were in those days because everybody used to be poor. Within the framework of our community I suppose we were sort of average, so there were no inhibiting factors in the sense that you had a bad image of yourself. We were very self-confident and I think that we were generally quite happy. We enjoyed playing, but we didn't enjoy studies. At school I played rugby. I'm kind of sorry today that I didn't take up any other sports, but in those days if you played tennis the other boys saw you as a sissy. You play *rugby* if you're a boy, a South African.'

When he was a child there were still coloured families living in houses in between those of the white people, but they were being gradually removed to the coloured township adjacent to the white town. Government policy directed towards preserving jobs in the western Cape for the coloureds meant that few blacks were seen in the area. The coloured and white people shared the Afrikaans language and Gawie remarks on their cultural similarities. 'Children accept things much easier than adults and we never really realized when we played together that we were any different. The distinctive coloured Afrikaans accent came later, probably when they were separated from the whites. When I was small, and even now, you still had coloured people who spoke with a perfect Afrikaans accent.' His parents never voiced any objection to his playing with coloured children.

It was a religious household and discipline within the family was strict. 'My father was, and still is, a very soft-hearted person; his anger built up slowly and then once we'd pushed him over the edge, then he'd not just give one of us a hiding, but tackle the whole lot. A tall order and a big job and he got it done with and then everybody behaved for another week or so. Of course with nine children around the house,' Gawie pauses to enjoy the humour of the situation seen in retrospect, 'if you *didn't* do that . . .' He has the feeling that parents in those days regarded the rearing of their children in a less pecuniary fashion than is common today. 'Nowadays, if you talk about children, the very first thing people do is to start doing sums and see whether they can afford it or not. So many whites tell you that their wives have to work because they can't afford the cost of living. And then, often, you look around and find the person telling you these things drives a BMW, he lives in a 100,000 rand house, he has a pool in the back yard, he goes on vacation once or twice a year and he can afford lots of luxuries which my mother and dad never could afford. We never went out to eat because my mother was an excellent cook; there was no pie she couldn't bake. Anyway, how do you take a bunch of kids along with you and have a quiet time at a restaurant? Not that there were what you would call restaurants, just little general cafés, or if you wanted to splash out you could eat at the hotel. We never felt that we were missing anything. We didn't know any better. Mother did the cooking, and for most of our lives she did the housework herself, though occasionally she had a young coloured woman servant in for a few hours in the day.

'An important factor which many people overlook is the parents' vision for their children. I would have felt very bad if I had disappointed my father. He put education first. His meagre income was spent to raise nine children. We didn't have a motor car for most of the time; it was only during later years, when there were only four children left in the household, that my father bought a little *bakkie* as a form of transport. The priorities were different.' All nine children matriculated and five have university degrees. Those who grow up in Swellendam tend to marry in the district and to stay in the area; Gawie is the only member of his family who has moved away.

There were no family holidays for, as Gawie points out, to get nine children on the road would have required a tremendous amount of administration, not to say expense. School vacations were spent on the farm belonging to his elder sister Ina's husband where he 'helped out' by milking cows and learning to do other chores, so that the days were a blend of play and work: 'If you have to open a gate regularly for someone, then in the meantime you ride the gate (which you're not allowed to do).' Harvesting potatoes, he reserved the tiniest ones for his war games, 'I used an old blade to cut them up into soldiers. A little spear could penetrate them. I remember I played with them a lot.' Games were improvised and developed under their own momentum. 'We didn't have a lot of toys and so made do with substitutes. We could be playing in the mud somewhere and talking and building castles in the sky. We let things go their own way. I don't know whether it's like that in Europe, with children more spontaneous than adults.'

He went to an Afrikaans-medium school in the town and matriculated in 1971, emerging able to express only a few basic essentials in English. 'I cannot remember encountering English-speaking people. There never was any feeling against the English as such, but amongst the group of Afrikaans-speaking kids we had this funny thing of making fun of each other when it came to speaking English. So it was a bit of a torture to actually stand up in class and speak English – that put us off quite a lot. I could read a book in English and understand it, no problem, because after I'd exhausted all the Afrikaans books in the little library I read English ones. I preferred non-fiction, books on biological subjects: animals, plants, biology, zoology – life is so short and there is so much to learn.'

There followed a period of compulsory military service. 'I was quite childish when I left school. I'm glad I went because I was used to the discipline at school; in those days corporal punishment was very much "in" still and we were strictly disciplined at school and I was disciplined in my household, so I could face the Army – just another form of discipline. We did our training in Potchefstroom, about 600 miles from home. That was the first time I had been away from home, removed from a very warm household, quite a psychologically traumatic experience for me at the time. Especially during that first week in the Army I missed my family a lot, but after that it was adapt or die. And after all these years now you tend to forget your family ... I won't say forget them, but you definitely don't think of them all of your spare time.'

Mediocre matric results having put paid to any prospects of furthering his education, Gawie's interest in biology prompted him to reply to an advertisement for a vacancy at a pathological laboratory in Cape Town. 'They dissected and analysed human tissue; it seemed rather a grisly job. Everybody there was English and my English, at that time, was bad. I was a total stranger in an absolutely alien environment. I talked to one guy there and he made it clear that I'd probably never become anything unless I furthered my education. I think that made up my mind.'

The Department of Education granted him a teaching bursary at the Afrikaans-medium University of Stellenbosch where he lived in digs with two friends. 'I enjoyed being a student, carefree and only working hard when you have to. When work was not demanding then it's just nice being out in the street, having a cup of coffee at a street café, talking with other students, enjoying life. Stellenbosch has a fine climate during spring and summer and it is such a beautiful place, although you don't always realize it when you're actually in the midst of it; only afterwards you realize you didn't appreciate it, didn't grasp the opportunities to exploit each and every little bit of that privilege.' It was generally possible to find someone with a car into which students could pile, sharing the cost of the petrol, and in half an hour to be diving into the huge rollers that crashed along a seemingly end-less stretch of beach. He played rugby and went to as many movies and plays as his pocket-money, 5 rand a week, would allow. 'Life was much cheaper and you don't need much when you're a student. Beers were occasional luxuries. I remember once I went on a blind date to a *braai* [a *braaivleis*, where meat was cooked on open fires]. 'I had to cater for her needs as well, so I bought a few lamb chops, a piece of sausage, a bottle of wine and firewood and I got quite a lot of change from my 5 rand.'

Student politics failed to interest him. 'I actually felt a sort of revulsion from politics because it becomes so nasty so easily. Mostly, it is totally illogical. The history of this country and of other countries demonstrates the amount of illogical develop-ment that has gone on during the years. If someone from outer space had to look at our political records on this planet and try to deduce our intelligence coefficient from that, we'd score low indeed. Even now, during our last elections, this ugly thing is rearing its head again. Among Afrikaners it seems (this is only an opinion, a feeling, I don't state facts) this sort of thing is starting to appear where people can't tolerate each other because of different political opinions. They're breaking up meetings. I was wary of subjects where you couldn't stand up and say, these are the facts, the cold, analytical facts, as we do in science. You can't do that in politics.'

Increasingly, studies absorbed him and following his gradu-ation and a year of teaching, he returned for a post-graduate degree. 'Then I started to like it, went on to do an M.Sc. in physics.' He was looking for a job at the time and wanted to stay in the Cape, but found that he was over-qualified for the few vacancies that existed in his field. 'I was approached in 1979 by a guy from the Atomic Energy Corporation, a semi-government organization, at Pelindaba, in the hills between Krugersdorp and Pretoria, and I had to take the job he offered because I didn't have any other options.' He was subjected to the customary security checks, but doesn't believe that these are influenced by politics. 'We have people of all sorts of political opinions working there.'

In December 1979, his final year at university, he married Katherina Petronella Maria Taljaard, whom he calls Petra. She was a qualified primary school teacher, two years younger than he and a companion of his childhood. 'We went on holiday for one solitary week, rushed back to Stellenbosch, submitted my thesis, had my oral examination. The very day that I heard I had passed the examination, we packed our few possessions and made for the Transvaal. Very much of a rush.' Full-time study was a luxury; he would do his Ph.D. while engaged in thermo-nuclear research at the Nuclear Development Corporation at Pelindaba. After a year in Pretoria where Petra worked at the Council for Scientific and Industrial Research, the Nothnagels bought the house in Gordon Grey Street and moved to Krugersdorp. Gawie travels the 50 kilometres to Pelindaba by bus each day, during which time he does most of his reading. There is still a lot of basic research to be done in his field of tokamak (the Russian acronym for 'torroidal magnetic chamber') plasma physics and he enjoys the challenge. 'The problem is that one tends, in South Africa, to be hampered by technology. You've got to order some of your equipment from overseas and the exchange rate is against you and politics is against you. Sometimes it takes six months to get a piece of equipment here.'

'Being a scientist nowadays means that you have to work very hard in a rather specialized field. Science has become a monster. It is an exceptionally bright or great scientist who can master all fields. The normal scientist is usually a hard worker who is very dedicated to his specialized field.' The experiments on which Gawie is working are of the huge, thermo-nuclear variety, aimed at a new means of generating electricity, using the same methods that the sun uses, to create, as Gawie puts it, a little artificial sun down on earth.

His father had been a National Party member for as far back as Gawie can remember. 'Politics in South Africa has for many years been an inherited thing, an emotional thing. Like in the case of the Germans, the Afrikaner was dictated to by that same sort of feeling, a *volksgevoel*. Now "*volk*" means nation, but has emotional connotations; a nation can be heterogeneous; a "*volk*"- can never be heterogeneous. There is a triangular relationship', he explains, 'between the Dutch Reformed Church and the National Party, with Afrikaans at the centre. The binding factor in the "*volk*" is the history and the suffering.' He says he is 'very much a non-political type of person. I cast my vote every now and then for what I thought was right, but I never got involved with politics at all. In fact, I thought that most politicians were rather stupid and therefore I never considered political issues, like whether it is the correct thing, for instance, to move poeple from one location to another. I never gave it much thought. I kind of just accepted that that was an acceptable political practice, and that's it.'

He bought his house in Gordon Grey Street in 1982. 'It was an established fact that the people of the nearby black township of Munsieville were to be moved to Kagiso, the larger black township south of Krugersdorp. You could have phoned the government then and they would have told you that Munsieville is moving. It has been OK'd. Everything was ready for Munsieville to move. The infrastructure had been created in Kagiso. There was no indication that Munsieville was going to grow or expand into a major black township.' Had he known, at the time of buying his house, that Munsieville was to remain in much the same form, he believes he would have had no objection. 'You know, they never bothered us. We never bothered them. And we lived as neighbours for quite a few years without any confrontation, without the slightest sign of friction. They walked through our residential areas to and from work. As far as I have seen, no white man has ever interfered with them.' There have, on occasion, been incidents of whites attacking blacks, blacks attacking whites, but these, Gawie believes, should be viewed as crime, not as a major political trend.

Early in 1985 the government, pressured by the international opprobrium that its forced removal of black communities had occasioned, declared that such removals would be suspended. In October the Deputy Minister of Constitutional Development and Planning, Mr Sam de Beer, a relatively enlightened member of the National Party, announced that Munsieville, under threat of removal for twenty-five years, would be allowed to remain and would be upgraded. He explained that he was aware that this decision might not meet with approval of all parties, but urged its acceptance in 'a spirit of goodwill and co-operation', Such a turnabout in government policy was not palatable to all of its supporters; for those who stood towards and beyond the right of the ruling party, perhaps half the voters of the area, it was anathema.

Gawie is critical of the response the situation elicited from the media. He speaks precisely and gently, sometimes hesitant, searching for the right English word. 'The press appears to be in agreement that the Munsieville/Dan Pienaarville situation can be seen as a model for South Africa as a whole. Therefore one expects reporting of a calibre that suits such a grave topic. One would expect good, factual reporting, taking into account the views of people of different communities and groups. The people of the rest of the country, to whom this matter is one of concern, could then see the problem from various angles so that they could appreciate the difficulties and the desirability for a solution that is acceptable to both the black and the white communities. Instead, the way the press has handled the issue has served to exacerbate dissension and any latent violence.

'For the first time in my life I was in a position to evaluate the factual content of press reporting in our country and I must say that it is extremely sloppy.' He refers to logical incompatibilities, factual errors and 'figments of imagination' in some accounts in various newspapers and mentions a story about white hooligans in balaclava helmets invading black townships in the area, leaving, 'a path of bloodshed and destruction' in their wake. 'You know one absurdity about the whole situation is that the reporter there mentions that the whites went into the black township, Kagiso, by bicycle, at night. That is the most absurd notion! Can you tell me that a white man will go at night-time into Kagiso by bicycle! He doesn't know the township; he doesn't know where to go – it is totally impossible! A reporter must be able to separate fallacy from truth.' It would appear, Gawie maintains, that the press is bent on highlighting confrontation and disinclined to explore important, but less sensational aspects, such as the views of those who would prefer to work towards a peaceful solution.

Most people, he tells you, are scared. Weapon caches found in the vicinity were given sensational press and television coverage. A petrol bomb was thrown into the house four doors up from Gawie's. 'People's nerves got worked up and they were grasping at straws and in the end, every human being seems to be rather selfish. What matters is what is going to happen to his pocket. And the right-wing parties and other groups exploited this confusion, basically to get votes. They maintained that the government had broken its promise to move Munsieville. There was an *Aksie Groep* [Action Group], and the Afrikaner Weerstandsbeweging and political groups that involved themselves in this for their own ends. That exploitation of the situation harmed the people of Dan Pienaarville more than they will ever realize. In the process they devalued our houses by kicking up the dust, making this an issue which was reported even in the *Los Angeles Times*, for instance – all over the *globe* the story went – so that everybody knows that the people in Dan Pienaarville expect their houses to fall in value. It's the old vicious circle: now who's going to buy here?'

In 1986 Gawie, together with Ronnie Standring and Anton Wilkins, both of whom own houses in Gordon Grey Street, formed a committee whose purpose was to preserve good relations with the people of Munsieville. The committee members do not know to which political party the others belong, nor are they linked to any of the other groups that, as he puts it, lurk in the shadow of political parties. They had resolved that they would act non-politically, simply as white residents. 'We wanted Munsieville upgraded so that we don't have this huge disparity between the average standard of living of two neighbouring groups. At the moment there are a myriad of squatter shanties spread all over the back yards of the registered premises in Munsieville. And particularly in the winter, they build open fires so that when we have temperature inversions (which happens quite often in wintertime in this vicinity) the whole area is covered in a thick blanket of smoke which comes right over our houses. The soot particles in the air make it impossible for my wife to hang out the washing. To an outsider such things might sound like mere trivialities, but they are practicalities. Most people don't see these things from a political vantage point.'

There are people who cannot accept the proximity of blacks and, he surmises, those who feel much the same about whites. 'But let's not talk about extreme opinions, because I do believe that extremists tend to be in the minority,' a shadow of a smile, 'I'd *like* to believe it, let's put it that way.' It is practicalities, he reiterates, and not politics, that concern him and his fellow property owners. What is going to happen to the value of their property? A four-lane highway – not, Gawie hastens to interpolate, a kind of Berlin wall, but a necessary conduit for traffic, planned four or more years ago – is being built parallel to and 60 metres away from Gordon Grey Street. The people of Munsieville will then be permitted to build their houses to its western border. 'That will bring them within 60 or 70 metres, while at present they are 300 metres away. Immediately, people might think that racism is gradually creeping into the conversation. That has nothing to do with it. It's an absolutely practical issue. There are basic socio-economic differences between those people there and us.' His fear is that this extension of housing for blacks will bring with it the accompaniment of backyard squatters and increased problems of pollution. 'If the government is to keep its word then it may not move any people. The squatters will stay. They are very much a practical reality of Munsieville and every other average black township in this country today and there are going to be *more* of them as they come to the metropolitan areas for job opportunities.

'Now the only concern of the people of Dan Pienaarville is that that kind of housing, shooting up within sight, with the proportionately increased pollution and of course, visual pollution – without being nasty – I mean, you look out on a shanty town, on . . . quite a camp, from your back door. The question is, will that not make Dan Pienaarville an unacceptable residential area for future buyers in general? Will not property owners lose more of what is probably their only material asset of any real worth?

'Obviously, if one wants to set an example in Krugersdorp, and if one wants to devise a system that works, where blacks and whites can live as neighbours, close together, without annoying one another, then the solution must involve satisfaction for both groups. The government must put its money where its mouth is and immediately start to upgrade Munsieville and eliminate pollution of all kinds, including visual pollution – that's a word I just created; I don't know if it's an acceptable term.' From time to time Gawie has meticulously repeated himself in order, as he explains, that he may not be misunderstood.

The little committee would seem to have been largely replaced by a study group, consisting of Gawie and Mr Wilkins (representing the residents of Dan Pienaarville) and four others. Mr Hayden (Gawie thinks he is a member of the Conservative Party) together with Mrs Botes, represent the Ratepayers' Association. Dr Pretorius, a local businessman, representing the National Party, is the group's chairman. Initially the two parties to the right of the government, the Conservative Party and the Herstigte Nasionale Party, nominated representatives to the group, but they later withdrew. 'Eventually the CP and the HNP didn't want anything to do with it because they maintained the standpoint that Munsieville had to go and they would participate in no further discussions on the subject.' The study group members planned to talk to the city councils of black Kagiso and white Krugersdorp and proposed a thorough survey of the main problems such as pollution, the expansion of Munsieville, the squatter problem, the devaluing of their property. They explored the possibility of creating a mutual facility for sport or leisure on the present vacant stretch of ground between the two communities.

'Munsieville must be restructured in such a way that it makes some sort of social sense. Within any community you have your areas where your poorer people stay and where your richer people stay. All that I'm trying to achieve is to have the richer people in parity, closer to the richer people on the other side, the white side, instead of a social inversion, which makes it unacceptable to one of the parties. One must try to work out a win-win situation.' Eddie Moketsi, the mayor of Kagiso, with whom Gawie once discussed the problem, readily understood and expressed his own distaste for the socio-economic climate of Munsieville, saying that that was the reason he himself did not stay there.

The squatters who have erected their shelters in the Munsieville back yards constitute the most serious problem in that their dwellings are an eyesore and it is chiefly the smoke from their fires that creates the sooty smog. They are part of a community of scores of thousands that squat in what is known as the PWV (Pretoria, Witwatersrand, Vereeniging) area. Makeshift shelters in open areas have been regularly demolished by the authorities, but as they have nowhere else to go the people rebuild the structures. One researcher estimates that an area twice the size of the present Soweto is needed to rehouse squatters in the PWV area. As the government at last lowers its previous impractically high housing standards, authorities in some areas have begun to introduce feasible low-income housing schemes.

The Nothnagels, who attend the Nederduitse Gereformeerde Kerk in the adjacent suburb of Rantendal, are unconcerned about their Church's recently pronounced 'open-doors' policy which admits people of all races to the congregation. 'In fact we have a black child, adopted by white parents, in our church at the moment, so she is a member of our congregation and we accept it that way. I don't think that most people are worried that black people can become members of the congregation; it's just that some people, I believe, are just a little bit scared that, with their huge numbers, the whole traditional outlook of the Church might eventually change. But I don't share these fears of the Church being swamped by black people because I believe that you would go where you feel welcome and where you feel at ease.' In his opinion, the considerable number of people who have left his church as a result of the 'open doors' policy, 'are just transplanting their problem in time and space. Their new church is going to come up with the same problem in a couple of years' time, that's for sure. And after all, there'll be no moving to another suburb when you get to heaven and find all the black people there.'

In Gawie's view, the emergence of an integrated society is absolutely inevitable: 'There are more blacks in the first two grades of primary school in South Africa at the moment than there are whites in all the educational institutions in the country. Could you imagine for one moment that an integrated society is going to be warded off by a white minority group? But people, particularly those with a conservative viewpoint, need time to adapt their views and beliefs. Now obviously, you don't have decades of time left, but on the other hand, if you force things on to people too fast, what you build is not an understanding of the problem, but a revolt against change. When it comes to people's pockets there is resistance; when one group is asked to pay for political change in the country as a whole, without any return of any kind, except a kind word and a plea to understand – people don't respond to that.'

History, Gawie maintains, shows that almost all attempts to create peaceful reform have failed, 'but if the history of this world has to be the law that governs the future, then I don't want to live here. So I am positive, and I believe that history is there to learn lessons from and not to govern the future of mankind. We just *have* to make this thing work in South Africa because there is no other solution. There is only one solution, and that is that everybody should create some space, living space, for other people. If the whites don't do it now for the blacks, then what chance do they have to demand that from the blacks at a later stage?'

He abhors violence, whether from the right or the left, but

sees no immediate prospect of its cessation. 'While the govern-ment is busy with reforms the people will demand more and they will grow impatient. The radical groups will misuse this for personal political ends, like so many groups misuse our situ-ation here, and violence will be with us for quite a spell yet, I'm sure of that. I think that what will stop it is a dispensation in which blacks have a say in political matters, where they can start to rule their own people and solve their own problems.'

Questioned as to how he would feel about blacks being given a vote in the central parliament, Gawie pauses. 'I'm not very *fond* of politics in the sense that I would make it my pastime to think politically, but I do think about it more and more as my children grow up because now I have some sort of investment. There really is only one way out for this country. We *have* to find a political system or structure wherein all people can partici-pate and we must find a way to satisfy all the groups in this country so that we can live together within the same country as different culture groups without any artificial laws eventually that separate these groups from one another. In fact, I foresee that in the future the government of this country will be multi-racial, including the blacks, because we know now that creating countries within countries is not going to solve the problems of South Africa in the long term. I suppose that everybody has realized that except for . . . I know that there are quite a lot of Afrikaans-speaking people who are against this change because they are afraid that the Afrikaner will lose his identity alto-gether.'

Gawie pursues his life with apparent equanimity. His property is unfenced, the lawn is mown, the flower beds trim. There is no noticeable burglar-proofing, no electronic anti-theft devices. The front door is not particularly sturdy. Upon being questioned, he said he owned no firearms, but volunteered, almost apologet-ically, that he had recently bought two fire extinguishers. 'That is only a sensible precaution.'

The Nothnagels' sitting-room has been furnished with natural pinewood and carefully chosen bric-a-brac. There are many pieces of heavy ecru lacework, little cushions covered in pastel satin and silk, and an assortment of exquisitely dressed, old-fashioned dolls sit on the dresser, on shelves, or inside open cupboards. Petra's clear colouring, wide eyes and dark hair falling in curls to her shoulders, accord with the setting. Gawie says, 'My wife has very much an opinion of her own, but in general we have the same views, not', he hastens to add, 'because *I* have those views. She formulates her own ideas or modifies some to suit her purpose.'

How does he see the future? 'I have no choice but to be positive. I can feel the change in attitude amongst people. And the few blacks I meet are the same.' Research opportunities might lure him overseas for a time, but he would always return. 'Africa grows on you. If ever I *had* to flee, it would probably be to another African country. I'm an Afrikaner, meaning I am a resident of Africa. I have no inclination or tendency to move anywhere else. This is why one must be tolerant. We have to learn to be more tolerant. We must discuss these things: attitudes, not politics. I always respect other people's opinions even if I can't go along with them. I still try to find out why that guy feels the other way and what makes him afraid and what makes him believe it's not going to work.

'I can see this country generating enough wealth if only we can start a system where all groups have a say and are satisfied with preliminaries – the majority of them; you'll never get all people being satisfied. Then you can start to build this country economically. There's a vast potential among the Third World blacks. They are sitting there, waiting to be trained, waiting to be utilized. The inhibiting factors must be totally removed. I'm afraid that many radical blacks see the future of this country as some radical whites see it, that it is meant exclusively for their faction.'

BILL WILSON

THE ROAD FROM Nelspruit to Malelane runs eastward along the valley of the Crocodile River whose waters, bountiful by South African standards, irrigate the citrus, pecan-nut and avocado orchards. Half an hour out of the town the mountains of the Crocodile Pass, studded with huge rocks, rise steeply on either side for a mile or so and then give way to sugar cane and banana plantations. In the river, which now forms the southern border of the Kruger National Park, crocodiles lie immobile on sandy banks in wait for the antelope who come to drink.

Independent Swaziland is south of Malelane, through the Jeppe's Reef border post, a country of mountains and fertile valleys, watered by many small rivers. Neat and whitewashed general stores with names like 'Lomsayi Nkaba Bhungane Vukane' and 'Phophonyane Jakiza' occur at intervals as the road climbs towards Piggs Peak. This is Swazi country. Approved white people are given permission to live or trade here.

At a turnoff a gravel road crosses the Phophonyane River as it falls over a series of flat rocks, potentially fatal when wet to any but the sure-footed goats. After passing through the bluegum plantations you enter the hillside land owned by Bill and Pidie Wilson. The deeply thatched roof sweeps down from above the upstairs bedroom to below the shining expanse of the leaves of the Swiss Cheese Plant and the massed blue of the petrea creeper. From the front terrace there is a vista of mountains jutting and falling towards the horizon and a wide valley between. Most of the indigenous bush near the house has been cleared, leaving the finest specimens of trees which, in response to their new-found light and water, have grown in strangely beautiful shapes. Water conducted from the river gurgles into a large pond, fringed with reeds and blue water iris; a Muscovy duck is tail up, diving for plants. A family of three geese and three goslings patrols the lawns and paths, warning the chickens to keep their distance and lowering their heads, beaks agape, to pursue any dog who ventures near. In a large open area under the soaring thatch wide sofas which can be converted into beds are backed with mounds of huge cushions, covered in mohair woven in a variety of jewel colours by Swazi women in a workshop on the opposite mountain. Tables are cluttered with books, papers, seeds and country paraphernalia.

Bill Wilson has just returned from an early morning climb with his dogs through the grassy avenues that intersect the plantations and up to the summit of Kobolondlo, a mountain of ancient granite. His shoes are strong, his country clothes comfortably worn. He is kindly and courteous, a tall man with a high forehead and greying, receding hair. He has breakfast with Pidie at the long wooden table that stands on the terrace with benches on either side. Pidie is tall, with high cheekbones and large, dark eyes, given to wearing casual combinations of clothes. A woman of verve and originality, she spends time painting in a wooden hut on the hill behind.

Bill, christened William Douglas Wilson, was born on 31 July 1915 at 54 Richmond Avenue, Auckland Park, an unfashionable suburb with wide, treelined streets in the western part of Johannesburg. It adjoined artisan and working-class areas. His father, Douglas Wilson, a Scot from Dumfries, had left school aged fourteen after the death of his father. He was articled to a firm of solicitors there and after qualifying came to South Africa. Within a few years in Johannesburg he became a partner of a Mr Routledge. Routledge and Douglas Wilson was to become a highly esteemed legal practice. His mother, also Scottish and born Jessie Frances Purves, came out to South Africa to visit old friends. She met and married Douglas Wilson in 1911. Bill describes his parents as 'Down-to-earth; honest, straightforward; very much part of what I suppose you'd call a bourgeois type of thinking that professional Scots people have. Absolutely excellent, but without any pretension. They didn't lack taste, their taste was quite good, but they didn't have money to spend on luxuries.' There was little emotional overspill. 'Both of them kept their problems and difficulties to themselves and my brother and I did the same. This was not a calculated, carefully thought-out policy, but more a custom amongst Scots which had advantages and disadvantages; the principal disadvantage is that communication is reduced. On balance, as between this approach which does lead to one's taking responsibility and initiative for oneself and the close communication found in other families, I think the latter is preferable. I am sad now that I know so little about how my mother and father felt and that there is no way of finding out.' He is proud of his Scots ancestry and remarks how, whenever he finds himself in Scotland and hears the accents of his father and mother he feels at home, happy and secure. They were good, square Scots, Bill remarks, who lived an austere life, both in a fiscal and a social sense. 'I was greatly influenced by their attitudes. We were never in the slightest doubt that they would make any sacrifice to secure us good educations, and they did, in fact, make considerable sacrifices.'

Bill's schooling began at St Katharine's, a kindergarten and early primary school for boys and girls in Escombe Avenue, Parktown. He describes Mrs Fielding, who ran the well-known school for so many years, as a 'fierce and outstanding woman'. 'In 1922 the first shots from the armed white miners' strike, which was nearly a civil war, were fired from the Brixton Ridge, half a mile from our house, at the Police Station and Transvaal Horse Artillery headquarters a couple of hundred yards away. Great excitement. For two or three days we were forbidden to leave the house. A soldier was billeted with us and a machine-gun sited on open ground opposite.' Bill was seven years old. He and his brother watched the final artillery and aerial bombardment on entrenched striker remnants in Vrededorp and later the defeated strikers being marched under guard along Kingsway to Milner Park. 'They were haggard, unkempt, unshaven, exhausted, demoralized.' The violence of the experience and the misery and despair left a lasting impression on Bill. Wages of white miners were cut by 25 to 50 per cent and many lost their semi-skilled jobs to blacks working for less pay.

At the age of eight Bill went to St John's, an Anglican boys' school whose fine stone buildings merge into the rugged beauty of the Houghton Ridge. Together with his elder brother, John, he would bicycle the five miles each way from Auckland Park to school. He became aware of and opposed to violence on a different level from that of the miners' strike. The last part of their ride home was through Richmond, the home at that time of unskilled manual labourers, mostly Afrikaners. 'The children there were a lot of very tough young men who, I suppose, not unnaturally, had a profound contempt for these English *rooinek* children who were not nearly as tough as they were.' The *rooineks* (literally, red-necks) would also have been seen as rich. 'They used to gather in small groups up a side street, with their bicycles at the ready, and wait for victims.' The two young Wilsons, not yet in their teens, developed a strategy. 'We would pause at the Sans Souci Hotel to get our breath, get all geared up and then ride as fast as we possibly could through Richmond and into the Country Club which was a sanctuary, for the various black guards would come to your assistance. But they did catch my brother once and gave him quite a beating-up.' Rides to town on the tram were fraught with the same kind of danger. 'We referred to them [the Afrikaners] as *jaapies* and would sit as far away as possible from them and try to avoid getting into so much as a conversation with them because it would invariably end in the threat of physical violence. I was frightened and I dare say my brother was too. I seemed to be rather better at escaping it than he because he got beaten up twice.

'They were rough diamonds, the Afrikaners I'm speaking of. Many had been *bywoners* [sharecroppers] who'd been forced off the land, drifted into the towns in search of work, and become poor whites. They were not equipped for industrial work, didn't have the training or the educational background to earn a decent living. I remember, in one of our Afrikaans matric set books, reading of the appalling hardships these people, driven off the land, had faced and how they had had to come and work competitively with people who were much better equipped for industrial life in Johannesburg than they.' English-speakers dominated the trade unions at the time and generally excluded Afrikaners.

Years later, in the Middle East, Bill was to come upon an Air Force officer. Swapping notes about their background, they discovered that they were the same age and that the officer had lived in Richmond. 'I asked him, "You weren't, by any chance, one of those thugs who used to chase us?" And he said, yes, he was. And here he was, Commander of a South African Fighter Squadron, with a DSO and bar and a DFC and bar, and a famous South African pilot.'

At thirteen, having become a prefect at his primary school, Bill went to Michaelhouse, the Anglican boarding-school set among the rolling hills of the Natal midlands. 'Michaelhouse was a wonderful period in my life. I liked the country enormously, the greenness and the mists and the rain and the cold and the streams; I thought it was a kind of paradise. The school itself, in those days, was quite primitive. During winter it was perpetually bitterly cold; there were hardly any fires and very little hot water. The food was almost exclusively mealie-meal porridge, except for lunch where stale bread and cheese broke the uniformity. We had extraordinarily poor food, but it didn't seem to do us any harm. I was enormously happy there.' It was at this time that he first became involved in religion in a way he describes as deep and secret. Compulsory twice daily chapel attendance, loathed by many, gave him an opportunity to practise his religion without drawing attention to himself. 'I think if there had been a perspicacious chaplain when I was at school I might easily have gone into the Church. It was never suggested by anybody and I was dedicated to the idea of following in my father's legal footsteps.'

On Sundays the boys were given a packet of sandwiches and allowed to go anywhere they liked; no one was permitted to remain within the school bounds. He and his friends would run over the hills as far as the Karkloof Valley and back, a considerable distance.

One of the few difficulties which he encountered early on at school was the system of initiation. 'It was quite rough,' he remembers. The boys were not physically hurt, 'but they were scared stiff. It took place on Saturday evenings and I used to go out of the school, into the fields and lie down in the long grass and come back when the bell went. That was an entirely effective method of escape.'

His skills and enjoyments ranged widely. He became head prefect and because of his distaste for violence did all he could to stop the initiation process and declined to exercise his right to administer corporal punishment. He gained a first class matric, did well at all games, was captain of rugby and played cricket for the school. He had a deep regard and affection for Kenneth Pennington, his housemaster. 'Ken Pennington was one of the Michaelhouse heroes; he was a fine games player in 1913/14 and he gained distinctions in the Royal Air Force Flying Corps in the war. He was awarded a Rhodes Scholarship and, after qualifying as a barrister, terminated what seemed to be a highly promising career in favour of teaching. He felt it to be his vocation and he was certainly an excellent teacher, maths and history. He was loved or hated.' After leaving school Bill became a personal friend of Pennington and his wife Ruth, often staying with them. Years later, in 1975, he was able to discharge in part the enormous debt he felt he owed to Pennington by helping to publish Pennington's *Butterflies of Southern Africa*, a book based on a manuscript left by Ken Pennington on his death.

Bill's father was doing well but 'we didn't have a lot of money splashing around. In 1928 we had a stroke of good luck because in that year the Californian citrus crop failed.' The small citrus farm Mr Wilson owned at Olifant's Nek near Rustenburg and which up to that date had hardly ever made a profit, suddenly produced a huge crop which sold very well on world markets. 'My father made something like 6,000 pounds, a lot of money by our standards. It paid for my brother and me to go to

Cambridge.' So, in October 1933, at eighteen, having stayed on in a post-matric class for the first half of the year, he went to Trinity Hall, Cambridge, a college with strong legal ties. He is not aware of there having been any problems in gaining admittance to Trinity Hall, but supposes that his record as head boy and captain of rugby at Michaelhouse, together with the recommendation of the rector, Donald Currie, a well-known Rhodes Scholar, must have been factors. Ever mindful of his commitment to follow in his father's legal footsteps, he knew he would go to the Bar. 'It was towards the end of the great depression. At that time one didn't have a lot of career guidance, but simply worked out how you could get a job. Your choice of a career was bound up with "How the hell can I make enough money to live!"'

Bill arrived in England with very little experience of life outside his boarding school; too young, he feels, to understand how to take advantage of the considerable range of opportunities which Cambridge offered. 'The impact of arriving in England for a country cousin like me was really very considerable, particularly in a place like Cambridge where you had these ancient and wonderful buildings.' He missed the space and sunshine of South Africa, but he was far from unhappy and made some good friends.

During the 1930s there were a considerable number of communists at Cambridge. When Bill got into the Trinity Hall cricket team in his first year. Donald Maclean was captain of the side. 'He caused a sensation because he resigned from the Trinity Hall cricket team. Such a resignation meant that his life had changed in a dramatic way. I imagine it was because he had been recruited and cricket was no longer a suitable occupation for him. I didn't know him well.'

In 1936 his father died and this meant that he had to exert himself to finish his studies as soon as possible in order to be able to help care for his mother. Having passed the law tripos, he sat for the examinations for the English Bar and then the LL B at Cambridge. 'That was exhausting. About six months of that year, October till the following March 1937, I lived in London in a bedsit and it was one of the loneliest periods I've had in my entire life.'

In June 1937 he returned to Johannesburg, having passed his Bar examinations and having been called to the Bar at the Middle Temple. While waiting to write his statute law exam for admission to the South African Bar he collected debts for his brother's office. Once admitted to the Bar he settled down to occupying himself for the ten years it was generally accepted in those days it would take to become established. He furthered his legal proficiency by 'devilling', writing legal opinions for barristers who might or might not use them. 'You got nothing for it. One didn't expect it. What they would do, they would discuss your opinion with you and they'd rewrite it if they didn't agree, so that you learnt an enormous amount on the way through.' He became secretary of the Bar Council which he enjoyed and he would get small briefs from his brother and friends of his father. 'I've always had the highest regard for various firms who briefed me in those days. I can still remember them, so you can see how important a brief was to me.'

War came in September 1939. 'Surprisingly, perhaps, I was prepared for it. During school and university I had been strongly anti-war because of the destruction, the loss of life, the futility; not a pacifist because I did not believe wars could be avoided totally and that, in certain circumstances, one might have to involve oneself. I had also been to Germany several times, had liked some Germans greatly and had been impressed by their achievement in emerging from hopeless despair and decay to a confident people of ability and energy, moving towards economic recovery. However, some of those I knew in Germany were Jews and I had a friend from childhood who was at Cambridge, Martin Greenberg, son of the distinguished Appellate Division Judge. During my visits to Germany with Cambridge colleagues I had experiences where the apparently cheerful outer crust was torn off to reveal what seemed to be both sordid and sinister. Also, the aggressive insatiability of German demands made me totally supportive of Great Britain though extremely doubtful about her military capability and preparedness. I had joined the artillery section of Cambridge Officers' Training Corps for a couple of years when I was at university because it provided the cheapest riding, and had been to annual camps at Larkhill on Salisbury Plain where we were drilled by regular army sergeants and practised galloping into action like Colonel Long in his disastrous manoeuvre at Colenso in the Boer War.

'So the decision was easy and the day after Chamberlain announced war found me with many others at the headquarters of the Transvaal Horse Artillery, a few hundred yards from where I was born, clamouring to join up. You could only go part time then, but after Dunkirk in June 1940 I sold my law library and furniture to get some cash and went into the army full time. There was nothing to stop me. My old mother was all right financially and there were no clients to disappoint.'

After the appropriate course, he was appointed to the Air Liaison Section of the 1st South African Division which was posted to Marsabit in Kenya in December. From there he moved with the squadron to Moyale, in southern Abyssinia. 'In the mess in the evenings Air Force pilots, most of them only eighteen or nineteen years old, would begin the argument which got as boring as hell, about how the Air Force could win the war on its own. Of course they were baiting me and got a bit of fun out of it because I would explain again and again the essential part played by the Army. One night, when I made my usual speech defending the Army, to my amazement one of the Air Force people said he absolutely supported me and that the others were talking nonsense. That's how I met Keith Acutt and we became very good friends. He was a chap who became important wherever he was, a bright and entertaining character.' It was a friendship that was maintained as they found themseves stationed near one another at various times during the war.

The campaign in southern Abyssinia was over quickly and the South African troops moved up through the Red Sea to Alexandria where an Australian division helped to repair and service their battered transport vehicles. They assisted in the evacuation from the Alexandria docks of the British forces who had escaped from the German attack on Crete. 'It was a terrible experience. The ships and men had been under constant attack not only by parachutists but by virtually unopposed German aircraft for days. The

Orion was one of the ships most damaged by German attacks, suffering a direct hit which penetrated the mess deck at mealtime with frightful consequences.' Not many days later, the 1st South African Division moved into the desert.

'Through my readings in the Bible, of the lives of the desert fathers, Muhammad, the Sufis, *The Seven Pillars of Wisdom*, Saint-Exupéry's *Wind, Sand and Stars*, I knew and had long been attracted by deserts. During our eighteen months or so in the Western Desert, much of which was spent in relative inactivity, my understanding of the spiritual and historical richness of the Sahara expanded. It suited my temperament, the desert – those nights with very bright stars that looked extremely close; an extraordinary sense of mysticism.'

There being little for an air liaison officer based with the 1st S.A. Division to do, Bill obtained an attachment to the Eighth Army where officers of his category were urgently needed. The work was demanding and the company good. 'One of the things that I look upon in retrospect as having been of enormous value and importance to me was being in the Army and thrown into contact with all sorts of people who, in normal circumstances I was unlikely to meet at all. And because you ate and lived largely in messes, distinctions in terms of wealth and poverty were really not there. Everything you needed in order to survive was provided. There was not much use for money; generally speaking, people used it on beer and cigarettes. There was nothing to buy out in the desert. It was a kind of egalitarian type of life of a really extraordinary time. Many of the prejudices that you find in ordinary life in peace time didn't exist and one made friends with whomever you happened to be near.'

In the Western Desert the South Africans, many of whom had made friends with British and Australians, found that the antagonisms between English and Afrikaners in their own forces seemed also to disappear. Most of the commanding officers and many of the senior staff officers were Afrikaners. 'You had people like Dan Pienaar who was really a great, very rugged, very tough sort of fellow who had the devotion of everybody, whether English or Afrikaans. They knew he would not have them killed if he could possibly avoid it.' When in 1948 the Nationalist government came into power in South Africa, with its racist policies that divided not merely black and white, but English- and Afrikaans-speaking South Africans, people like Bill recoiled in dismay. 'In the S.A. Divisions we had an incredibly happy relationship between English- and Afrikaans-speaking people. When 1948 happened it came as a real major blow and surprise. It was a shock to us after what we had felt was a breaking down in the Army of all the hostility that had been harboured for the previous forty years. We could not believe that men from the Army would have voted Nationalist.'

Bill was not to remain with the Eighth Army. 'General Pienaar, commander of the 1st S.A. Division, became incensed at the frequency with which his men on the Gazala line were being bombed not only by the Royal Air Force (which he regarded as offensive but understandable, seeing they were incompetent pommies) but even worse, by the S.A. Air Force: this he regarded as unforgivable. He instructed one of his staff to demand my return to the Division. I came back and explained how difficult it was for pilots to bomb with the extreme accuracy called for when opposing forces were in close contact in static positions and whilst the pilots were being harassed by enemy fighters and anti-aircraft fire. He cooled down, but I was out of a job.'

Within a few weeks the great German outflanking attack on the Knightsbridge area behind the Gazala line began and led remorselessly to the collapse of the line, the investment of Tobruk and the exhausting and morale-shattering withdrawal to El Alamein, the last defensible position before Alexandria and Cairo, themselves indefensible. 'Upon arrival at El Alamein the 1st S.A. Division was one of the few reasonably cohesive units left in the Western Desert. Because I was jobless I became one of Dan Pienaar's personal liaison officers and thus was close to what was going on.'

After a four month course at the British Senior Staff College at Haifa and a couple of months at home in South Africa, Bill returned to the South African forces in the middle of 1943 and was appointed to the Staff of the 6th S.A. Armoured Division.

His position as Air Liaison Officer he knew to be no particular challenge, so he leapt at the opportunity offered to him of joining the Yugoslav section of the SOE (Special Operations Executive) of the British Army. After painful interviews with his senior officers who viewed his proposed move somewhat sourly, he obtained permission to transfer to the British Army. 'I soon learned that I had become a member of an intensely interesting unit, surrounded by secrecy, playing a role of major importance in the war. The political and military significance of Yugoslavia was receiving increasing attention and the SOE organization, dealing with it from a British point of view, had already moved from its original clandestine character to a more regular, though still eccentric, operation. It was a small organization and even as a junior officer one was part of a team and was fully informed on everything that took place.'

'The original contact between Britain and Yugoslavia had been made by exceptionally brave Canadian Croats, jumping blind by parachute, in civilian clothes, at night after an eight-hour flight from Cairo; no weather forecasts and navigation by dead reckoning. There were no reception parties. Radios were strapped to their backs, phials of poison in their pockets to enable them to handle the situation if captured, gold sovereigns for trading or bribery in their bags.'

'Soon after I joined SOE the Yugoslav section was turned upside-down, totally changed its character and mode of operation. Convinced of the great political and military importance of Yugoslavia during and after the war, Winston Churchill intervened and stipulated that a new military mission to Yugoslavia be established. It was to be under the command of Fitzroy Maclean, a brilliant man in his early thirties who had had some years' experience in the Foreign Office before the war, partly in Russia, and who was promoted overnight from the rank of captain to brigadier, the cause of no little resentment. Under him were an extraordinary group of men ranging from Randolph Churchill (Winston's son) and Evelyn Waugh, the writer and a close friend of the Churchill family, through some outstanding professional soldiers. James Klugman, a British communist, who in his teens

—— 137 ——

had met Chairman Mao and was later identified as a Russian spy, was one of them. It was a strange set-up but worked astonishingly well, largely because Fitzroy had a direct radio link with Churchill, bypassing all the usual channels. This, too, was deeply resented, but no one was prepared to challenge Fitzroy or Churchill – in fact, one or two people who opened their mouths too wide had got their marching orders within twenty-four hours.

'I had never been a politically minded person. I was neither pro nor anti capitalism or socialism. I had a kind of romantic hero-type feeling about the partisans. I knew and liked James Klugman, who eventually, in the 1970s, was labelled a communist spy. He used to talk a certain amount about communism, but I was very busy and on one occasion he said, "You're just politically muddled." I was simply a staff officer, getting supplies into the field in a way that would be most effective in countering the Germans. I also went round some of the refugee camps in Italy with General Velebit, who eventually became the Yugoslav representative at the United Nations. He interviewed commissars, in English part of the time, and afterwards went out of his way to explain what he was doing, organizing the active communist elements in these refugee camps and getting the right people in office. So I got to know quite a lot about communism and the way they acquire and order power. I was never very keen on that. I didn't like that sort of manipulation of people.'

Within Yugoslavia there existed what amounted to several civil wars. Mihailovich, Minister of Defence under King Peter of Yugoslavia who headed a government in exile in London, operated chiefly in Serbia. He was opposed by Marshal Tito who, with his partisans, was stronger in the rest of the country. Tito had been trained in Russia and had, before the outbreak of war, returned to Yugoslavia where he had organized an effective underground communist network. In May 1944 the British government withdrew its support from Mihailovich and his Chetniks and thereafter concentrated upon Tito who operated in a more belligerent fashion. 'From a purely operational point of view it seemed right because the partisans were far more aggressive, holding down something like eleven German divisions, some of which would otherwise have been on the Russian front at a time when Russia was near exhaustion.' Bill was distressed at the abandonment and ultimate execution of Mihailovich whom he considered to have been a brave and loyal man.

'The Russians, sensing the importance of the operation which was being conducted by the Royal Air Force and British liaison officers (with, oddly enough, one or two South Africans), arranged to have a Russian squadron with its own commander and commissar established at Bari in southern Italy. The supplies which they flew into Yugoslavia were all British, but they would replace the "Made in England" labels with ones that read, "Made in Moscow", or something of the sort. It was an extraordinarily bizarre set-up.'

By mid-1944 most of the country outside Serbia and major towns were under the control of the partisans and it was possible to land on the strips which had been created by Royal Air Force units. Bill conceived a great admiration for the courage and endurance of the partisans. 'For a period of three years they had lived a life that almost defied description. The conditions under which they existed were not merely austere, but continuously harsh. The Germans mounted major, highly organized attacks on their positions at intervals of three to six months and they had practically nothing in the way of food, clothing or medical supplies, other than the very limited amount that we could drop into them or that they captured. They practised a simple, but complete form of communism. Everything was shared totally. It was fine. Round about the middle of 1944 this started declining, that is, the spirit of idealism, as the battle to strengthen and entrench their positions in the post-war power structure for Yugoslavia began to predominate.'

Tito, as a result of help given to him by the RAF and the United Kingdom, had become close to Fitzroy Maclean. Nevertheless, when it came to the relief of Belgrade, he played what Bill terms 'a very dirty trick' on Maclean. He allowed the Russians to gain honour and score a coup by flying him into Belgrade. Maclean, who had not been taken into Tito's confidence, nevertheless learnt of their plans. 'He was flown into Belgrade in an RAF aircraft, arriving almost simultaneously with the Russian plane. These sort of one-upmanship tricks were practised in those days. A very interesting period. We always felt that we were doing something enormously important; that was one of the satisfactions of this particular job. But as you can imagine, it was a shambles in many ways with many conflicts between people. We made a lot of personal friends among the Yugoslavs and we believed that Fitzroy Maclean had done a wonderful job with Tito. He liked and respected Tito and wrote about him. When the war was over the Russians attempted to dictate to Tito, but he stood up to them and took a courageously independent stand.' Bill believes that this may be attributed in no small part to Fitzroy Maclean and the 'eccentric sort of circus that he ran'.

Peace came to Europe in March 1945. By that time Bill had been appointed Assistant Adjutant and Quartermaster General of the Mission with the rank of Lieutenant-Colonel, and had been mentioned in despatches. He was asked to contribute to the history of the Yugoslav section for the SOE records. He observes that while it would seem that he had had a very successful war, he was not in a good frame of mind when it was all over. 'I was deeply depressed and not at all well physically. I think we all realize that we live several different lives. One leads one's working life and then you have other lives as well, interior lives that don't always fit together comfortably and which often lead to inner conflicts and unresolved paradoxes. This was certainly my situation at the age of thirty when I ended the war. I suppose that most people, at that sort of age, have the same experience. And of course, generally speaking it's not discussed and can be quite painful.'

He returned to South Africa in November 1945 and, after being discharged, returned to the Bar. But he found the fighting of minor cases unfulfilling. Keith Acutt had told him that Anglo American, the company in which he worked, would be opening new gold mines in the Orange Free State and would be needing 'a lot more people'. He introduced Bill to Harry Oppenheimer whose father, Sir Ernest Oppenheimer, offered him a position in the Anglo American Corporation which he headed. This seemed to be the opportunity he yearned for to do something constructive, so he accepted. He knew nothing about business and was uncertain as to whether the step he was about to take was a wise one. Certainly, in the beginning, his mother objected to his descent into what she saw as commerce. In time she accepted it and followed his career with interest and enjoyment.

Soon after joining Anglo American Bill became engaged to and later married Pidie Buchanan, the daughter of Dr George Buchanan, deputy director of the Institute for Medical Research. He was somewhat concerned about her relative youthfulness, 'because I became thirty-one in 1946 and she was nineteen and that seemed a prodigious difference in ages. This worried me and I made some surreptitious enquiries to make sure that she wasn't still at school.' He is amused at himself: 'I was relieved to find that she was at the Technicon doing art.'

Illustrating his ignorance of business, he recalls that one of the earliest jobs given to him was the drawing up of a debenture trust deed for the first three of the Anglo American gold mines in the Orange Free State. 'I didn't wish to disclose my ignorance and so rang up an old lawyer friend and asked him, "Now what is a debenture?" and he told me.' But he learned rapidly, both from the wise old lawyer, Ben Friel, who had kindly allowed him to share his office, and from the executive committee whose secretary he became. As all matters of major policy in Anglo American were discussed in that small and select committee he learned a good deal.

Harry Oppenheimer had also served with the South African forces in the Middle East and it was not long before Bill found himself working with him to establish the Orange Free State goldfields. The north-western Orange Free State became a familiar landscape. 'It is absolutely flat, the only pimple to mar its uniformity being Koppie Alleen [the little hill on its own]. There were no trees then, other than a few stunted bluegums around Odendaalsrus. With every gust of wind great clouds of dust rose hundreds of feet high, reducing visibility to a few hundred yards and providing striking evidence of the reality of the dustbowl threat which was then causing considerable worry in the Orange

Free State. Over the next decade or so this country was to be transformed into twelve large producing gold mines, six of them under Anglo American management, bringing with them roads, railways, towns and industries and even lakes, filled with water pumped from underground, attracting flamingoes and duck. The local farmers, Afrikaners who had worked the land for generations, found themselves overcome by events they were unable to resist. They sold their farms and moved away to remote areas, trekking away from things they did not altogether understand and did not like at all.

'This particular province, the development of the Free State gold mines, which appealed to me enormously, had been allocated to Harry by Sir Ernest. Three of us worked on it – I'm talking about the financial, administrative and non-technical side. Harry, who was chairman, Keith Acutt and myself, very junior. We worked together extremely happily. I think that it was partly the effect of the war, its egalitarian atmosphere that had appealed to me so enormously, that led to working together in this extraordinary way. The excitement and challenge of the huge undertaking was heightened by the fact that it occurred immediately after those years of killing and destruction. We were full of ideas which were not always approved by others, either in Anglo American or in the mining industry. Harry was obviously the boss, but he never even slightly took that sort of attitude. If you disagreed with him, you said so frankly, and he listened. It was a very happy relationship. People were amazingly ungrasping and little attention was paid to status or hierarchy or salaries. Certainly I was not well paid in those days, and one had to accept the responsibilities of senior office long before receiving the appropriate appointment.'

These three relatively young men, together with others working on the project, introduced many concepts new to the mining industry. These were not simply random products of rebellious thought; they were the outcome of serious, sometimes passionate, debate on the role and justification for huge companies disposing of very substantial sums of money and technical and administrative resources. 'We felt that private enterprise was inherently better equipped for the purpose than state control with its inevitable injection of political thought and interference, leading ultimately to reduced efficiency and flexibility, as well as less revenue. On the other hand, it seemed to us that major companies must take on exceptional responsibilities in relation to their own employees and the community of South Africa at large. The various new concepts then started emerging automatically from this line of thought.' Previously black workers had been housed in huge barrack-like compounds. To replace these, they employed Francis Lorne, a well-known architect who had designed Anglo American's head office, to design attractive double-storey buildings around quadrangles; these would be called hostels. The whole nature of accommodation and eating facilities was upgraded.' Concrete bunks, one above the other, were replaced by beds, 'admittedly sometimes tier beds'.

Joane Pim, South Africa's leading landscape gardener, was employed and given a free rein to exercise her talents for natural layouts of grass, indigenous trees and shrubs. She designed the gardens of the hostels and the mine managers' houses, as well as the environs of the mine. Changes were made, too, in the kind of houses built for mine officials. 'Before this particular period I don't think that a single house on the mines of the Witwatersrand or Klerksdorp had been designed by an architect. They were always designed by mechanical engineers. Mechanical engineers built houses that would never fall down, but they were usually very, very ugly. So we introduced a new aesthetic regime.'

Numerous other innovations occurred. 'The most important in a social sense – I am not going to deal here with technical avenues which were of major significance too – was to be the provision of family housing for migrant labourers. Up to this time all migrant labourers had been housed in single-sex compounds. Within the South African system the concept of family housing for migrant workers was revolutionary. From the beginning we had all agreed – and had been supported by Sir Ernest – on the importance of this development. Ground was bought on which to situate the housing, and building began. Then Dr Verwoerd, who was later to become the Prime Minister of South

Africa, took the file home for the weekend. He came down the following Monday or Tuesday with an absolute cast-iron decision that this would not be permitted. We had, by this time, built on some of our mines enough houses to accommodate 3 per cent of their complement. And that was how it came about, with his sledgehammer decision, that the Orange Free State mines were permitted to house 3 per cent of their complement of black workers and no more. If it had not been for Dr Verwoerd I think that we would have succeeded in dealing with migratory labour having family housing.'

Bill found the pioneering work in the Orange Free State exciting and fulfilling. 'It was a very happy period in my life and I think it was also a very happy period for Keith and for Harry himself; indeed this spirit infused all those working on the Free State project, either at head office or on the mines. We all got on very well and you felt that you were doing something important, not only from a financial and mining point of view, but in creating thousands of new jobs, paying much better – all these things – but somehow also you knew you were participating in something that was setting up new standards.' In 1948 Harry Oppenheimer, while retaining his position as chairman of the Orange Free State gold mines, became Member of Parliament for Kimberley. Keith Acutt and Bill continued with the work they had started and met with Harry Oppenheimer when he came up for the weekends. The development of the new mines was a great success, but it was not without difficulties and technical setbacks. Huge amounts of money were required to bring the mines into production. 'We were developing seven new mines, one a year; it took roughly three years from starting a mine for it to come to production. It was looked upon by some as questionable whether we would be able to handle this technically, financially or administratively. One of the most difficult areas concerned the finding of the huge amount of money that was required; it was plainly beyond the capacity of the South African institutional set-up and stock exchange, so we had to get money from other places. This was Sir Ernest Oppenheimer's field and he never for a second doubted whether it would be forthcoming. We, in turn, had complete faith in him and so had no doubts either.'

Fortunately the gold-bearing reef was wonderfully consistent and, of the seven mines that Anglo American established, five were extremely good and one was moderate. The seventh was mothballed after sinking a shaft and doing limited underground development. 'A pretty good average, I think. I suppose the major factor in the success of the whole Orange Free State gold-fields was the uniformity of the reefs and their consistent good value. In other words, it was not anything of our doing, it was something that nature had provided. There was a good deal of feeling, I think, during those early days in the Orange Free State that we lacked the experience and, in particular, the breadth and depth of technical and administrative ability to bring seven mines to production in seven years.' A Canadian mining company which had been thinking of taking an investment in the gold-fields declined to do so on this account. Then there was the man from a major French company who did some calculations and proved conclusively that none of the Free State mines would be profitable at all. 'He refused to participate,' Bill suppresses a smile, 'a grave mistake, I might tell you.

'Sir Ernest Oppenheimer died in 1957 at the age of seventy-five, having founded the corporation in 1917 and been chairman ever since. He had seen it and De Beers through the dark days of the great depression and the post-war years of rapid growth. It was a great loss. Sir Ernest's affection and unshakeable confidence in Harry had been a major factor in the development of the Orange Free State mines.' Harry Oppenheimer retired from parliament to become chairman of the Anglo American Corporation. Keith Acutt became deputy chairman and Bill was appointed Managing Director. These changes meant that all three men had regretfully to sever their close connection with the Orange Free State mines.

Bill had always taken the view that senior people, both young and old, should take on responsibilities outside the corporation, not so much in a business as in a social or charitable sense. He had become particularly interested in schools and had been appointed a governor of his old school, Michaelhouse. Another appointment was that of chairman of the Standing Committee of Associated Church Schools whose central role was to support, at governor level, the independent (that is non-State) schools. In addition he persuaded Harry Oppenheimer to take the chair of the Industrial Fund, which raised over a million pounds to update laboratories in major independent schools and some of the Roman Catholic ones.

Following the massacre at Sharpeville in 1960 when some 5,000 unarmed black supporters of the Pan Africanist Congress were fired on by about 300 police, resulting in 69 of the PAC supporters being killed and 180 wounded, there was a major loss of confidence in the government. Many white people emigrated. There was a withdrawal of foreign funds and support for the country, resulting in an economic slump. 'The government responded by introducing more and more control methods. One of the bodies some of them wanted to tame was the private schools. The independent school movement was out of line with the whole concept of apartheid and was in outspoken opposition to the government which in 1962 introduced the Education Advisory Council Bill. The Bill looked innocent enough, but careful examination revealed that it could be used to deprive independent schools of their independence. So we put up a fight and gave evidence before a select committee.'

Believing that the best form of defence was not only to be critical, but constructive as well, he set about establishing the 1961 Education Panel, whose members were vice-chancellors and professors of education at English-speaking universities, and prominent businessmen and heads of private schools. Under the chairmanship of Judge Schreiner, one of South Africa's great liberals, the panel produced a blueprint for South African education, an imaginative document which attempted to forecast economic development in South Africa over the next twenty to twenty-five years. The South African education system would have to supply the qualified people to create this economic development. 'It became plain during these discussions that one of the major necessities was to introduce radical changes in black education. Of course now we are reaping the reward of not accepting these things and not having made the changes.'

Black musicians and singers, a number of whom have subsequently achieved fame and international recognition, had up to this time been heard by only relatively few whites. In the late 1950s Bill became chairman of Union Artists, the company which financed and presented *King Kong*, the first large-scale musical to be presented in South Africa with a black cast. Miriam Makeba was the star of the Johannesburg production in the Great Hall of Witwatersrand University. The show was an enormous success in South Africa and a modest one when it was transferred to London. 'That,' he laughs 'was an interesting sideline to my business activities. Rather hair-raising at times, but exciting. We lived from hand to mouth. It was a hazardous sort of operation because if you had a performance, say, at eight o'clock, you were never certain, until five minutes before the curtain was due to go up, who was going to be there, because people used to get arrested. It wasn't always the police's fault, either; very often people just didn't arrive,' and he laughs again, recalling the kind of carefree irresponsibility of which he could never be capable, 'the African attitude to these things. And so people had to step into all sorts of extraordinary breaches and we were lucky to have people like Ian Bernhardt and Robert Loder to handle these crises.'

Bill had been Managing Director of Anglo American for about seven years when he was asked to take on a major role in the Corporation's London office. 'The understanding was that I would replace Keith Acutt who had not been in good health. My primary task in conjunction with the Hon. Hugh Vivian Smith, chairman of the British South Africa Company (the Charter Company), and Derek Pollen, Managing Director of Central Mining, was to bring about the merger of these two companies and a smaller London-based company of the Anglo American Group, Consolidated Mines Selection. The merged company would have very considerable assets and with the aid of technical services from the Anglo American Corporation was expected to become an important factor in international mining. The Charter

Company (Rhodes's vehicle for his Rhodesian activities) and the Central Mining (established before the Anglo-Boer War by Wernher and Beit and for many years the parent company of the largest gold mining group in South Africa) had distinguished pasts.'

The Wilsons left for London in September 1964 with their four children. 'Our family had always been a close one, but when we went over to England the bonds became infinitely more tight. For the first few months, even year, I should say, we lived uncomfortably in temporarily rented houses, having to move every few months before we found something satisfactory. In fact the house we did eventually find was a beautiful place in Phillimore Gardens, off Kensington High Street. It had a gate through its wall into Holland Park which meant that the children could go for walks in the park without having to cross any streets. That was a very happy period of all our lives because the bonds between us had become extremely strong and at the same time Kelane and Monique were very attractive girls and Sarah and Simon, although tiny, were amusing creatures.'

After some months of negotiation and quite difficult and complex reorganization of the staffs of the three companies, Charter Consolidated became operative and involved itself in mining undertakings in distant parts. The first was the Tronoh group of tin mines in Malaysia and the second Somima, a copper mine at Akjoujt in Mauritania. There was also the Cleveland Potash Company, established jointly with Imperial Chemical Industries to mine potash in Yorkshire; this was regarded at the time as a major coup for Charter Consolidated. Bill was especially interested in the Mauritanian venture, not least because it meant that he was once more back in the desert which he loved.

Thus by 1968 Charter Consolidated, superficially at least, seemed to be doing well. It was involved in two new mining ventures and the acquisition of a third, and the mining and industrial interests inherited from Central Mining in the United Kingdom were performing reasonably. The price of Charter Consolidated shares on the London Stock Exchange had appreciated substantially. But there were underlying problems and tensions.

Towards the end of that year changes which included Bill's replacement in London were made in the most senior levels of Charter. He was told he could either take another senior appointment abroad or return to South Africa. He and Pidie decided to return. 'It was as much her decision as mine. She ran the house and looked after the children and so on. We had enjoyed many aspects of London enormously, but we were really South Africans, and you don't easily get out of the South African and African role. It does grab you.

'Pidie and I went off to the South of France with the children. I felt like a holiday. We rented an old rectory at Menerbes in Provence that belonged to the Gimpels, the art dealers, and we lived there for three or four months. That was a wonderful period. During the period at Menerbes our family ties, always extremely important to us, were further strengthened. We were together on our own, living quite an isolated life, although various people did come and stay with us.'

Readjustment upon his return to South Africa at the end of 1969 was not easy. The ground he had occupied previously had been taken over by others. 'The family was very important indeed to me during the first few months after our return to South Africa when my life at Anglo American was unsatisfactory and not altogether happy. Then in May 1970 we had the most terrible disaster. Kelane, our eldest daughter, was killed in a motor car accident on her way back from Johannesburg to the University of Cape Town. This affected both Pidie and me dreadfully. We went over to England for about three months. It was a tragedy from which I think we will never properly recover.'

Later that year they returned to Johannesburg. Bill had always taken a keen interest in the welfare of blacks in the organization and was less than satisfied with the corporation's performance in this regard. 'So we established a committee which we called the Employment Practices Committee where we took a serious look at what we were doing in these fields and increased pressure for major changes and in particular the elimination of discrimination between black and white, both in wages and in conditions of service, pensions and so on. That I found very interesting, though quite hard going. Men in charge of Anglo American companies and divisions are strong-minded people, very much involved in the profit motive, the major motive of any commercial concern. Naturally they look long and hard at proposals for social change from a cost point of view and turn a jaundiced eye on moves which will reduce the profits of their companies. People sometimes think that it would be easy to wave a wand inside Anglo American and change immediately all the social and personnel policies, but this is not the case. You can only progress by means of patient and persistent persuasion if you want to succeed in making changes that will stick without ruining companies.' In 1970 he was made deputy chairman of Anglo American.

'Earlier on I mentioned the discussions we used to have on the business philosophy of the Anglo American Corporation and the need for it to concentrate not only on profits, but also to provide a fair deal for the people working for it and to play a role in society as a whole. The principal method of fulfilling its role in society has been through the De Beers and Anglo American Chairman's Fund to which all the companies of the De Beers and Anglo American groups contribute percentages of their profits. The amount is very substantial indeed and has an enormous impact on charitable work. I think it would be fair to say that hardly any major educational or charitable operation in South Africa has started or operated without aid from the Chairman's Fund. Indeed I know of no organization of a similar kind anywhere in the world that has resources so large and operates with such efficiency, effectiveness and concern. Amongst the activities that we were supporting in the earlier 1970s was a clinic near King Williams Town named Zanimpelo which was run by a young woman doctor, Mamphela Ramphele, who was a close friend of Steve Biko and eventually bore his son.'

In the spring of 1976, accompanied by Paul Henwood, the manager of the Chairman's Fund, and for part of the time by Father Aelred Stubbs CR, Bill went to visit various projects in the Eastern Cape which Anglo was supporting, including Zanimpelo, certain agricultural undertakings run by the University of

Fort Hare and a new agricultural college. They spent the evening at the clinic with Mamphela Ramphele, Steve Biko and some of their friends. 'It was a most wonderful occasion. We discussed everything with frankness, openness, good humour, optimism. I had the highest opinion of Steve Biko, though I saw too little of him to become a close friend.'

They met again when Steve Biko came to Pretoria to give evidence in a court case. 'Steve rang and asked if he might come over for the afternoon. Again, we had an extraordinary afternoon. He told me a lot about his past life, what he'd been through, what he'd been struggling for and what his aims were. He was full of humour and lightness and cheerfulness. He also spoke about his previous interrogations by the police and security services.

'And then – I don't know how they knew about it – we were down in Swaziland and a man from *The Star* rang one day in September and said, 'Are you aware that Steve Biko has been killed?' I remember this very clearly indeed. Absolute shock. I thought this could happen to him because he'd told me about aspects of interrogation he had undergone which he felt might earn him the hostility of his interrogators. I had a feeling that he might get beaten and I suppose that this was, in fact, what happened.' Bill has related this with almost bated breath, so softly that it is difficult to catch his words. 'I had a feeling at the time that that was an absolutely extraordinary, amazing story. I've remained firmly of the opinion that that was one of the real disasters in South Africa. This was a man of extraordinary charisma and ability and kindness and strength and courage, a most lovable sort of person, and big and strong. The killing', he repeats, 'was, I think, one of the disasters of this country.'

He also met Nelson Mandela, in about 1961: 'There again, I was very deeply impressed. I thought he was a really wonderful man.' Mandela had wanted to speak to someone from Anglo American and a mutual journalist friend had invited Mandela, a friend of his, and Bill for dinner. Nelson Mandela had read the last couple of annual reports of Anglo American and asked a lot of questions. 'Most of the evening was spent on the question of the nationalization of the mines to which I was totally opposed. I certainly did all that I could to get this concept out of his mind because I am certain that if the mines are nationalized profits and technical and administrative capability and standards of safety will decline. Many mines will be out of production in no time.'

These views were reinforced later by his experiences on the boards of the Zambian copper mines at the time when the government took control and political appointments and decisions and influences began to override economic considerations, with disastrous consequences.

'It would seem that the pleas against nationalization fell on deaf ears because the African National Congress still talks of nationalizing the mines.' He found it interesting that when the man who accompanied Mandela said that after Sharpeville Harry Oppenheimer ought to have shut down the mines, Mandela immediately responded that there was no way in which Mr Oppenheimer could have shut down the mines. 'He didn't expect people to do absurd and foolish things as gestures of some kind. That was my only meeting with him, so it's a pretty flimsy basis to go on, but I certainly got a fine impression of him.'

In July 1975 Bill turned sixty, and having warned Harry Oppenheimer of his intentions some months earlier, stopped working full time for the Anglo American Corporation. He wished to be available for his family. 'We had another problem which concerned the sometimes unstable health of our second daughter, Monique. After an attack of glandular fever she had never quite recovered her health and in August 1975 they took her to New York for treatment. From there they returned to stay in London where, upon her recovery, she went to an art school where she gained first class honours in illustration.

Throughout the period since the return of the family to South Africa in 1969 until the present, Bill has renewed and continued his involvement in activities outside the Anglo American Corporation. Chief of these has been non-racial schools. 'My enchantment with such schools has been a long and enduring one and is due to my feeling, supported by many years' experience, that children are able to handle racial issues unselfconsciously. Grown-ups get involved in all sorts of problems and competitive situations and anger and so on, whereas young children just get together and play and talk and work together without any of these problems.'

Waterford, in independent Swaziland, of whose school council Bill is a member, was the first non-racial school in southern Africa. 'Simon, my son, who was there doing his A levels for two years, has got friends, boys and girls of all races, who were at Waterford and who still come together when they are any-where near each other geographically.' The second of the non-racial schools was Maru a Pula in Gaberone in Botswana. 'It was founded by an old friend of mine, Deane Yates, who had been headmaster of St John's College. We had encountered each other when he was chairman of the Conference of Headmasters and Headmistresses and I was chairman of the Standing Committee of Associated Church Schools in the early sixties. When I came back from England he asked if I would come on to the school council, which I agreed to immediately and was one of its original members and remain one today. Maru a Pula is a very happy school and successful academically. One of its former students, Liyander Lekelake, was the first black girl Rhodes scholar and is up at Oxford now. The most important point is the extraordinary happiness and joy there is in that school. We had to raise large sums of money for its buildings and establishment and I asked Harry Oppenheimer to become chairman of our original fund-raising drive which was extremely successful.

'I think it was in 1980 that Deane, after ten years as headmaster of Maru a Pula, felt he should return to South Africa in order to investigate the possibility of starting non-racial schools here. Quite early on Steyn Krige, who had established Woodmead, north of Johannesburg, a school which could by that time claim to have become non-racial, joined in discussions. The result was the establishment of NEST, the New Era Schools Trust, under the chairmanship of Professor G. R. Bozzoli, the former Vice-Chancellor of the University of the Witwatersrand. The board of trustees is non-racial and drawn from various parts of South

Africa, about twenty-four in number, of whom I am one. They worked unremittingly from 1980 to get permission to establish these schools – no school which has not been officially registered can operate within the republic of South Africa. This was resisted and obstructed by politicians and civil servants for a period of about five tedious years, delaying the establishment of the first school, Uthongati, at Tongaat, north of Durban, till January 1987. Only 25 per cent of the students at Uthongati are white and up till now it has been an outstanding success. The second of the four schools NEST hopes to establish will open its doors in the Kyalami area, north of Johannesburg, in January 1989 and we hope that we will be able to raise the very considerable amount of money needed for two further schools, one in Grahamstown and one near Cape Town. The establishment of a school like Uthongati costs something of the order of nine million rand, so NEST has to collect thirty-six million rand establishment costs plus a considerable amount for bursaries. I believe that these schools have an enormous part to play in the future and that they should be supported in every way possible, both inside this country and outside.'

In about 1970 he had taken on the chairmanship of SACHED, the South African Council for Higher Education, devoted to the development of correspondence and tutorial courses at the higher level of school and early university education. Its focus was black students. The organization, run on a small staff, was always on the brink of bankruptcy and from time to time in trouble with the authorities who disapproved of its direction, radical in the South African context. In 1978 both David Adler, one of the founders of SACHED, and Clive Nettleton, a co-worker, were banned. 'We certainly had some hair-raising experiences, but today SACHED, since 1982 under the chairmanship of Archbishop Buthelezi of Bloemfontein, has a multiracial staff of over two hundred and makes a vital contribution to the raising of educational standards, particularly in the field of black education which continues to lag so far behind.

The Ernest Oppenheimer Memorial Trust of which Bill remained chairman until 1987 provides scholarships and bursaries for university students, mainly for blacks. It also grants travelling fellowships for leading academics which enable youngish professors of promise from universities all over the country to travel abroad, something that is of particular importance with the isolation of South Africa internationally. It has also awarded scholarships to musicians, several of whom have become internationally known. He remains a member of the Board of Trustees. A more recent interest is SHAP, Self Help for African Paraplegics, based in Soweto. 'The medical treatment of paraplegics and quadriplegics in the hospitals, particularly at Baragwanath and Natalspruit, was good, but there was no post-hospital care for them and the small government grant they received left them living below the breadline. 'Under the leadership of a remarkable man, Friday Mavuso, himself a paraplegic, and some help we gave them, a factory employing eighty of them has been established in Soweto. It is allied to a sports facility for disabled people and hopes to double the number of its employees in the coming year if it can get the funds.'

The value of his work in the fields of education and labour relations was recognized in April 1974 when Bill was awarded an honorary LLD (Doctor of Laws) by the University of the Witwatersrand.

Bill and Pidie now spend part of each year in Newlands, an old suburb of Cape Town which lies near the foot of the mountain. Oaks, planted by the early settlers and lining many of the narrow streets, have flourished in this area of heavy winter rainfall. The Wilsons have converted one of the old foresters' cottages so that the kitchen now forms the end of the dining-room. An old Italian screen hangs on the far wall. Pidie now has time to paint. 'She has had this problem,' Bill explains, 'that her creative nature was overlaid by her strong sense of responsibility in caring for her children. That occupied so much of her time and energy that it was only sporadically during our married life that she was able to get down to some painting.' They spend long periods in Swaziland. In intervals between attending meetings connected with his educational interests, Bill reads and climbs the mountains either alone with his dogs, or with friends.

What about the future of South Africa? 'Well, we live in an explosive atmosphere, highly explosive, primarily because of unjust and unacceptable political and economic policies, but fanned also (and often irresponsibly) by powerful institutions inside and outside South Africa. That does not mean there is going to be an explosion. I don't think there will be. The mounting forces against it are too strong. I don't mean only the police and the Army. There is something more important than this: the massive and widespread social, psychological and economic advance occurring amongst hitherto disadvantaged people, the removal of humiliating restrictions, the opening up of avenues of progress. I think this will help to avoid an explosion; but the slow rate of change and its limited scope is bound to lead to continuous and heated conflict.

'We must develop common horizons that overarch division, and that can't be done without negotiation during which leaders emerge and real issues are tackled. At the moment there are false impressions about causes and what can be achieved, leading to a sterile concept of transfer of wealth through loot rather than development through ability, initiative, inventiveness and hard work. And an alarming capacity has been developed amongst radicals for persuading ordinary decent people to support things they know to be mad and wrong: preventing children from going to school, killing your opponents by the most terrible means, sanctions, disinvestment. We watch and live apprehensively, rejecting both optimism and pessimism.'

'No, we won't be leaving southern Africa. We have been through that thought process and here we are. I can't take a high moral line on the issue, though. I am afraid too many able young blacks and whites have already left and the head-hunters are around. I understand the reasons for people going and the reasons for leaving will remain until a probability emerges of a South Africa with challenges and opportunities for all: a South Africa not likely to blow up in one's face.'

MARIA ELIZABETH VAN NIEKERK

IT IS NINE o'clock on a summer morning and Maria van Niekerk, a small wiry woman, bright and loquacious, has already mown the patch of front lawn with the motor mower, put the household wash in the machine and hung it up. The suburb is Ridgeway, ten minutes' run south of Johannesburg, and the Van Niekerks' single-storeyed house, separated from the street by a low diamond-mesh fence, is similar to many others in the district. Two small dogs bark at passers-by. She unlocks the iron-grilled gate at the entrance to the house, leading the way through the hall and kitchen. At the back is a large swimming-pool and an adjoining paved area with chairs and an iron container for *braaivleis*. The Van Niekerks own this house, the one next door and another in which their daughter and her husband live in a nearby suburb. They also own a seaside house which Maria bought with money left to her by her parents. 'I could have used it to go overseas – we haven't been overseas – but I thought it was better to buy a house.' Both she and her husband Ebenaezer came from impecunious families and she is proud of what they have achieved. 'In getting these four houses I never had a servant in all my life and I had six children, all born at home, and I brought them all up.' She collects stamps and helps the neighbourhood children set up their own stamp collections. One of her greatest joys is reading the romances published by Mills and Boon. 'I *love* them! I've got *dozens* of them.'

She was born Maria Elizabeth van der Merwe, in Sidwell, perhaps the least affluent of the white suburbs in Port Elizabeth, on 16 July 1929. During the Anglo-Boer War at the turn of the century, the ox-wagons of her Van der Merwe forebears, ostrich farmers in the Steytlerville district of the eastern Cape, were commandeered by the British; they would depart, loaded with food, but would emerge from the deep mountain passes empty; this was almost the only way in which the Afrikaners of the Cape could express their solidarity with their compatriots fighting in the Transvaal. Some men did slip away across the colony's northern border to join the Boer commandos and members of the family, questioned as to where Piet or Jan was, would give evasive replies about his having gone to work in Port Elizabeth.

After the war the slump in the feather market terminated the prosperity of ostrich farmers. 'My grandfather, François van der Merwe, walked out of there with his wife, Maria Elizabeth, his nineteen children, his wagon and sixteen oxen, loaded with a few remaining household possessions. Ruined. They came to Port Elizabeth because it was only there there was money. They wouldn't *think* of coming up to the north because that was Sodom and Gomorrah.' Maria's father, Johannes Jacobus Leonard van der Merwe, the youngest of the nineteen children, was born in Steytlerville in 1905, brought into the world, like his siblings, by a black midwife. He left the little school at Kleinpoort aged eighteen and became first a glazier and then a fitter and turner.

Maria's maternal relatives were Goosens, proud of their distant relationship to General Louis Botha. They owned farms in the Alexandria area, north-east of Port Elizabeth, a part of the Eastern Province referred to by Maria as 'the old world'. Her mother, Maria Elizabeth Charlotta Goosen, was born there in 1908. According to Maria, it was the martinet grandmother, Sara Helena Goosen, who drove many members of the family to the desperation of abandoning their farms and trekking to the Transvaal. There being no telephones in the early days, the old lady would summon her sons by shining a mirror in the sunlight, 'They reckoned when she lifts that mirror they had to be on the farm within five minutes.'

The Van der Merwe family lived in one of the small houses with a little front garden in the Port Elizabeth suburb of Sidwell. Maria remembers the sound of rain on the corrugated iron roof and the sash windows which, when the cord broke, had to be propped open with a stick. There was an outside lavatory where the bucket was regularly removed by the 'night cart', driving along the little back lanes between the rows of houses. 'No burglar proofing, thank the Lord, the doors stood open night and day and sometimes when family came in from the farms they went and made coffee in the kitchen until we woke up.' After the death of her mother in 1930 she and her sister, Sara, continued to live in the house with their father. Later their grandmother told her how each morning he would dress them, give them breakfast and take them to her house, redolent with the aroma of freshly ground coffee. Here they would be joined by cousins whose mother worked in the shoe factory. All the children were dosed each week with castor oil, 'to clean your blood so that you get no boils or pimples. Then once a week coconut oil was put on our heads to stimulate our hair, make it grow better. You see, it had to be done that way.' On Saturdays Maria and Sara would accompany their father to work where they would play with the little pieces of glass he had bevelled for them. 'We weren't allowed to run around like mad. My father was strict, but he was just. We just knew we had to listen.'

There were occasional visits to their maternal uncle, Stoffel Botha, at his farm, Doringkloof, in the Alexandria district. The little girls were intrigued with some of Ouma's rituals; the daily airing of her sheets and pillow-cases, the folding and unfolding of blankets, the placing and removal of the counterpane, all done by herself. No servant was ever allowed to touch the bed. 'And I always remember her with this long nightdress and I thought, I wonder how Ouma would look in a pair of pyjamas?' In their uncle's and aunt's bedroom there were forbidden escapades of throwing themselves into the depths of the feather bed. They gazed at the evening line-up of the *volkies* (the coloured workers), each with a jam tin to be half-filled with wine. This was the *dop* system whereby a daily wine ration was sometimes given in lieu of money.

The children were inculcated with respect for the coloured people, generally referred to by Afrikaners in that area as 'hotnots'; they encountered few blacks. Feelings, however, for their elderly coloured servant, Mina, were spontaneous, 'Oh, I *adored* her! I *adored* her! She was big and fat and I used to kiss her. Ach, she was Mina, she was mine!' They were taught to address older people of colour as *aia* or *outa*, forms of 'aunt' and 'uncle'. Had they referred to a coloured woman as *meid*, 'Grandma would have smashed us, really given us a good hiding.' Swearing was forbidden as it was 'against the Lord's wishes', but Maria remarks tartly, 'I could say a few nice words, I remember, like "hell" and *donder* [thunder] and my auntie tried to catch me and put pepper in my mouth, but I pushed behind the old collie dog and she couldn't get me.'

According to Maria, Afrikaners can work well with blacks, but not necessarily with coloured people, 'because we believe it's a bad black man and bad white woman, that's why coloureds are there.' (She neglects to mention the more common situation of a white man and a black woman.) 'If you had had any pride in your colour you wouldn't have mixed with something below you.' She recalls, as a child, finding Mina sitting sobbing on the steps. The cause of her grief, which she revealed to Maria's grandmother and which the grandmother tried to keep from Maria, for it was unsuitable for a child's ears, was that her son, working in the merchant navy, had 'taken' a white woman in England. 'She was crying, disgusted, because they were suffering already because they can't fit in anywhere. They don't want to be with the blacks, and the whites don't want them. Now their children marry a white woman and bring more suffering.'

'I spoke only Afrikaans and a Bantu language – I can't remember it – up until the age of seven.' The language referred to would have been Xhosa, most commonly spoken by blacks in the Cape. 'In my childhood memory they were wonderful days.

My "godfather" was Dr Zinnebach; he was our family doctor and like a father. He was a Jew. And our dominee was Dr Minnaar from the Dutch Reformed Church. Those were the people who ruled our lives. When something was wrong either Dr Zinnebach knew about it, or Dominee Minaar knew about it.' Maria denies hotly there being a prevalent prejudice among many Afrikaners against Jews. 'My grandfather was "done" by the Jews over the ostriches – they knew in advance that the price of ostrich feathers had fallen in London and yet they still lent the farmers money to buy more ostriches so that eventually they took over the farms – but Dr Zinnebach was our doctor, equal to the *predikant* [pastor].' The children were obliged to learn a verse from the Bible to recite to the dominee on his regular weekly visits. 'I remember that one of mine was, "God so loved the world that he gave his only begotten son so that the world could be saved."' There was a little tin, the *Sendelingbussie*, kept in a prominent place on the kitchen dresser for the 'missionary money', to be used to build churches for the blacks. Visitors were expected to contribute a coin.

Wages in Johannesburg were higher than in Port Elizabeth and so, despite its evil reputation, at the end of 1935 Johannes Leonard van der Merwe found himself a job there with Excelsior Shopfitters. He had promised his dying wife that their daughters would always be with her mother, but she would not accompany him. A plan was therefore devised and agreed upon whereby Johannes would marry Elsie, his late wife's sister. In 1936 the couple were married in Johannesburg, a marriage of this order of relationship not being permitted in the Cape Province. His chief purpose, it would seem, was to have a mother for his little girls. 'My father got work here, still in glazing. Lubner Grunow was his boss; my father adored him. My father didn't jump around from firm to firm. He worked for Excelsior Shopfitters all his life.'

The family lived in a small flat in the centre of the city, opposite the Marshall Square police station. With regard to her stepmother Maria confides, 'I only liked my father. I had to tolerate her; she was there.' Yet she was later to name one of her daughters Elsie, after her stepmother. There was a school within walking distance, but it was not to Mr van der Merwe's liking. 'My parents were very choosy; having nothing, they still wanted their children to have the best.' So the children travelled by tram to the preferred Johan Rissik School in Jeppe. Maria and Sara were not allowed to play after school with other children, but had to stay in the flat during the afternoon. 'Naturally, we slipped out. If you tell a child he must sit there for an hour and he sits there – well, he must be sick. So we slipped out. *Skelm!* [deceitful]' Her eyes sparkle.

Mrs van der Merwe was one of the Afrikaner women, many of them young and from country districts, working in the clothing industry. Through its general secretary, Solly Sachs, the Garment Workers' Union had been instrumental in improving working conditions and raising wages in the Transvaal. The Union was also attempting to assist the introduction of coloured workers into the industry. Some Nationalists, strongly influenced by Nazism, saw the coloured workers as 'the black menace'; they were supported in their aim to destroy the Union by certain pastors of the Afrikaner churches. Maria's stepmother was deeply resentful of the coloured workers, calling them 'lazy and incompetent'. 'The white women', relates Maria, remembering the complaints of her stepmother, 'were paid very little, *very* little. I remember one day she said that in Port Elizabeth our servants weren't as badly paid as they were, and the servants got their food, which they didn't. The white women had been in the factory longer and so should have got a bit more.' They resented working on the same premises, even though the coloured women might be in a different room, 'not because [if] you're white you're better than somebody else, but because [if] you're white you've got a different culture and you want to be with your white friends; you can't speak about the same things to the coloureds.'

In 1938 Mr van der Merwe bought a small, square, single-storey house in La Rochelle, a suburb to the south of Johannesburg where, because of the proximity of the dust from the mine dumps, property was a good deal cheaper than in the north.

In Maria's childhood the eastern Cape was predominantly English and English words crept into the language of Afrikaners. She recalls her elders referring to 'cousin' Elisabeth or 'cousin' Jan; she could never think of calling her father by the Afrikaans, *pa*. 'We called our father "Daddy"; he treated my sister and me as equals, but we had to have manners. At the beginning of the meal there was a prayer and he wouldn't start if we weren't all there, and you couldn't leave the table before the final prayer was said.' Children were not allowed to speak at the table. 'We had our native girl (she got the same food), but we had to work with her. We had to take everything off the table and she started the washing and one of us dried, and my mother in between. We were strictly brought up. I don't think a glazier used to get much, but we always had decent food on the table. I suppose my mother made it decent. Money was never there that we could buy new cars.' A seamstress made the girls' everyday dresses and their church dress. They wore uniforms to their local Afrikaans-medium Junior High School. 'In the afternoons the native girl looked after us. There were one or two English-speaking families in La Rochelle, mostly Jewish. We kids spoke a bit Afrikaans, a bit Jewish and a bit English. Children can understand each other and we learnt from each other. I learnt to swear nicely in Jewish. I also had the loveliest memories of my life with Dianne Cohen, Henry Cohen and Julie Cohen and on the Jewish holidays I used to eat matzos with them and we even used to pinch the Jewish wine, we kids, all together. In my childhood we were strictly Afrikaners and strictly Dutch Reformed, but not for one moment must we think that we were better than anyone else.'

As was customary among Afrikaners, the children were taught to call older women *tante* (auntie). Whilst, earlier in the century, many Afrikaners had spoken excellent English, by the 1930s a strong movement against anglicization was developing. 'If you spoke to Afrikaans-speaking people in English, then you got a good smack because our father said you're low-class if you want to make out you're English and you're really Afrikaans. That's not done.' On Sunday afternoons, after morning church-going and lunch, Johannes van der Merwe would take his daughters out into the *veld* and the *koppies* that lay to the south. 'When we were thirsty he would warn us, "Don't drink standing water. Watch it. If it's been over seven stones you can drink it." He knew all about the trees and if he didn't, he would take the leaves away and tell us later.' He interested them in stamps, 'because you learn about people through their stamps', and encouraged them to learn languages. 'He wanted us to learn, learn, learn and be observant: "Never pinch with your hands, but pinch with your eyes. Your hands are there only to better yourself and to work with." The main thing we had to learn was music. A lady makes music. I used to love piano lessons and drawing, but never in my life have I liked to cook.'

In 1938, the centenary of the start of the great trek, the Van der Merwe family spent the week, culminating in the most sacrosanct of Afrikaner days, December 16, on the little hill just outside Pretoria where a monolithic monument was to be built, a tribute to the *Voortrekkers*. 'Cousins and friends came from all parts of the country and we stayed in tents pitched around the *koppie*. The comradeship was fantastic! You've all got something in common to talk about. We all wore *voortrekker* clothes and we girls wore *kappies*.' The picture Maria presents is congenial, of groups gathering around the camp fires in the evenings to sing Christian songs and ballads idealizing the *Voortrekkers*. Conventions were strictly observed. If a young man wished to speak to a girl he had first to ask permission of her father.

Maria left school, aged fifteen, in Standard 8. Having learnt typing and bookkeeping at school, she soon found a job at a wholesale chemist and went on to work in the office at Randles Brothers and Hudson, a large soft goods wholesaler. 'It was a British firm with the head office in Manchester. It was a wonderful firm; the James brothers who ran it were fantastic people.'

In 1945 Elsie van der Merwe rented the little shop on the corner of their street and converted it into a tearoom and confectioner's. Sara and Maria helped to serve the customers in the afternoons and at weekends. 'My mother was a real Jew – we used to tell her that – she was a businesswoman.' At that time it was the practice in most shops and cafés to serve white customers first; blacks had to wait. The Van der Merwes, according to Maria, served first arrivals first, irrespective of their colour.

It was at a youth meeting of her church that eighteen-year-old Maria first saw 'the long-legged guy' who, she resolved, was to be her husband. They did not meet until some weeks later when she found him there again, now in his police uniform, and learnt that his name was Ebenaezer van Niekerk. He accompanied Maria and her red-haired friend, Johanna, home, wheeling his bicycle. She was not allowed to speak to a man unless she had been introduced by his parents, but on this occasion she knew that there could be no objection as she had met the young man at *church*. Her parents granted him permission to visit her again. 'Ebenaezer wasn't allowed to come more than twice a week and, poor man, he had to sit there while I worked in the tearoom.' After they had known one another for six months, he invited Maria to come with him on a visit to his family who farmed near Calvinia, in the north-western Cape. She was sure her father would refuse to let her go but, to her astonishment, he agreed. 'I could have fainted. He said to me, "I want you to go and see if those people have got a 'stripe' in them, if they've got coloured blood. We must be sure. Look at the children; the mother might have nothing wrong, but don't be mistaken, in the second, third, or fourth generation the 'stripe' will show."'

Ebenaezer van Niekerk's late father had been a *bywoner*, working for the owner of the farm, but given a portion to farm for himself. His first wife had died after giving birth to her eighth child. Ebenaezer, born in August 1926, when his father was sixty-five years old and his mother forty-five, was the last of the eight children of the second marriage. The children went to school and stayed at the school hostel in the little town of Brandvlei. Both school and hostel were subsidized by the NG Kerk and farmers who could afford it gave produce; no payment was expected from those who could not afford it. Once a month the children were allowed home for the weekend, some travelling by car, but most being fetched in donkey carts. At three-monthly intervals there would be *nagmaal* in the town and farmers would travel in and stay in their *nagmaal-kamer* or *kerkhuisie*, the room or little house made available in the town for that purpose. The children from the hostel would be allowed to join their families on these important occasions. When not at school the Van Niekerk children herded their father's sheep (there were no fences), or earned a little money working for neighbouring farmers. The children of the first marriage did what they could to help with the education of their younger brothers and sisters.

Maria and her husband-to-be left Johannesburg on the evening train: 'From here to Hutchinson, on the Cape line. At Hutchinson you get off, wait till eight o'clock at night for the train to Kootjiekolk and you get there in the morning. It was so cold; they had big iron containers filled with hot water to keep you warm. It was all just sitting, no sleeping places. You arrive at Kootjiekolk and wait for the railcar at four o'clock in the afternoon. It takes you to Sakrivier and the family met us there.' They stayed with Ebenaezer's older brother, and visited other brothers and relations, all sheep farmers. Grazing was so sparse that only four sheep were allowed to a hectare, and the farms have to be vast. Ebanaezer's parents' house, which had fallen into disrepair, was on another farm; it was built of clay and had the remains of a thatched roof. The baking oven was outside.

They should never, their father had taught them, imagine that they were above doing even the lowliest work. Before paying someone else to do a job, they should try to do it themselves. So it was not altogether surprising that Maria and her sister, when their brother was building his house, undertook to cart bricks in a wheelbarrow from the bottom of the hill up to the building site. One put a rope, attached to the wheelbarrow, around her waist and pulled from the front; the other pushed from behind, with intervals for applications of plaster over their blisters and a good deal of laughter. Therefore when Mr van der Merwe gave Ebenaezer van Niekerk permission to marry his daughter, he advised him, 'She's not dull; she's a happy girl. We do many things together. You shouldn't break her spirit. She's the kind of woman, if she wants to get on the roof and fix something, she'll do it, and I won't stop her. She's even helped me to do mechanical work on the car. She's got a star for shooting. Don't stop her from doing anything because then she'll be dull and empty.' The 'star for shooting' and 'a hang of a lot of cups' had been gained in competitions at the Booysens Ladies' Pistol Club. 'I didn't do it because it's useful for defending yourself; it was just something I love.'

Maria and Ebenaezer were married at the Dutch Reformed Church in Rosettenville on 2 December 1950. 'I had a beautiful dress made of chantilly lace, a flower-girl and a bridesmaid, and another policeman was best man. That night we had a little party for friends and relatives at my parents' place. Instead of going on a honeymoon we used that money to buy a bedroom suite for our room in Fortuna Street, Mayfair – it was another policeman's house.' In the evenings Ebenaezer studied in order to become a 2nd class sergeant. Throughout their marriage he tackled a number of courses, succeeding eventually in obtaining two diplomas in Public Service by correspondence through the University of South Africa.

Maria stopped working in September 1951, a month before their first child was born. There followed, over the next 15 years, five more children amongst whom the names of all family members have been distributed. After the local Afrikaans primary school they were all sent to the prestigious government Helpmekaar High School on the northern and more affluent side of town. Maria thought that they would get a better academic education there than in the local high school where she feared that her girls might learn domestic subjects. 'My husband is not a man who drinks or who goes out spending money; he gave me his money and I *made* it work. I worked night and day and made all their clothes. Every jersey they put on I had made. I've never had a native girl to touch my house. I had one once when I wasn't well, but she was such a disappointment I never took another one again. Never.' The children helped with the chores and her husband bought her a washing-machine. 'My girls can all make their own dresses and any of my three sons can fix a car.

'When they were still young, my husband used to tell the

children, "Listen, when I'm in the police offices, or when I'm out, I'm always a policeman. And I will help a person, no matter what his colour may be." That's the way he brought up our children. All of us can't believe in the same thing; each one has a different idea in life. I brought my children up to be *free-thinking*. That's why, in our house, each child of ours has his or her own idea and they speak it out and fight it out; but they must never forget their manners. No matter if they had to marry a different colour . . . we'll *never* allow a different colour to come into the house, but we'll never chase our child away. Their coloured children wouldn't be allowed in the house either.'

The family's annual holiday was often spent at the police rest camp at Port Edward, on the Natal south coast. 'It's gorgeous! In the early days it was more primitive; now all the houses have their own toilets and bathrooms. And what's so nice at the police camp is that there are English, Greek and Jewish policeman and they all come down there and the kids all play together.

'There you don't ask about your father's rank; your rank doesn't count, whether you're a constable or a general. The late State President, "Blackie" Swart used to come into my house and eat my biscuits and so did "Lang Hendrik" van den Bergh, chief of police.' The Van Niekerks later built a two-storey house for themselves, facing the Indian Ocean and near the police camp.

Turning to politics and to General Smuts, she believes that he was a 'brilliant man', 'but he spent too much of his time overseas. We reckoned he should have stayed here with his old wife that needed him more. Things like that put us off the government. Many of our family joined the Army, but where we didn't agree was that they sent the coloureds and the blacks up to Italy. We said they should have kept them here in South Africa because when blacks go there they go with the white girls who do anything for a little money. They would make more coloureds in Italy and those coloureds and blacks will bring their wives here and we're sitting already with the problem of the coloureds.'

Maria's father had been a supporter of General J. B. M. Hertzog's National Party until 1934 when Hertzog joined General

Smuts's South African Party to form the United Party. At this point they turned their allegiance to Dr Malan's breakaway 'purified' National Party which rejected links with the British empire and with the capitalists. One of their chief grievances against the United Party was its upholding of the voting rights of coloured people in the Cape province: 'The Nationalists promised that the hotnots, the coloureds, would be on a different voters' roll as their culture is different.'

During the 1948 general election she and Ebenaezer, not yet married, worked for the National Party in the area, registering voters. They sat up through most of election night, exulting, almost incredulously, over the results as they came through on the radio. One United Party seat after another fell to the Nationalists. Then came the announcement that General Smuts had been defeated in Standerton, the seat he had held for twenty-four years. 'As we came from the Eastern Province the first thing we thought is that the hotnots will now be taken off the voters' roll.' Maria herself had not voted in the Eastern Province. Her grandmother, who was 'so honest and upright that she would never tell a lie', told her something that 'made a hang of an impression' on her. 'We knew how our people there couldn't dare to vote because the hotnots would be standing there, waiting to vote in the same place as the whites, and they had a different way of life and it was easy for them to swear. If you were white you had to go very early to vote, otherwise the hotnots curse you out of line. They'll start from your toes and go up and swear about your mother and your father. And that's what we didn't want. What belonged to our parents was holy to us. So we were pleased when Dr Malan came in.

'I'd promised the Lord that I will never smoke again if the National Party comes in, so that night I left off smoking. I told Mr Rymer, my boss at Randles Bros, that I'd promised God that if he brings us in I'll never smoke again. "I'm sorry, I know you belong to a different party from mine and I'll never let my party interfere with my work, but I'm telling you I'll never smoke again." And he used to bring me boiled sweets because I was biting my fingernails.'

Maria considered joining the right-wing Herstigte Nasionale Party, the HNP, and helped its local candidate in the 1981 elections. She was, however, unhappy over the HNP's rejection of the English language. 'I've got daughters-in-law who are English and a son-in-law who is German, and they're good, lovable children; they're the white race and it doesn't matter what language you are, if you belong to the white race you're good enough to marry my children.'

When Dr Andries Treurnicht broke away from the National Party in 1982 to form the Conservative Party, she was one of the first to join. She maintains that the CP is really the genuine old National Party of Dr Verwoerd, the architect of separate development. 'We are modern; we are human; we are Christian. Every mother wants what is best for her child: education, health, good living. We say that it is their right as a human race for the blacks to have these things, but they must be separate. Now we call it "partition" because America made the word "apartheid" sound so horrible, so cruel, which it wasn't.

'This blue sky is everyone's, no matter what colour you are. God gave it to all of us. But *we've* got the belief that God made us different because we are different, otherwise he would have made us all the same. If you are a proud black you wouldn't want to mix with the white people. You're proud of your black children, their shiny little black faces and white teeth. Black is beautiful. White is beautiful. Mix the two: make bastards. And that is God's truth. That's why we never have respect for the low-class coloureds.'

Maria has also joined the AWB, the Afrikaner Weerstandsbeweging. 'Now you'll say, you belong to one party, why join the other party? The difference is that the Conservative Party is to do with parliament, whereas the AWB stands only to bring the white people together, to remind them that they are a minority and that if we allow the government to go on doing what it is doing now, we will be no more. It will be a bastard race and we don't want that.' She is concerned over accusations that Eugene Terre'Blanche, the leader of the AWB, is a Nazi and a racist. 'If they say you are a Nazi or you are a racist because you stand up for your few white people, then I'm certainly one, too. We only stand for what is our own. We are only fighting for our children. I wouldn't like to see my beautiful daughter with a little black baby. I could never feel the same. . . . Good God! I'm never a racist!' She supports Terre'Blanche in his call for a territory to be set aside for whites, pointing out that areas have been designated specifically for other groups such as the Tswanas, Vendas and so on. The territory he claims for the *boerevolk*, the Afrikaner people, is the 'two old Republics', Transvaal and the Orange Free State, as well as a portion of northern Natal, settled by Afrikaners in the last century. 'We ask it for the Afrikaners, but the English and Greeks can be there, too. It doesn't matter what language you speak; as long as you're a Christian and you're white, you're welcome to stay in that part.' Jews, if they 'continue in their Jewish faith', will not be admitted. Blacks would be admitted to the white areas only as migratory workers. 'We are fighting for our culture and our heritage.'

Mr van Niekerk belongs to neither the CP nor the AWB. 'For peace in the house, he never ever speaks politics, he just tells me, "When I was a policeman I had to serve *everyone*."' Two of the children have followed their mother's political line. But her youngest daughter, Andrea, who is a post-graduate student at the English-speaking University of the Witwatersrand, is more independent. She has expressed the opinion that people who love one another should be allowed to marry. This is an aberration that her mother attributes to the mistake of social mixing: 'If you think you want to marry a different colour then you must go and look in the Bible. God didn't want it. He would have made us all the same if he'd wanted it. He wouldn't have made different nations and different people.'

The repeal in April 1985 of the Mixed Marriages Act of 1949 and the Immorality Act of 1957 was a great shock to many Nationalists. 'We stand for not bastardizing our land, our people. It's got to be pure white, pure Indian, pure blacks and the coloureds must be proud of what they are now. And here P. W. Botha comes along and takes away those laws. That's just giving an open letter to carry on, mix and marry with one another. We couldn't believe it! It was the shock of our lives!' Together with many Nationalists, they had imagined that the reforms for which the Prime Minister had elicited the support of the electorate in the previous election would be to make racial laws stricter, 'And here he throws everything open! It was a horrible shock, especially for our old people.'

She condemns the idea that the Group Areas Act might be repealed. 'My culture is that I have been brought up to respect you, no matter what colour you are, and my children have been brought up to respect, but the black man's culture is different, his way of living is different. He'll shout from one end of the street to the other. I'll be always on the needle. Instead of a happy, Christian person, I'll be a ball of hatred.' The introduction of black and coloured supervisors and managers in some super-markets does not perturb her. 'If he wants to work, he should work. He's also got a family; if he can't work, he can't feed his family. But I believe they should stay among their own people.

'And another thing, you must never, never refuse somebody bread in your house. If a native girl or a black man comes to my door and he asks for food, I give him food. But when a child comes, I tell him, "No, go and ask for work, because you're just loafing around. Go and look for work; there's many people who will give you work in their gardens." One of my sons cut the neighbour's grass for pocket money. It's nothing to be ashamed of.'

The Afrikaans Protestant Church was formed in 1986 as a result of the displeasure of Dutch Reformed Church members at the decision to admit worshippers of all races. 'I don't believe in throwing my church open. Why must they come and sit right by me?' She would not object to the blacks using the church *building* and the bibles and hymn books, but believes that their services should be at a different time. Soon after the resolution had been passed, three blacks walked into her church in the suburb of Kroonrand. 'My neighbour, Mr T. S. du Plessis, a deacon in the church, stood up and like a gentleman he told the black lady, "Please, this is for the white congregation. You will disturb the people." People were looking, especially the kids –

it's something unusual. The kids were not giving their attention to the dominee; they were all peeping behind their mothers' backs.' A church member bought the disused Dutch Reformed Church in Brixton, a mile or so west of the city and there are already 12,000 in the congregation of this Afrikaans Protestant church. Upcountry farmers have contributed 60,000 rand, the result of a livestock sale they organized for the purpose. Maria, anxious as to the future of her children and grandchildren, is happier in her new, segregated church.

Asked what would happen if blacks tried to join the congregation, she replies, 'As civilized people we will go and ask them to please go out. "Do you want to have a service? Our priest will always welcome you to tell you about the Lord. But here we, as Afrikaner South African whites with a culture of our own, we want to have our church." Fighting is not for us.'

Just as abhorrent to Maria is the participation of the Indians in the tricameral system of government. 'We believe that our parliament is the house of our Lord, so how can you have Hindus and Muhammadans there! We believe that they can have their own House and make their own laws, but we don't want them to do it in the House where the Christians are.' She excuses the inclusion of some Jews in parliament because they come from 'the land of our Lord', Israel, visited by many of the newly affluent Afrikaners.

SAMUEL GOLDBLATT

CONSIDERABLE NUMBERS OF Eastern European Jews, anxious to escape the pogroms, came to South Africa in the final decades of the last century and early in the present one. Between 1880 and 1910 some 40,000 Jewish immigrants entered South Africa. The discovery of diamonds in Kimberley and the surrounding district in the early 1870s and of gold on the Witwatersrand in 1886 drew many of them to the country. The first Union census in 1911 showed a count of 46,926 Jews, 3.7 per cent of the white population. Some of these were English and German Jews who were generally better off than the Eastern Europeans. The latter would send the men first, who once they had gained some kind of foothold, would summon their families. Most were impecunious and spoke only Yiddish.

Solomon Goldblatt, born in about 1890 in Trisk, a little village in White Russia, arrived in South Africa in the early years of this century and travelled up to Koffiefontein in the Kimberley district. He began like many other Jewish immigrants as a pedlar, or as the Afrikaners said, a *smous*, plodding from farm to farm until he could afford a pack-donkey and later, a horse and cart. His history, as he progressed to trading and then to setting up a '*kaffir* store' in Senekal, is almost lost because in later years, when his life continued to be a struggle, he was silent concerning earlier hardships.

His first wife, Sarah Wainstein, who was perhaps a second-generation South African, died giving birth to their son. In 1925 he married Cissie Dreyer, an Irish Jewess of German origin who, with her mother and brother, had arrived in South Africa in 1909, following her father who had come, as a grandson was one day to remark ironically, to make his fortune.

By the time that Samuel, the couple's only child, was born on 23 March 1927, Solomon Goldblatt had bought two small farms of 800 and 1200 morgen respectively, just outside Senekal, a town in the eastern Orange Free State. A Mr Klopper managed these farms for him, endeavouring to raise cattle and to grow maize; but Solomon Goldblatt's entry into farming was ill-timed, for the early 1930s were the years not only of the depression, but of a particularly severe and lengthy drought. He also operated a mill where he ground mealies brought to him by small farmers, chiefly blacks, of whom a few were still being permitted to farm on a sharecropper basis. His chief source of income was from the 'kaffir store' in town. He sold blankets, rolls of material, tinned foodstuffs, maize-meal, sugar, hats, mainly to the blacks. 'He considered himself', Sam observes drily, 'to be an all-rounder, but he wasn't a very successful one. Men like my father had a major problem in producing an income for their families and their whole life revolved around business, around earning a living under very difficult conditions.' Joseph Goldblatt, Solomon's elder brother, either more astute or more fortunate, developed a successful grain business in Bloemfontein.

The house in Senekal in which the Goldblatt family lived was the usual functional square structure with a *stoep* in front which, together with the high ceilings, helped to keep the house cool in summer. The roof was corrugated iron. At the back was a cabbage patch and the *kleinhuisie* (little house), the euphemism for the long-drop lavatory. 'There was a coal stove and no geyser – that came as a luxury, later on. You heated a four-gallon paraffin tin of water on the stove and carried that through to the bathroom. Water came from the windmill and the rainwater tank, but during the early 1930s when eventually our dams on the farms dried up totally, it became increasingly scarce, so my brother and I would have to bath together.'

The household was run on strict kosher lines, 'my mother saw to that. The Irish Jews are like the Irish Catholics, rabid and intense. I was brought up in the orthodox Jewish fashion, going to synagogue, observing the various Jewish rites, not allowed to carry money on the sabbath, that kind of thing. There didn't seem to be any class consciousness; poor and wealthy Jews shared. In these small communities if a Jew didn't go to synagogue he was singled out as being the exception, because it was the practice for everyone to go. We were taught', Samuel comments, a little grimly, 'that we had to go to *shul* so that non-Jewish people would recognize that we were Jewish. That was one of the rationales.' Observance of the sabbath, however, was superseded by the necessity to earn a living, so although the family attended synagogue on Friday night, the store remained open on Saturdays. (This was a source of continuous spiritual discomfort to Cissie Goldblatt.) The language in the house was English, but the boys, whose friends were all Jews or Afrikaners, were more at home in Afrikaans which was also the language the servants were expected to understand.

According to Sam, Jewish families in predominantly Afrikaans-speaking country towns such as Senekal contended not only with the economic perplexities, but also with considerable anti-Semitism. His recollections are mostly unhappy. 'There was no English-medium school in the town and I think that at my Afrikaans-medium primary school, of about 300 predominantly Afrikaans-speaking children, eight or nine must have been Jewish. In typical historical tradition there have to be scapegoats and the Jewish children were, to a great degree, the scapegoats.' He was constantly aware of the potential threat. 'If you went to a movie you might have your hair or your ears pulled, or be hit on the back. There were occasions when I had physically to fight my way out of school because I was Jewish. I would have preferred to have gone to school in more —' he searches for a word, '— more comfortable surroundings.' There was little help from the masters, some of whom, in Sam's opinion, capitalized on the predominant prejudice. There was a good deal of corporal punishment, and it seemed to be the Jewish boys who were singled out; the fact of their tending to be among the brighter pupils added rather than detracted from the problem. 'One teacher by the name of Van den Bergh who, I expect, would have been an extremely successful Nazi, took great delight in beating the Jewish children. And of course we would never tell our parents. One night my father happened to walk into the bathroom while we were in the bath. My half-brother, Issy, had had a caning by Van den Bergh and he had weals across his backside, actually open cuts.' It took a little while before the boys revealed the truth. Issy was taken to the doctor who reported his findings to the headmaster. Nothing further was heard of the incident.

Jews were subjected to a variety of pejorative names. Sam's brother played in the first rugby team as hooker. 'The only support he ever got was when we were playing schools in one of the other towns and they would all shout, "*Hak! Jood!*" which meant, "Hook! Jew!" And if there was a Jew in the team, he was the one you went for. City people were generally unaware of the anti-Semitism in the *dorps*. It was a state of affairs hardly conducive to the development of self-confidence; one continuously felt threatened. I certainly did. I always felt threatened.' His father's taciturnity concerning pogroms led him to believe that parents might have been aware of anti-Semitism, but that they didn't feel it to the same extent. 'They weren't subjected to it the same way the kids were.'

Not all Afrikaners were anti-Semitic, but such prejudice, amounting sometimes to victimization, appeared to be almost part of their culture. Jews were associated with the *smous* of the old days, speaking broken Afrikaans. It is not improbable that the success of many of the Jewish general dealers lent an edge to attacks.

The Goldblatt boys played in the Zand River in Senekal and tried to model the clay into oxen as the black children did; as they grew older there were 'rugby' games with the blacks on a flat, sandy area. The children rode horses bareback and stole fruit from neighbouring orchards at night. During holidays Sam sometimes visited cousins in Johannesburg, 'I was the kid from the Free State, speaking English with a heavy Afrikaans accent, so I'm not sure that I was the greatest asset to have in the home. We rode on the trams and looked at the shops in town.'

Mixed bathing was not permitted at Senekal's municipal swimming-pool – men and women used it on different days. Sam, vulnerable to ducking once he was in the water, confesses to having been 'dead frightened' of swimming. 'And you, as a Jew, knew that if you left your clothing in the changing-room it could be stolen by the time you came back. But you learnt to live with it. It was an accepted part of life.

'There were some Afrikaners who refused to shop at Jewish shops, who refused to do business with Jewish people. In the Afrikaans communities anti-Semitism was drastic, but I don't think you could say that if you were Afrikaans, you were anti-Semitic. I expect there were, even in those days, some relatively liberal-thinking Afrikaners who were maybe broader in their outlook.' Sam thinks that the success that many Jews achieved in their businesses fuelled envy and dislike. Although there were a few English-speaking families in Senekal, he cannot remember having any friends who were English-speaking and non-Jewish.

The Jews were not the only butt of derision; in the early 1930s there were also considerable numbers of poor white families, many of them with six or eight children. 'The poor whites were frowned upon by the more affluent Afrikaner, the successful farmer, accountant, doctor, store-owner – I'm talking about their kids. My contemporaries would victimize the children of the man who drove the night-wagon (there was still the bucket system of sewage disposal), or the guy who did any kind of menial job, like being in charge of a black road gang.' Jewish children suffered far less at the hands of the poor white children who themselves were victimized. 'The poor whites were generally less intelligent, probably simpler in their attitudes and had other problems, whereas the ones who were more comfortable could afford the luxury of having a go at the Jewish people.'

In the hot summer evenings after supper Solomon Goldblatt would sometimes take the children down to Paxinos's café. Throughout South Africa the little neighbourhood shop, open at all hours, has generally been a Greek family business. 'That was a really big thing, to walk down there with your father and he would buy you an ice-cream, which cost a tickey, the equivalent of threepence.'

Jewish families in the *dorps* were closely knit, not only by their religion, but by a strong community spirit. The original synagogue in Senekal, on the bank of the Zand River and now a national monument, was the one that Sam attended on the sabbath and high festival days. By the time of his bar mitzvah the congregation had shrunk and there was no regular rabbi to take the services. Sam's preparation was with the rabbi who lived in Bethlehem. Sundays were often spent with friends in towns such as Paul Roux, Ficksburg, Kroonstad, or Bethlehem which, though they were twenty miles or more away, were considered to be neighbouring. Anti-Semitism was not discussed at these gatherings. 'It was a way of life. You just didn't talk about it. You accepted it, the fact that we weren't the most popular people in the town. And our counterparts on the Afrikaner side were being brought up in a culture that taught them that Jews are no good, so have a go at them if you can.'

In 1940 Solomon Goldblatt died of coronary thrombosis, a not uncommon cause of death in the Jewish community at that time. His son believed that their poverty and the cold in Eastern Europe had contributed to the diet of Jews generally being extraordinarily high in fats; in the long, hot summers of the Free State, however, such dietary habits were dangerous. 'He was a physical man, used to carrying the bags of mealies up and down the stairs to the mill. He died of a second coronary, just six weeks after his first. He had no life insurance, because he was one of the chaps who was going to make it, but he didn't live long enough. The Land Bank, at that time, owned just about all the farms in the Free State and his farms were mortgaged to the hilt. There were just about no assets and he was insolvent for the amount of seventeen pounds.'

Following Solomon Goldblatt's death, his widow, accompanied by thirteen-year-old Sam, moved to Johannesburg to stay with her brother and sister-in-law in Greenside, a middle-class suburb largely composed of golden face-brick houses.

'My half-sister, Jeanette, had already left Senekal because when a child left school they went to the big city, either to university or to work, and generally lived in one of the many boarding-houses in Hillbrow, Yeoville and Berea that catered for people from the country. Some Jewish families took in boarders. A useful situation. It created the ghetto environment all over again.' His brother Issy matriculated later that year and established himself independently in Johannesburg. Sam was sent to Parktown Boys' High, a large and well established government school. He describes the period, in a tone of grim understatement, as one of 'some discomfort'. His mother went to work, making lampshades at her brother's lampshade factory in one of the southern suburbs. At night he shared her room. There was scant communication between them and Sam conjectures, 'I imagine she had her own major problems in dealing with that situation where she must have been completely unwanted by her sister-in-law. I'm sure it must have been an embarrassment for her to sit at the dining-room table and she must have gone through some excruciatingly unhappy experiences.'

At school he found himself in the company of boys from a relatively affluent background. He was no longer subjected to anti-Semitic attacks, but his small-town background and Afrikaans accent set him apart. 'So there I became the star Afrikaans pupil and the buffoon in the English class. The English teacher would call me a lump and the essence of stupidity which didn't do my self-image, already battered in Senekal by Afrikaners, much good.' The compensations were sympathetic Afrikaans and Latin teachers. Furthermore, freed from fears of anti-Semitic victimization, he began to enjoy rugby and got on well with the rugby master, Frikkie Marais. 'In Senekal I'd been dead scared to play rugby because it was just natural, if there was a Jewish guy in the team, that he would be beaten up. I was very frightened and would only go so far as maybe a practice match and run like hell if I saw a few guys coming at me.' In Johannesburg, he and one of his friends would swim at the municipal swimming-baths or in Emmarentia dam and go to the cinema on a Saturday afternoon. There were occasional parties at private houses. 'I had my first relationship with a girl in my last years at school. She went to Barnato Park and I used to help her with her Afrikaans.'

In 1942 Sam's mother married a widower from Senekal and he remained with his uncle and aunt. He matriculated in 1943 and it was suggested that he be articled to his aunt's brother, a leading Johannesburg accountant. Sam's desires lay elsewhere. He wanted to join the Air Force and become a pilot, 'because so many people I knew were joining the Army, I wanted to join. It was the "in" thing to do. It was quite a shameful thing to be walking around in civvies. There was a certain amount of glamour in wearing a uniform, and having a basic interest in photography, I thought I might do a navigator's course. There was a strong desire to be identified with all the others, not to be out on a limb.' With weary resignation he explains, 'I was only sixteen and my mother wouldn't sign the papers. That was another great disappointment in my life.' So, as an articled clerk, he began the tedious matter of adding up endless columns of figures. On Friday and Saturday nights he worked downtown in the wholesale business area at one of the two intriguingly sleazy nightclubs, the Savoy, where from a narrow doorway one climbed, almost in the dark, a steep flight of stairs to the dimly lit room with a small dance floor surrounded by tables. Customers brought their own liquor, but if you knew Red Webber, the owner, he could fix you up. 'There were some fine musicians like Cyril Jenks and trumpeter Rabinowitz. The popular meal there was steak and eggs and sweetcorn. I could make maybe 5 or 10 pounds a night in tips, whereas my salary with the firm of accountants was £3.17s.4d. and they deducted a penny for the stamp you had to sign across.' At this time he was sharing his room with his aunt's nephew, a medical student, and the two young men got on well. But the year was a gruelling one. 'I didn't really want to do accountancy. I was keen on sport and didn't have the opportunity of playing because of my job, early morning and evening lectures, and I was working to become financially independent. Didn't enjoy too many luxuries. If I went visiting it was on my bicycle. I suppose I had the compounded problems of an adolescent.' Shortly before the exams at the end of his first year, overwhelmed and close to collapse, he went to his aunt, Minnie Dreyer, the only person in whom it seemed he could confide. 'She gave me sympathy. It was the first time that I realized that she was aware of my being there. We became close to one another, good friends; she became my confidant.' He gave up accountancy.

The year was 1945 and Samuel had to compete for employment against demobilized soldiers. He found a job in a motor spares business, owned by gentiles and with one or two Jewish employees, where he worked himself up to become one of their travellers, his fluency in Afrikaans being an asset in the country areas. 'I worked the Free State and the western and eastern Transvaal. It really wasn't my style. I hated it, but I worked on commission and it was a way of making some money.' The weekends, when he returned to the small rooming-house in Berea, near the city centre, provided him with a brief respite and an opportunity to go dancing which he loved. He had taken lessons in ballroom dancing and become a teacher. 'But I used to get a Sunday night depression; it was a most disturbing experience, contemplating the early start the next morning to travel endless stretches of dusty dirt roads and sleeping in a different hotel every night.'

After the move to Johannesburg Sam had attended the Berea synagogue, and in accordance with the Jewish teaching, walked the considerable distance from his home. 'Then I kind of got over that and went to the Greenside synagogue which was much nearer.' He had also become involved in the Jewish Youth Movement, 'a middle-of-the-road one', designed to create an awareness of what was then Palestine, and Zionism. When the War of Independence broke out in Israel in May 1948, 'a number of us were canvassed as to whether we'd be interested in going to Israel to do a particular job. Most agreed. We were involved in some very basic training here in South Africa on certain days of the week and were aware that the police had noticed our activities because we had the numbers of their unmarked police cars. So it was, to some degree, a bit of an undercover operation.'

Previous groups had been successful in leaving South Africa, but when the *Sunday Times* broke the story of the secret mission just before the departure of Sam's group the government forbade the venture.

The Immigration Quota Act, drastically restricting the flow of immigrants from Eastern Europe, had been passed by Parliament in May 1930. Although Jews were not named in the Bill, introduced by the Nationalist-Labour government in power at the time, it was clear that it was aimed against them. It met with scant opposition from other parties. Over the years the Jews had been accused of being unassimilable. Furthermore, it was alleged that because the Jews had monopolized the commercial field, leaving no room for Afrikaners, they were thus responsible for the poor white problem. Jews were accused, too, of crowding gentiles out of the professions. 'There were many instances of attacks on Jews, on Jewish businesses, synagogues. The swastika was a very popular insignia in this country at that time. News of what was happening in Germany filtered in from Germany in the early 1930s and seemed to be a licence for anti-Semitism to be pursued in a much more brazen fashion.'

In 1933 there had emerged the most powerful of a number of Nazi-style movements, the South African Christian National Socialist Movement; its activist spearhead was the Uniformed Greyshirts with cells throughout the country and a fortnightly bilingual newspaper. Among its aims was a Jew-free state, to be achieved through the revocation of South African nationality from all Jews, and the protection of South Africans against being ousted by Jews from any trade or profession. One Afrikaner expressed regret at not being able to eliminate the Jews as Hitler was doing, adding that they could, however, 'make it impossible for them to live here.' The anti-Semitic movement resulted from grassroots pressure and public manifestation was discouraged when the National Party came to power in 1948.

The National Party won the 1948 general election by a small margin of seats, although the United Party, owing to the system of delimitation, polled more votes. 'I was in shock at the result as most of the Jewish people in this country, I expect, were.'

The news that the Prime Minister, Field Marshal Smuts, had lost his Standerton seat was the culminating blow. 'It seemed to be the death-knell and more so in view of Eric Louw's anti-Semitic pre-election platform and campaign.' Louw had been the South African Minister Plenipotentiary to the United States, England, France and Portugal, during which time he had become deeply influenced by Nazism. 'It was a very frightening experience because Eric Louw's verbal threats had been that he would rid the country of Jews if the Nats got into power. So the Jews were very frightened when the Nats won the election, anticipating that there would be a purge of the Jewish communities throughout the country. But one never heard a word after that. It disappeared entirely. From an official, governmental point of view I don't recall having heard anything further about the Jews or anti-Semitism. So the whole thing kind of settled down.' From the age of eighteen Sam voted for the United Party, 'Not so much for them as against the National Party,' but never became involved in politics.

In 1949 Sam Goldblatt started his own motor spares firm at Odendaalsrus on the new Orange Free State goldfields, in partnership with Teddy Cohen who already had a business on the East Rand. 'I sold my car and borrowed 250 pounds from an uncle (not the one I was living with). He was an accountant and thought it sounded like a good proposition. It was an opportunity, and we thought that we could do OK, and of course Afrikaans was no problem to me. When I got there Welkom had a bottle store, a pharmacy, a café and a couple of general stores, and that was it. Odendaalsrus had the old Commercial Hotel with its swing doors into the bar. The miners and the shaft-sinkers earned good money and there was a lot of money around, lots of drinking and drunkenness.'

On the goldfields Sam served as a committee member of the Jewish congregation. 'It was a growing community and we were all young people. There is the Jewish Helping Hand and Burial Society, called the Chevra Kadisha, and we young men had to prepare people for burial because there was no one else to do it; quite traumatic for some of us.' He speaks of the pioneering spirit at that time with people coming from all parts of the country to open outfitters, jewellery stores, garages; and doctors, accountants and lawyers. 'There was a large English-speaking community. We played golf and were members of the Oppenheimer Golf Club. It was a young, vibrant Jewish community and we had a lot of fun. Danced, had parties, got drunk. The anti-Semitic aspect seemed to have almost disappeared. Here and there you knew that somebody was an anti-Semite, didn't like Jews; he probably wasn't shy to talk about it, but he didn't do anything.'

On holiday in Cape Town he and his friends discovered that they, as somewhat prosperous bachelors from the Free State goldfields, were regarded not unfavourably by the young women of the town. It was in February 1953, in a party at a restaurant, that he met Betty Kramer, private secretary to the manager of Woolworths. They were married in August that year at the Vredehoek Synagogue in Cape Town. Max Kramer, Betty's father, was a 'gent's hairdresser' who had come out to South Africa from Moscow in the mid-1920s: Rose Riesin from Vilna had followed in the same year and they were married in Cape Town.

Sam and Betty returned to Welkom where she had no difficulty in finding secretarial jobs. For the first two years of their marriage they shared Sam's bachelor flat. Then they bought a house in Odendaalsrus. His eyes light up as he describes the weekend golf tournaments and the 'fantastic social life' with its succession of parties in the growing community of the goldfields. He had bought out his partner and established another little business in Glen Harmony, but his mounting prosperity failed to satisfy him. 'I really couldn't stand business. I'm not the right kind of person for it. I thought there was more to life than buying from A and selling to B. It just didn't appeal to me.' In 1957 he sold his concerns and moved to Cape Town where he had always wanted to live. 'We had made good friends, still keep in touch with many of them. But I hated the work I was doing and hated the people I was doing business with. I realized I wasn't a trader. I was pleased to get out of the Free State, didn't even look back when I pulled out.'

Before Sam could find the small motor spares business that he wanted he was persuaded to join the Sun Life Assurance Company of Canada as an insurance salesman. It was with some reluctance that he agreed. 'I didn't know anybody in Cape Town and I had to learn the business the hard way, which is probably the best way to learn it.' His interest was soon seized by the possibilities of the enterprise and he studied and took courses at the head office in Canada. Mutual funds and life assurance were his particular interest. 'I earned quite a reputation in Cape Town for being a good life insurance man and so it became easier as I went along. I got working with a number of firms of accountants. The easier it got, the more interested I became.' He derived 'tremendous satisfaction' from the job and the growing esteem in which he was held. 'I liked working intimately and confidentially with people and somehow I earned the confidence of the people who became my clients, so I liked that level of communication. I became very interested in personal development and in training on sales courses. The motivational aspects of all those things interested me and I found a niche and obviously, if you find a niche, you become good at it. The Dale Carnegie course which he attended helped him to overcome his diffidence. 'I learnt to stand up on a platform and talk without the words sticking in my throat. It was a tremendous achievement.'

He was assigned to 'cold canvassing', calling on strangers to discuss life insurance. 'It was a painful experience for me, but I had to do it because I was determined that I would succeed. I didn't want to give up. Despite my tremendous shyness, I pushed myself to make these calls. But I developed a particular approach that enabled me, when I telephoned people I didn't know, to get appointments.' He went on to do a Dale Carnegie sales course and became one of their assistant trainers at evening sessions. This led to his appointment within his company to a position where he was in charge of recruitment and training. The creation of a successful sales team was a further source of satisfaction.

Throughout this period Sam's interest in Israel grew. 'I think it was my desire to identify with what I thought was "my people", and I felt that the only place that I could really do that in a fulfilled fashion was in Israel.' A visit he made in August 1961 elicited some job offers from life insurance companies there and strengthened his resolve. Betty was not in agreement, but finally submitted and left Cape Town, where she had been brought up and where her parents were living, with great reluctance. The year was 1962 when the country had not yet begun to recover from the slump caused by the Sharpeville massacre two years previously. The depression had not, however, affected the life assurance business.

The Goldblatts' first four months in Israel were spent at an Ulpan, or absorption school. They lived, with their two small sons, Saul and David, in a very small flat. 'The food was terrible, the conditions alternately muddy and dusty. Miserable.' In the vicinity were some low class north African Jews, 'very unpleasant people', who stole anything that was left outside. 'Conditions were a bit primitive, but fortunately there were, in addition to the families from the USA, Mexico, Poland and France, a number of South African families with whom we developed quite a spirit.' Parents attended Hebrew classes each morning while their children were cared for in a crèche or a school. 'In the afternoon some of us studied and other chaps started looking round for jobs or housing. It was a busy time and you had to become accustomed to the life-style and environment. We went out every Saturday, touring the country and saw a helluva lot of Israel during that four-month period. The evenings were spent socially, studying together, playing bridge and having a bit of fun.' Sam, jolted by the change from a westernized business and professional community to the culture of Israel, pronounced the four months in the Ulpan to be necessary shock-treatment. 'If you go into a bank in South Africa, or to the Post Office, or if you get on a bus, there is a certain amount of civility, there's a certain rapport. But you don't have that in Israel. You have to fight for everything. You've got to fight on the roads, you've got to fight on the bus, you've got to fight in the queue and you've got to fight at the Post Office or the licensing department. You have to fight your way through because', he gives a little bark of a laugh, 'that's how the people are. So that's quite a culture shock. It was literally starting all over again, but that wasn't a real problem. It was, again, the pioneering spirit.'

Sam was employed by one of the largest insurance companies in Israel, Migdal Insurance, Tel Aviv, to develop a sales force similar to the one he had created in Cape Town. As many of the men he trained could not speak English, his own mastery of Hebrew grew. Finally, after nine months, the men he had trained were ready to write up their own insurance; Sam explained to the management the necessity for a contract between the salesmen and the company. The company was not prepared to issue a contract. If there was to be nothing holding those whom he trained to himself and to the company, Sam saw no purpose in continuing. 'If somebody else offered them an extra 5 per cent they would take it.' Despite this divergence of views, he was urged to remain with the company and he continued for some while to occupy one of their offices and to sell for them.

Sam and Betty had bought a house in Herzlea, north of Tel Aviv. They developed close relationships with many of their neighbours who came from Russia, Poland, France, Germany and Egypt and continue to correspond with them.

However, in February 1966, having been away for exactly four years, they returned to Cape Town. Betty, a warm friendly woman, was as reluctant to return as she had been to leave. Their emigration experience had been disrupting, but 'interesting and wonderful' and had cost them almost their last cent.

Sam joined the first mutual fund company in South Africa and opened the Sage offices in Cape Town in March 1966. The concept was new; he strove to persuade accountants and attorneys of the value of unit trusts. The Stock Exchange boom in 1967 and 1968 was helpful in boosting unit trusts upwards, but they fell disastrously in the slump a year later. In the early 1970s Sam opened his own brokerage firm which he called Personal Financial Planning, devoted to the planning and analyses that accountants did not do for their clients. When, in 1974, Liberty Life, a large insurance group, took over the company with which he had originally been associated, Sun Life of Canada, Sam was persuaded to join them, on the understanding that he could run 'his own style of operation'. In 1978 he moved up to their head office in Johannesburg. His most recent development has been to take over responsibility for the sales and marketing of Guard-bank, a mutual fund in whose management company Liberty Life and First National Bank are joint shareholders.

There are three Goldblatt children, all of whom have been educated in Jewish schools. Saul, the eldest, born in 1957, became involved in the computer world but, frustrated by his com-pulsory military training and the annual camps he was obliged to attend, left South Africa for Hong Kong where he is prosper-ing. David, born in 1960, is specializing in paediatrics at the Great Ormond Street Hospital in London. 'He has not emi-grated. He loves Africa. He would return', Sam pauses for em-phasis, 'under different circumstances.' He will not amplify his meaning. Mia, seven years younger, has been inspired by the eight months she spent at the Hebrew University in Jerusalem on a special programme and inclines towards settling in Israel when she has obtained her Bachelor of Commerce degree at the University of the Witwatersrand.

The establishment of the State of Israel, Sam believes, has been effective in improving the image of the Jew in the eyes of the non-Jew. 'Israel is such a popular place with Afrikaners and Nationalists. They suddenly see a different kind of Jew and come back with a much healthier respect for the Jew in this country. Even some of the clubs which previously excluded Jews have opened their doors to them.' He is uneasy at the growth of the AWB (Afrikaner Weerstandsbeweging) which claims that it would exclude Jews, together with Indians and blacks, from its ideal state. 'The Jewish Board of Deputies is very aware of this movement, of its power and influence. We have no doubt that, should the Conservative Party become a dominant political force, there will be very, very specific moves made against the Jewish people. I have no doubt that there would be some marked emigration by Jews and English-speaking people.' He is alarmed at the similarities between the AWB and the Nazi movement. 'Their swastika-like insignia is only a symbol, the *herrenvolk* symbol, but it goes much deeper. I don't think that most people

—— 189 ——

in this country really know very much about what happened in Nazi Germany, whereas when you talk to people who've suffered that experience and been through concentration camps, you begin to identify the AWB kind of movement.'

Sam, lean and fit, runs early every morning on the cricket field at the Old Edwardian Sports Club. He has the opportunity of retiring in less than three years and judges himself able to afford to live overseas, but the final decision would be dependent on currency regulations and the value of the rand at the time. He and Betty would like to live in a country more accessible to their children. But for the climate, he would choose England. He has a deep love of South Africa, but foresees major problems in the form of emergent black power, industrial problems and strikes of 'huge proportions.' 'I think that there will be major problems among the black people, the workers and the anti-workers, the kind of thing that we have seen to some degree and which, I think, will escalate. I think we will suffer increasing acts of terrorism. You can see how easily people adjust. If a bomb explodes and kills a few people, nobody really reacts to it. There's a bit of shock and horror at the time and a little bit of nervousness, but twenty-four hours later people have adjusted to it.' He foresees people becoming, to some extent, shock-proof to increasing acts of terrorism and the possible emergence of a military state. 'I don't believe that you can live in a country with thirty to thirty-five million blacks and keep them suppressed *ad infinitum*, so that I'm not sure that one can predict with any degree of accuracy what is likely to happen, but I do see some very difficult times ahead, and I think they'll be interesting times. I don't have any doubt that, in time to come, there has to be a black government in this country. There just has to be. By force of numbers.'

'I would have no problem living under a black government provided it was economically viable – that's the final analysis for most people, economic viability.'

SUE DRUMMOND*

Parktown north is one of the older suburbs in Johannesburg, some of the bungalow houses in its quiet streets dating from the beginning of the century. The Drummonds' house is not one of those that have been modernized, but they have recently erected a ten-foot wall along its road frontage which, together with the iron gates, assures a greater degree of security and some privacy. The house, with its corrugated iron roof, is set well back from the road; a lawn stretches up towards the small swimming-pool, fenced around its perimeter to keep children out. Two Labradors, one golden, the other black, come bounding out, soon abandoning their ferocious barks for waving tails and a fussy welcome. Sue, tall and very slender, stands on the long, wide *stoep* below which the arum lilies cluster; three-year-old Emma's mop of black waving hair nestles shyly into her mother's side. Sue's clothes are uncontrived; her thick, chestnut-brown hair is wound up loosely at the back of her head, but strands keep escaping. It is only when she begins to talk that she is lit to a kind of beauty.

A stable door opens into the living-room, casual and spacious. Paperback books, whose titles tempt the visitor to pick them up, lie about. More books, records and tapes are stacked in shelves. On one wall is an original oil-painting of an English harbour, on another an Irma Stern print of a woman's head. There is also a

* The names of the principal characters in this story have been changed at their request.

print of a black woman against a background of diamond mesh wire, her eyes bound with a scarlet cloth. Over the fireplace is a picture in pastel crayons which, Sue explains, symbolizes the post-independence situation in Africa where an elite group takes over and establishes itself at the expense of the majority. The house invites exploration.

Suzanne Duceau (she prefers the abbreviation, Sue) was born into a Catholic family in Kensington, Johannesburg, in 1954. Her father, Victor Anton Duceau, was born in what was then Lourenço Marques in Mozambique in 1925. His maternal grandfather, an immigrant from Holland, had fought on the side of the Boers in the Anglo-Boer War. He had been captured and deported to Holland, but allowed to return under an amnesty. His wife survived a British concentration camp. Sue's paternal grandfather, Felix Victor Duceau, was French and one of the first electricians in Lourenço Marques. When he began, in 1917, electricity had only just come to the city and was installed in relatively few houses and buildings. He would travel about in a rickshaw to read meters and to discuss with property owners, over a cup of coffee, the problems they were having with their electricity.

Felix Victor Duceau died of malaria in 1931, leaving his wife, Kitty Bies, with little money to rear her four children. Sue sees her as 'an amazing woman' who, against all odds, started up a typing school in the city. There being no suitable school for them in Lourenço Marques, the boys were sent as boarders to the Marist Brothers College in Johannesburg. Victor, who was to be Sue's father, went on to gain a degree in electrical engineering at the University of the Witwatersrand. After graduating he travelled to Manchester to pursue his post-graduate studies, in the course of which he met Jean Mary Stuttard. Victor proposed to her and was accepted. He returned to Johannesburg, established himself in a job, and cabled for his fiancée to follow him. They were married in 1953 and set up house in Kensington, a prim, middle-class suburb to the east of the city. In due course Victor became a naturalized South African.

Sue, their first child, was born in 1954. Nine months later she lay on the back seat of the car in which her father was teaching her mother to drive. In a moment of panic there was a fatal swerve and a collision. Sue and her father survived, but Jean Mary died. Two years passed and her father visited Manchester leaving Sue in the care of relatives. He returned with his second wife from that city. Sue was three years old at the time and says she has some warm recollections of her early years with her stepmother, but the relationship deteriorated as her three step-brothers were born. She became 'a problem' and, aged five-and-a-half, was sent as a boarder to the nearby Bezuidenhout Convent. 'The older girls were very nice to me. I was the baby, so it wasn't bad. It was always tense at home. I didn't particularly look forward to going home.' But there were neighbourhood friends and as she grew older she read a good deal. Her childhood heroes were Robin Hood, Joan of Arc and Prince Valiant. 'Funny, it's mostly men,' she recalls.

At fourteen she was sent to the Notre Dame Convent in Kroonstad, a small town on the banks of the willow-fringed Vals River. 'I loved it! It was great! The nuns used to take us for picnics where we swam in the river; it was very muddy and the barbel used to tickle our toes. Lovely! They were terrific people, the nuns, quite a different sort from the usual in that they were very political. They had a world perspective and were very con-scious of the situation in this country. We were taught to be very critical about things and to argue. Some of the sisters of their order were working in South America with Paulo Freire who introduced a new system of teaching literacy and came over to speak to us about the Paulo Freirian approach to solving community problems by means of appropriate education. His concept of conscientization is an extremely valuable method of assisting people to gain insight into their own situation, into how the power structures work and what levels of intervention are possible by the people themselves. It teaches them to look critically at why they are oppressed and at the mechanisms those in power use to keep people in positions of poverty and ignor-ance. They must then discover what action can be taken to start counteracting this.'

Sue is struck by the incongruity of there existing, in the midst of that most conservative province, the Orange Free State, such a convent; some of the nuns had been educated at Oxford or Cambridge. 'Some girls thought the nuns were going too far in teaching us the things they did: others thought it was a good idea.' She is not sure whether the parents were aware of the extent to which their daughters' horizons were being extended. It was the nuns, she believes, who made her own perspective different from that of her family and from the majority of whites. The convent closed in 1973, but recently there was a class reunion which Sue attended. The chief concern of most of her peers, she says, seemed to be how to find the best place to which to emigrate.

The nuns also taught comparative religion. 'I was, of course, a Catholic, but I lost my religion at the age of fifteen. Learning about other religions made Christianity seem not special; other religions such as the Buddhist and Muslim faiths seemed to have a lot to offer as well.'

In her final year Sue considered studying medicine, but doubted her academic ability. However, after an aptitude test confirmed her leanings, the convent gave her a small bursary which, together with a State loan, set her up in the Medical School at Cape Town University at the beginning of 1973.

For five and a half years she lodged in Rondebosch with a Mr and Mrs Jaffee. Sue speaks affectionately of the old couple. 'They were not orthodox Jews. They had been committed socialists in their youth in Lithuania, and she was a member of the Black Sash, a woman's political organization.' Rondebosch is one of the older suburbs, sprawling at the foot of the mountain on which the university stands. There are many solid little cottages, relics of the foresters who once lived there, which are eagerly sought by the buyers of today. The Jaffees' house, once the residence of the mayor, was both imposing and rambling. It was filled in a random fashion with treasures from Europe and also from South Africa; pictures, mostly originals, crowded the walls. Sue's quarters consisted of three rooms and her own cooking facilities in the upstairs section where leafy branches tapped at the windows. In her final year first Mrs Jaffee died, followed soon after by her husband. In his last days Sue and his grandson, a medical student in her year, looked after him. She had become very fond of the old man and relates how, before he died, 'he took my hand and said, "I will always remember you."

'I enjoyed university. The first couple of years I was terrified that I wasn't going to pass and I worked extremely hard and got good results. Then I realized that I didn't have to work that hard to get through and I started socializing a lot and joined NUSAS [the National Union of South African Students]. It was great fun!' Holidays were spent earning money to pay for the coming year and the jobs which Sue found ranged from promoting Stellenbosch Farmers Winery products to selling damp-proofing for houses and to working in bookshops. She also tried selling encyclopaedias. From time to time her father helped her, but 'on the whole I paid for my own education and now I'm repaying the State loan.'

The NUSAS project which she helped to establish was one involving a coloured community at Lourdes Farm, near Crossroads, a squatter settlement. Here, in among the scrubby Port Jackson willows, the only plant that will grow in that sandy terrain, were other squatters. Most of them were farm workers, chiefly from the wine farms, who had been displaced by mechanization. They had organized their own committee, headed by a fiery and articulate woman called Mrs Pretorious. 'I don't know what work she did. I think she received some disability grant. She was hyper-thyroid and was under treatment for that and it certainly made her *very* active. She was a very powerful person. While she was involved in this project she split up from her common-law husband because he couldn't tolerate her being so dominant. He'd been supporting the family up until then and when he left there was a problem.'

At the outset there had been a multi-disciplinary team, all of them students, consisting of literacy teachers, lawyers, engineers concerned with water supplies, architects who looked at housing. A good many of the volunteers fell out but the medical and social worker group persevered. 'We learned far more than we taught them, in terms of what is practical and what is real. Teaching people about the five major nutritional food groups, that one needs a certain amount of protein, fat, carbohydrates and so forth every day – and then seeing what can actually be purchased with their incomes. What can be bought to go round a large family.' The students tried to arrange for a non-commercial organization which sold low-cost, high-protein foods to bring its products to sell at the camp, but there were practical difficulties. They believed that the people should be 'conscientized', educated to view their problems within a political context. 'We started with tuberculosis. Why do they get it? The answer is that it's related to their poor living conditions and unless those conditions are changed, people will continue to get tuberculosis. Malnutrition, violence, all problems can be traced back to where they are rooted in socio-economic conditions. But I think what I learned most is that that sort of analysis doesn't actually help, doesn't lead one anywhere unless there is positive socio-political action that can be taken at the time. We would say, "What are we going to do about it?" And they said, "Well, if we had guns we'd go out and fight now and throw the government out. But we don't have guns so we can't do it."'

The project extended over some three years with the students coming during weekends and sometimes on weekday evenings. The winter rain flooded the area and when it dried cars became trapped in the deep sand. A few students persisted, funding was obtained and a crèche built. Sue was astounded at the level of violence in the settlement, related mainly to gang warfare, 'We'd come there and somebody's house would have been burnt down; people we'd had in health care the week before would be dead.' There was a formidable alcohol problem attributable, in her view, to the fact that many of the people had been farm labourers in the western Cape where they had been paid, in part, with the customary daily wine ration. 'Some days we used to arrive and find every adult in the house unconscious from drinking, lying on the floor and the children running wild. And then there were other times when a wave of righteousness would sweep through the community and they'd be bashing bibles, involved in great religious ceremonies, chastising themselves and trying to reform. And trying to drag us in as well. We didn't feel this was necessary.' Efforts made by the students to involve the residents in discussion concerning the socio-political causes of the drinking, or in withdrawal programmes, became relics of good intentions. 'However, we did succeed in setting up about six health groups and training them in first aid, child health, family planning and nutrition. And we produced a booklet, "Community Action Brings Health", which was later used by other groups.'

The December vacation job at a mission hospital near Nongoma in KwaZulu, at the end of 1976, was unpaid, but gave her valuable experience. 'I was still a student, just finished my fourth year, so I just generally helped out and did whatever the doctors allowed me to do. I saw the less serious conditions and sutured people and helped with operations.' Almost all the able-bodied men in the area were migrant workers and most came home on leave at Christmas. 'The amount of wife abuse was horrendous! Women coming in really cut up badly. You can imagine the tensions from the migrant labour system, men coming back and suspecting infidelity. Sometimes there were clashes over authority. The women came in – awful! awful injuries! Severe! The missionary doctor there was quite used to it, but it appalled him, too. He'd say to the women, while he was sewing them up: "When you get home, make your husband drunk and when he's drunk, grab a bottle and break it and cut him up." And apparently', Sue added, laughing bitterly, 'this used to cheer the women up, just the thought of doing it. If these women went to the local police station to report being assaulted, they were turned away. The police refused, said it was a marital problem and not their business. One saw old workers who'd been dumped, coming back with tuberculosis and occupational diseases, no longer considered fit to work.'

In her elective period at the end of 1977 Sue chose to go to Zambia, 'It is poor, with a really shaky economy; yet their priority seems to be providing access to health care for everyone. Clinics were run by medical assistants who, after passing their O levels, have a three-year course based at Medical Assistant Training Schools. After passing exams they gain certificates. These people are trained to diagnose and treat conditions and to refer to doctors those they aren't sure about or think are more complicated. They can immunize, do antenatal care and deliveries; they know about water supplies, sanitation, nutrition – so they're all-round health workers. They're very good. The general policy towards providing health care I found quite extraordinary, even in remote areas. It really opened my eyes to alternative ways of solving problems in the health sphere. The infrastructure exists to make health care accessible to most people.'

During the two months she was there Sue met and became quite friendly with South African exiles. 'Some were ANC people and I learned from their perspective as to how they saw South Africa. It certainly changed my political thinking. What impressed me most was their cheerfulness and their determination. They said: "We are right. The struggle is just. We will win." There's absolutely no doubt in their minds. I was very impressed.' The Zambian experience was a good one for her, 'quite mind-opening'.

As it was not possible at that time to fly direct from Lusaka to Johannesburg Sue and Ian, a fellow student, decided to return via Malawi. Having fallen out with one another they agreed that she should travel north and Ian south, to meet up three weeks later. 'I hitched around up to the northern part of Malawi and then boarded this boat – locals refer to it as the "steamer" – that goes up and down Lake Malawi. I was determined to go third class with the people. Other whites looked at me and said, "No, no no! You can't do that!"' Firm in her purpose, Sue bought her third class ticket and found herself in the cramped quarters in the hold. People, goats and chickens were squashed together. 'It was dark and stinky and the minute the boat set off people started being sick. I then changed my mind and bought a first class ticket. And when I got up on deck and into the open air, people said, "We told you so!" I had to swallow my principles. Certainly, the conditions in which the blacks travelled were horrendous.'

She enthuses over Malawi's tropical, lush vegetation, 'It's almost like paradise, so fruitful, bountiful and green. People are quite poor, but there seems to be fish, and fruit and things growing everywhere. It's a pity it's such a reactionary political system.' Whites whom she met cautioned her, 'For God's sake don't talk any politics! Not anywhere; because there are spies everywhere and you'll be put away.' 'I listened to them, but Ian didn't meet people who told him that and he was put away. They imprisoned him for about three days. He was in prison on the day we were supposed to leave and I phoned his parents and they contacted the South African consulate there. It was a particularly unpleasant experience for him.

'Malawi was an interesting example of tyranny within an independent African state. I'd seen Zambia where the majority of the people did seem to support Kenneth Kaunda and there was a level of democracy even though it was a one-party state. And despite the economy being so shaky, things worked and were logical and the health services were good. There was a level of political repression in Malawi, although they were probably much more efficient in producing goods and running trains.' Health services in Malawi were not well organized, nor were the clinics adequately supplied with medication, drugs or equipment. 'In the rural areas I certainly saw a great many people with illnesses, children suffering from malnutrition and women with enormous goitres; there were people who seemed to have tuberculosis.'

During their elective period most of the students in Sue's class had gone to Europe or the United States looking, she surmises, for future jobs. 'Most of my medical school class of about one hundred and sixty has left this country. The major English-speaking medical schools export most of their graduates. At the moment I think that about 80 per cent leave within a couple of years of qualifying. I think that English-speaking white South Africans are the last people medical schools should train. Blacks and Afrikaners are much more likely to stay. It's an enormous waste of resources.' It costs the State something like 100,000 rand to train a medical student. 'I'm not concerned about the State's money. It's the country's resources that are important. Medicine is used in a public relations fashion in this country: it produces good doctors who go abroad and make a good impression. And they say, "Look at the level of technology and sophistication that we've achieved! We're part of the western world, a bastion of the western world. You can't abandon us!"'

There are photographs of Sue at her graduation in 1978, shining-eyed and with an abundance of chestnut-brown hair falling around her shoulders. She did her housemanship at Edendale Hospital. Edendale is a well-established black area some eight kilometres outside the Natal city of Pietermaritzburg. 'I chose it because I'd been very interested in rural black medicine and it seemed to be a hospital that would provide that sort of experience. I was rather horrified to discover, when I arrived there, that all the rugger-buggers in my class were also there.I hadn't realized that it was a sort of rugger-bugger hangout – well they were mostly Natalians, from that area. It was the main training hospital for white doctors.' Instead of gaining, as she had imagined, valuable experience in a black rural area she found herself launched into three years of battles with her colleagues. 'My colleagues regarded it as very much a training ground, a guinea-pig conveyor belt, a place where you see lots and lots of interesting pathology. The fact that the pathology belonged to human beings who had lives and problems outside the hospital gates didn't seem to occur to them. So there were lots of conflicts.'

She hardly fared better with the Zulu and Xhosa doctors who had been trained at the University of Natal. 'Most of them were very Black Consciousness oriented, hostile to any whites and particularly so to liberal or lefty whites – I don't know why, possibly because we were trying to *do* something.' Local trade unions and community groups would sometimes ask Sue and other like-minded doctors to assist their members with various projects. 'We would get up at the crack of dawn on Sunday mornings to go out and help them, but the black doctors wouldn't. My impression was that they weren't at all interested in offering any sort of service to community groups. So there was resentment with them as well because though they mouthed off a lot of rhetoric about being oppressed and whatever, they weren't prepared to actually put in the action that was required.

'It was very good training and I learnt a great deal – at the people's expense, obviously. I mean, one's thrown in the deep end and one makes mistakes. But I think that whereas I had a consciousness of this, most of the doctors there didn't at all. I don't have all that much faith in medicine as a whole, really. Most of our treatment doesn't have that much impact on people's health. Maybe 10 per cent of the conditions; the rest are going to continue as they are going anyway. Medical resources should be directed towards the prevention of disease and the organization of medical services. This is not easy to implement in South Africa.'

Sue became involved with the rape crisis group in Pietermaritzburg. 'I was very active in that. Although rape occurs in all communities I think it does tend to occur more where there is more general violence: it is a form of violence against women.' Members of the group visited both black and white schools, talking to the older children and to teachers. They sought to inform people, too, through newspaper articles and radio and television programmes. 'I think that we did have quite a good impact in changing community attitudes. It's still going strong, very strong. There was one programme on "Should rapists receive capital punishment?" We opposed this because it perpetuates the cycle of violence.'

After her year of housemanship and another as a hospital medical officer, Sue spent a year using the Edendale Hospital as a base for her work in community clinics, scattered about in the valleys and hills that surround Pietermaritzburg. 'The nurses running them weren't trained to do community work. They had been trained to be sort of handmaidens to the doctors in hospital wards. They weren't taught how to take the responsibility of diagnosis and treatment and they felt very insecure and unhappy about being sent there.' She had some success in organizing inservice training for the nurses, to equip them with the skills necessary to run a rural clinic. 'Nurses are an elite group in the black community. They're probably, on the whole, a lot more intelligent than white nurses because intelligent black women have two options: nursing and teaching. It's probably changing today, but certainly in the rural areas these are the only options they had and you get some extremely bright women. But they are frustrated because the system is so hierarchical. It's really an awful system.'

It was a toughening experience. 'On a Saturday night in surgical casualty there would be a whole row of stretchers with dying people on them – and racing from one body to another to see who is going to survive, who one can actually help and who is beyond help and should just be left to die. That sort of experience, which is certainly pretty common, hardens one. You can't allow yourself to feel: you would go mad.'

In 1981, when she was twenty-six, Sue was awarded a British Council scholarship to study for a Master's degree in Community Health in Developing Countries. The course was at the London School of Hygiene and Tropical Medicine. 'It was wonderful! I really enjoyed it. I was the only South African they'd had on the course for about eight years. They were very ill-informed on South African conditions because they had had no people from here and also because South Africa hasn't been submitting statistics to the World Health Organization – it left the body in about 1972.' Sue was one of thirty-three students on the course; they had come mainly from South America, Asia and Africa, but there were students from Denmark, Germany, Sweden and England. 'Just learning from my classmates about their experiences and the problems they face and how they try to solve them was so useful.'

Being in England evoked ambivalent feelings. London struck her as hostile, dirty and very cold: it seemed to her that foreigners were not really welcome. She stayed at first at William Goodenough House, in Mecklenburgh Square, near the British Museum, a hostel for students from the Commonwealth and ex-Commonwealth countries. Among the South Africans there was William Drummond whom Sue already knew from Pietermaritzburg. After three months she moved, with William and some of the people in her class, into a house in Highbury belonging to one of the lecturers who was overseas on sabbatical. 'It was lovely! We had a super time! William knew lots of very good Indian restaurants, and cheap ones, as well. The School of African and Oriental Studies which was across the road from the School of Hygiene had the most wonderful curry! I think the students insisted on it. We ate there a lot.' London continued, however, to depress her. She visited an uncle in Bolton and went for long walks on the moors. This would lift her spirits temporarily. There were also two happy weeks during which she worked as a locum in paediatrics in a small hospital in Banbury in Oxfordshire.

'Most of the people in my class who weren't British experienced an enormous culture shock, just as I did. And I thought, "My God, if I'm experiencing it, it must be ten times worse for them!" We formed a sort of African group and used to huddle together in the tea-room and reminisce about Africa and talk about what we missed about it. They included me as an African, which I liked.' There were jaunts with William and friends in the holidays to Portugal and to Spain where they hired a car. 'There was a chap from the London School who was doing a course there and we stayed with him. He was a real communist and took us on a tour of various places and showed us the fascist architecture. Since I've come back here I realize we've also got it, like the Johannesburg Civic Centre, archetypal fascist architecture.' She spent time, too, with her father's sister who had married a Portuguese colonel and worked in the South African embassy in Lisbon.

In the summer of 1982 Sue and William were married in Westminster Town Hall. For the reception they rented a sixteenth-century house in Highgate, 'where Marx is buried'. William was English by birth, but had been educated in South Africa, latterly at Waterford, a non-racial boarding-school in Swaziland. Upon completing his A levels, he had left for England where, after a succession of jobs as bus-conductor, milkman, baker and painter-decorator, he obtained an educational grant that enabled him to go to the School of Oriental and African Studies in London. There he majored in African History and Geography and went on to gain a Ph.D. in development economics at the London School of Economics.

In between his studies he taught at a school in London, but

abandoned it after an Asian friend of his had been beaten up by his pupils. 'Real toughies, these kids, and no corporal punishment allowed,' comments Sue. William then registered for his Ph.D. His area of interest was South-East Asia where he intended to do his field work, but the lecturers urged him rather to go to South Africa. 'They said there was practically nothing coming out of South Africa and that as he had good connections there that was where they would prefer him to do his field work. And that's how he ended up coming to KwaZulu and meeting me.'

It had been a year of extremely hard work. Sue was awarded her Master's degree in Community Health in Developing Countries and passed a diploma course in Public Health. She also passed the British exam for Community Health specialization. 'I thought that, seeing I was there, I'd better have a go at everything. But it was hard work. Maybe I frittered away my time, sitting at books. I don't know.' In answer to an advertisement for doctors qualified in community health to work in Zimbabwe, Sue found herself entering Zimbabwe House which retained its fortified appearance from the Smith days. She felt that as a South African, she stood little chance of being appointed, but William had urged her to try. 'They were very nice. They said, "wonderful to have you! Come along! We really need people with degrees like yours."' Because she had learnt to speak a little Zulu while working in Natal, Sue asked to be sent to Matabeleland where the people belonged to the same Nguni-speaking group; her experience with the Zulu people had given her a degree of understanding of cultural aspects of the Ndebele people, something she considered very important. The man interviewing her seemed a little surprised and asked her if she was sure that that was where she would like to work. Sue, unaware of the problems that she would encounter, confirmed her statement.

They bought a house in Bulawayo. William became a training specialist with the agricultural extension services and Sue, aged twenty-nine, was appointed Assistant Director of Medical Services in the two provinces of Matabeleland, 'quite a responsibility at that tender age! But the person I worked with was a most tremendous chap, Alan Pugh, respected by everyone. When the locally elected provincial councillors had met after independence to appoint a Medical Officer he was unanimously approved. He ran the service so logically and well and I learnt a great deal from him.' Sue is enthusiastic about the health services in Zimbabwe, which were similar to, but superior to those in Zambia. In addition to the community health workers, there were village health workers and co-operation with the traditional birth attendants.

Soon after her arrival, Sue went to a meeting of the Provincial Council, made up of elected representatives from each district. 'They were very dignified. Some of them were chiefs who had been popular, some were ex-combatants.' There is mild surprise in her voice as she relates how nice they were to her, even after she had explained that she was from South Africa and coming to work with them. 'They were so gentlemanly. They treated me so well. They accepted me. They were so co-operative about things we needed done, like building clinics. A very positive and democratic system does exist, to a large extent, in Matabeleland. The ability of the community to participate and be involved in the health services was tremendous.'

After she had been there for nine months, Alan Pugh went away on holiday, leaving Sue in charge of medical services in the two provinces. The organization was sound and there appeared to be no problems in the offing. All the health staff spoke very good English. 'But the Fifth Brigade was knocking around Matabeleland and killing people in large numbers. The Fifth Brigade is Mugabe's special brigade. I was travelling round the rural areas and seeing the survivors in hospitals: small children who had been bayoneted, pregnant women who had been bayoneted and raped, old men who'd had straw tied round their limbs and been set on fire! It was too horrible! Just hearing from them what had happened to the non-survivors one could estimate the numbers involved. One can't really know how many were killed, but some people put it at as much as 30,000 in that year. And that's as many people as were killed in the fifteen years of *war*. I don't know if it's as much as that, but probably at least about 10,000.' Many of the nurses in the rural areas had, before independence, been members of ZIPRA, the armed wing of ZAPU, Joshua Nkomo's party. Being young, idealistic people, they were prepared to venture out to work in rural clinics. 'And of course, particularly as they were ex-combatants, they were seen as dissidents by the Fifth Brigade who picked on anyone who was seen to be associated with ZAPU.'

Sue felt that if she were to order these nurses back to their clinics it would be almost like sentencing them to death. At the same time, the health services were collapsing. She consulted a local brigadier who advised her to write a report, saying that when she had done so the authorities would certainly investigate the situation. 'And being young and naive I did as requested and got affidavits and that sort of thing and wrote the report as quickly as I could – and the next think I knew, I was transferred to another province! Apparently this report had gone to the Minister of Defence who'd passed it on to Mugabe who said, "Get rid of her!" This is what I've heard.'

Sue was sent to Masvingo province, the old Fort Victoria, on the Mozambique border, to run a field hospital. 'I felt horrified! Disillusioned. Not so much that they had transferred *me* – I mean I was disillusioned when I saw what the Fifth Brigade was doing. It was so senseless, so stupid. I couldn't understand *why*. They'd fought this war against Smith's regime. They'd won the war. Everything was going for Zimbabwe. Donors were falling over each other to give money. They already had a very good infrastructure – and yet they were killing people. And for no reason that I could understand. It was so tragic. And I think it's given Zimbabwe a bad name and jeopardized their standing in the world community.' Initially, Sue said, the international community had been interested in reporting on the excesses of the Fifth Brigade. Reporters would be sent to the area and she would, clandestinely, take them round to show them what was happening, hoping that international pressure would bring a halt to the Fifth Brigade brutality. 'But the world lost interest after a while and nobody asked what was happening and the atrocities continued. One certainly loses faith in the media; it's newsworthy for a while and then people grow tired of hearing about it and the atrocities continue . . . Nobody *cares*, that's it.'

William, unable to get a job in Masvingo, remained in Bulawayo, some 300 kilometres away. 'I used to commute weekly on the local buses which were mostly diesel and very slow. It was fascinating; the people were always so nice. And no matter how packed it was – I'd usually be the only white on the bus – they'd always make room for me and push things aside and hold my suitcases on their laps. I really enjoyed it, just chatting to them.' In Masvingo cholera, brought in by Mozambican refugees, was rife. Sue's patients lay on mats beneath the trees to escape the heat. 'When they were pouring out diarrhoea we dug a hole in the ground and put the bedpan in that – they were on and off bedpans all the time and often we couldn't get to them in time. We supported them so that they wouldn't get pressure sores. It doesn't sound very nice, but it was the most comfortable and practical thing to do.' The health staff had an army tent and a very tiny caravan, but Sue, armed with mosquito repellent, slept where it was cooler, under the stars. She was the only white person in the area.

She found the health services inferior to those in Matabeleland. 'There's a lot more corruption and nepotism and misuse of vehicles. This may have been because the people in that area were from the powerful governing Shona group and did not feel the need to obtain the support of the masses.' In the end, she and William both resigned. 'We didn't feel we wanted to work for that government any more.' The experience had been disillusioning in terms of their faith in the government, but 'I have tremendous faith in that community in Matabeleland. Tremendous people to work with!'

The year was 1983 and there were rumours that South-West Africa (the name that Sue insists upon using while it is under South African control, believing it should not be called Namibia until it is independent) was about to receive its independence. Sue had contacted the administration who had offered her a senior job. When she and William arrived in Windhoek, however, the offer was withdrawn. 'They made feeble excuses such as it being impossible to expect a woman to go out into the field while there was virtually a civil war and that they couldn't have a man and a woman going out there together. But I heard later that they had a file on me; in it was a statement that I was more left than Mugabe. So they wouldn't employ me. I was unemployable, though I was more qualified in community health than anyone else in the country. The Secretary for Health hadn't half the qualifications I have, but they wouldn't employ me.'

William landed a job with the National Building and Investment Corporation, concerned with low cost and self-help housing. Sue found part-time work with a general practitioner. South-West Africa seemed a very strange country. 'Its population is just over one million and they have, I think, fifty-three political parties. They're so divided and preoccupied with stabbing each other in the back. An extraordinary place. And very interesting individuals, both black and white. I think their isolation makes them eccentric; they tend to become very strong characters.'

Kenneth Abrahams, for whom Sue was to work part time, was a general practitioner and a founder member of SWAPO (South-West African People's Organization). He is classified as coloured and his wife, whom he had met when they were both studying at Cape Town University, is of Herero German mixture. Abrahams had grown up in District Six, the lively, racially mixed slum in the heart of Cape Town. As children, he and his brothers and sisters used to visit their grandfather who was white and a postmaster. He told Sue of his torn feelings, looking at his grandfather and knowing that he must not say, 'Hullo, Grandpa.' They had to behave as though they were just any coloured children. Exiled on account of his political associations, he had worked in Sweden, England, Tanzania, Kenya and Zambia where he had been Kenneth Kaunda's personal physician.

Abrahams returned to South-West Africa in 1978 under an amnesty which many thought would lead to independence and to his being appointed Minister of Health. 'But the independence didn't happen. He is a quite extraordinary man, brilliant! Of course the government wouldn't employ him.' In addition to running his general practice he published a newspaper and was very active in community and development projects. He was a founder member of SWAPO, but later moved appreciably to its left.

Many of those who came into Dr Abrahams' surgery were Basters, descendants of early Dutch renegades from the Cape who intermarried with the Hottentots. Some spoke of the demeaning treatment meted out to them by whites and Sue wondered how whites were able to identify them as they are often very fair skinned. It could only be, as she put it, 'that it's a learnt attitude; they don't put themselves forward as arrogant and cocky, so are immediately sensed not to be white. Most are very proud to be Basters – it means bastards, really. If you call them coloured they get very angry. They have a special homeland, Rehoboth, and a town of the same name, some 89 kilometres south of Windhoek. There are class divisions within the coloured community and the Basters are at the top of the ladder.'

While in South-West Africa William and Sue put their names down on a list of parents wishing to adopt a child as Sue had found that she couldn't have her own children. The list was a long one, but the time came when a baby girl was offered for adoption and turned down by the fifty couples who preceded the Drummonds. They gladly took her. Emma, as they named her, is classified white, but her skin is a warm light brown. By what extraordinary leap or fall in the South African bureaucratic passion for categorizing people according to the colour of their skins this obvious mistake occurred no one can say. She is the product of the union in England of a white woman from a deprived community in the Cape and a West Indian father. The child had been born in Cape Town, but racist pressures, coupled with a shortage of money, had made it impossible for the mother to keep her. William's employers, once they gained news of the colour of his adopted child, demanded his resignation.

The couple moved to Johannesburg where community reaction to their brown child proved to be far less intense. 'When we were in Windhoek, just walking down the street with her in the pram, I used to feel that people wanted to assault me. I felt very defensive, very angry towards people who were rude and abusive. In Johannesburg we haven't encountered any nastiness at all. People are a bit curious; they look at me and they look at William and you can see they're trying to work out how this whole situation came about. No one is actually nasty, which is very nice. When we first took her to nursery school they said, "Oh, we're delighted! We always wanted to have black children but we weren't allowed to by the education authorities." She seems to be quite popular, she's invited to a lot of birthday parties.' Sue appreciates that Emma will undoubtedly encounter racism as she grows older. However, in the larger cities such as Johannesburg, there is a growing acceptance of day-to-day association with people of other races.

The Johannesburg City Council offered Sue a job and little else being available, she accepted. In her view the Council is very conservative. Its services are racially segregated; doctors are appointed to work in communities of their own race. For the first time Sue found herself working with a white community. Her clinic was based in the southern suburbs, an area of predominantly lower-income groups, working-class people, mainly Afrikaans-speaking, living in small houses.

All infants are required to be immunized against the six major diseases of childhood. Some of the immunizations are obtainable only at the clinics. Sue, at her clinic, finds that there are many parents who comply, but the inverse care law, a phenomenon not peculiar to South Africa, seems to pertain: parents who are oganized and responsible (and who often take their children to private doctors as well) are those who use the clinics the most. The ones who need it don't come. It is the task of the health visitors, generally from Afrikaans-speaking families, competent, pragmatic women in Sue's view, to visit homes where children have not been sent for immunization. On their recommendation Sue will also visit. All too frequently she finds pockets of severe deprivation and poverty. The parents are often working, leaving the children in the care of a black nanny who is exploited and underpaid. 'Even the poorest, down-and-out unemployed always have a black employed to do the housework. It seems to be an absolute necessity of life in the white community.' There are poverty-sticken homes with rotting floorboards, bedrooms stinking from unchanged laundry and children being fed white bread with black tea, the only food in the house. Many of these children suffer from suppurating ears and dental caries, while some have heart conditions. The clinic is free as is the dental hospital, but there seems to be an apathy that impedes parents from making use of the facilities.

One day a week is set aside for black patients at the clinic. Black nurses and doctors are brought in; the same rooms are used, but so as not to offend the whites (many of whom have not learnt to accept the use of teacups which, though carefully washed, have once been used by blacks, let alone medical equipment which has touched black skins), a different set of instruments is used. (In suburbs to the east and west of Johannesburg complaints by white residents have put a stop to the existence of a black clinic in their midst, even on one day a week.)

The separation of the races, however, despite the ardour with which those in power pursue it, is constantly breaking down. For instance, on the 'white' days the waiting-room of the clinic is crowded with blacks, the nannies of the children waiting for attention. Many of the nannies have babies on their backs (this is one of the reasons for their having to find jobs in the southern suburbs where pay is much less, but where babies on backs are tolerated as part of the bargain) and when the doctor has seen the white child she will often say to the black woman, 'Well let me immunize your baby, too, to save your having to come on another day.' And on the one day a week for black patients there are sometimes whites in the waiting-room, employers who have brought their servants and who expect to be given racial priority and not to be kept waiting.

Apathy and negativism seem to Sue to characterize the white community in the southern suburbs. Unemployment, particularly among young men, is high: they are threatened by jobs previously reserved for whites being made available to blacks. At a community hospital (for whites only) where she is on duty for two evenings in each month, one of the commonest causes of admission is attempted suicide by medicine overdoses and cut wrists, particularly amongst young men. 'Some return two or three times. The level of despair is enormous. Men are angry and their racism is intensified at jobs being taken over by blacks.'

—— 211 ——

Violence, both self-inflicted and that perpetrated upon others, accounts for many admissions, as do alcohol-related problems. There are also abortions (illegal in South Africa), mostly in quite young girls. 'It creates a picture of a deprived, violent society, where the cycle of deprivation is being perpetuated. I think that the underlying problem is unmet expectations: being white and having this promise of privilege which doesn't materialize. Trying to live with what they think they should have and what they don't have. And seeing blacks becoming more affluent.'

Most infants are admitted for gastro-enteritis, a shocking fact in a developed society which has excellent water, sanitation, food supplies and antenatal and perinatal services. Sue ascribes it to the failure of many mothers to breast-feed their babies. 'In the white working-class group bottle feeding is seen as sophisticated, very similar to black women who are becoming urbanized and aspire to sophistication. They also feel that breast-feeding's some sort of an animal function and it's "not nice".' A fairly high level of air pollution, particularly in the south of Johannesburg, could account for the large number of admissions of children and adults with bronchitis and pneumonia. Among the elderly there is evidence of malnutrition; many live in little rooms, some in their own houses which have often been allowed to deteriorate. 'Generally they are really terrified, living on their own, because they're vulnerable to attack. Very little is done for this group of forgotten, elderly whites who are completely inarticulate.'

Since the fall of the white government in Mozambique and the war in Angola there has been an influx of Portuguese into South Africa. Many have come to Johannesburg and large numbers live in the southern suburbs in houses that are almost always well painted and immaculately kept. They tend to keep to themselves. 'It's very rare to find one who is really down and out and they certainly take any opportunity that arises. One gets the feeling of an industrious group that are going places, whereas in the traditional southern suburbs community which tends to consist of some English, but mostly Afrikaans working-class people, there is the apathetic impression of not really being interested in going anywhere and certainly sponging whatever they can to stay comfortable. I do feel sympathetic towards them. I like many of them, but as a group within South Africa they're just going to have to pull up their bootstraps and do something because I don't think anyone will look after them much longer.'

When Steve Biko died in detention in 1977, the conduct of the doctors under whose care he was supposed to have been was investigated by the Medical Association of South Africa. They were exonerated. 'Many doctors felt that this was simply not acceptable, that these doctors had collaborated directly with the police and the State to cover up his death. They had not acted in the interests of Steve Biko as a patient.' As a result an alternative association, the National Medical and Dental Association (NAMDA), was formed in 1982. There are about a thousand or so paid-up members. 'Its aims are to remove apartheid from the health services and to create an equitable health service which, unlike the present system, does meet the needs of the majority of the people of this country.' Many of its members have been politically active and it aims to fulfil a role very different from the Medical Association of South Africa which Sue sees as a kind of trade union to protect the status and earning rights of doctors.

While at Edendale in 1982 she had been a founder member of the Natal Health Workers' Association, an organization which later amalgamated with other groups to form NAMDA. Since her return to the Republic she has been involved with those doctors who provide emergency services. 'Many township groups who've been under attack from the security forces have found that they have no access to health care because if they do go to the local hospital, they generally get picked up; simply being injured is regarded as enough evidence of having been involved in something suspect and they are interrogated, either at the hospital or in custody. So they're very much deterred from using the local health services.' Many people are known to have died or sustained severe disabilities because they were afraid to use the medical services. 'That is why we have undertaken to train volunteer township groups in first aid. The trainers place much emphasis on the greater strength derived from working as a group, rather than as individuals, but this is not always possible under the conditions in which the participants find themselves when they return to the townships.'

The need for physical healing is great, that for emotional restoration is hardly less. 'There is an enormous need for counselling skills. Groups like the Detainees Support Committees are always encountering people who are suffering acute anxiety and bereavement as a result of the State's repressive activities. Another organization with which we work is OASSA, the Organization for Appropriate Social Services in South Africa. OASSA is a group of psychologists, social workers and others in that field who have developed techniques of short-term training in how to help people in crisis situations, using listening skills and intervention techniques. They appear to have been remarkably effective under the circumstances.'

The white left does not always work together harmoniously, a fact that Sue does not deny. 'The conflicts that I have had working with colleagues in NAMDA with regard to first aid training are generally the sort of conflicts that arise in the white left in this country. Whereas people like myself feel that we ought to evaluate what we are doing very closely to see how effective we are in achieving goals that we set, others feel that we don't have the right to deny any community group which asks for these resources.' She considers the amount of personal time and effort that goes into these activities, 'Having a small child and leaving her with William to look after during the time when I'm doing the training, it's an enormous personal demand which takes up a great deal of time, energy and donors' money and I can only justify it to myself if we are achieving results.

'The left seems to get into such knots of conscience in trying to be democratic that it immobilizes itself. There are also personal power struggles. I have very little tolerance for that sort of thing – it makes me unpopular. I get really annoyed. I think, in a way, it's a heritage of us whites having been seen to be arrogant, sure, confident, directive – directive is probably the best word – in the past. Blacks level the charge: "You're so directive. You're so the-boss-in-charge" – whatever. In a way whites are trying to live that down.' Her voice becomes thin with despair. 'It doesn't always help.'

NAMDA runs a service for released detainees who have overwhelming medical and psychological needs. 'Many have been tortured and some have a need for their wounds to be attended to, though generally they are kept in detention until these have healed. They suffer from the trauma of enormous stress related to the solitary confinement and torture, which results in depression, anxiety and disorientation. But I am unable to see detainees because as I listen to them I know that the things that were done to them are being done to people *now*. I can't actually accept the thought. It drives me mad. I want to go out and start tearing things down. I've tried seeing them a few times and I'm on standby if other people can't make it, but I cannot see them on a regular basis. I'm glad there are people who can do it. Released detainees come and they sit down and they've got these wounds and injuries and they say, "Well, this was done to me and that was done to me," all with deadpan faces. If they collapsed and yelled and screamed and said how much they hated these people it would be almost cathartic – for me as well – to feel the anger and hatred. But they don't. I almost feel as though I have to react on their behalf – it's so terrible!'

She cites the case of a fourteen-year-old boy from a town in the Northern Transvaal. He was part of a group who resisted the demands of his schoolmaster for extra fees; they felt that the money was simply going into his own pocket. The schoolmaster called in the local police who went to the boy's home and beat him severely with a *sjambok*, in front of his parents. 'He had dreadful *sjambok* tramlines all over his body and they had broken both his wrists, in front of his parents, and dragged him off to prison. They left him for seven days with no treatment for the broken wrists. Can you imagine! Using the toilet, or eating, or dressing, or washing – the *pain* of broken wrists! And eventually he was taken to the local black hospital in the black town and under anaesthesia they put on these very ungainly plasters. He still can't move or do anything for himself. And then he came to us. Part of what we require is documentation of their injuries in case legal action is taken against the authorities. I sent him off to a local radiologist who X-rayed his wrists and said they were terribly badly set and that unless they were rebroken and reset he would have deformed arms for the rest of his life, wouldn't be able to use them. At that stage I'd just about cracked up and he was so cool, matter-of-fact, unemotional – and he's a child! I pulled out of that because I couldn't handle it – at the thought that this is happening all the time and we can't stop it. Other people, fortunately, are strong enough to carry on.' She reflects upon how hard the batons must have hit him to break his wrists. The words come reluctantly, almost drawn out of her: 'I get filled with helplessness and loathing. It's so . . . I have such hate for the people who do these things.'

Halfway through 1986 the City Health Department agreed to Sue's conducting a research project into the health of white pre-school children at nursery schools and at child minders. Children from the better-off and more organized families generally attend the subsidized nursery schools,while those from poorer families go to so-called private nursery schools or to child minders or nowhere at all. Sue is concerned about the unattended and un-diagnosed problems of the children in these latter classes. The child minders are aware of many of the problems, but they feel inadequate to deal with them. She has proposed, therefore, that she should run a training scheme for them. 'This will be linked to a randomized control trial which is supposed to be a scientific way of proving that something works.' One of the qualities that she will endeavour to measure is what, for want of a better term, is called the warmth factor, the caring for children. 'We certainly don't see child care as only custodial.' Particularly in the poorer areas she has encountered a high degree of hostility – parents become incensed and insulting. 'The poor white group tend to be extremely alienated, even from a government and administration elected, apparently, by themselves and supposed to be looking after their welfare. They react in a very hostile fashion if there seems to be any intervention in their lives.'

Several doctors of Sue's convictions are to be found working at the clinics in the black townships near Johannesburg. 'The reason why I'm not working at a black clinic say, in Soweto or Alexandra, is because, having worked in Zimbabwe, I realize that very little can be achieved in these present circumstances. One is simply doing patchwork. There really needs to be an enormous political change before any real improvements can be made. And I feel the white community needs to be prepared for change in the future. The work I'm doing in the southern sub-urbs, working with white community health workers, I feel can show that a different kind of health service, a different pattern of health care, delivered by groups who aren't particularly experts or specialists, is as applicable in the white community as it is in the black community. I hope that it will enable whites to live with a more egalitarian health service in the future.'

William and Sue are not thinking of leaving South Africa.

JOHANN FREDERICK
FARRELL AND JACOBUS
DANIËL FARRELL

WITH THE DESCENT into the lowveld, which begins towards Belfast, the terrain becomes increasingly hilly, grassland giving way to bush and low trees. After Waterval Boven commercial plantations of wattle and pine cover the slopes on either side of the Elands Valley gorge. Resinous fragrances, sometimes with admixtures of less pleasant chemicals, are emitted from the large sawmill near the point where the Elands and the Crocodile Rivers join to flow into the fertile valley which stretches onwards towards Mozambique. At the turnoff, Burnside, there is a dirt road running along the valley, the mountain slopes on either side mottled with outcrops of huge smooth 'whale-back' granite domes. A sign on a gate on the right-hand side reads 'Oklahoma', from where the drive proceeds in a series of curves up the mountainside, past a neat flat-roofed cottage and still further up to a sizeable bungalow, set high above the ground and roofed with brown tiles. In the garage is a Porsche and a four-wheel-drive vehicle. Two flights of steps lead up to the patio which overlooks the valley and the mountainside beyond.

Jacobus Daniël Farrell, generally known as Cobus, solidly built, wearing a safari suit with short trousers, comes out to welcome the visitor. At thirty-one years of age he is self-assured, but with that slight awkwardness that characterizes so many young South Africans. Glass doors lead to the living-room; everything is very new and tidy; there is an air of prosperity, but not of ostentation. Colour photographs of his children, their grand-parents and other members of the family hang on the walls. The Farrells are a very close-knit family. Cobus's sister, Madelize, who has a cottage on an adjoining plot, is one of several visitors who call during the evening, she is vivacious, dark-haired and married to Robbie Ward, a radio technician. He sells two-way radios, 'a big thing in the lowveld these days, with all these land-mines'.

Cobus's wife, Pauline, is a tall, slender woman in her late twenties, her natural shyness increased by being required to speak English. She is one of four daughters whose father, Paul Fick, was the manager of a large farming estate at Barvale, a few kilometres away. After leaving school she became a nurse in the nearby town of Barberton, but never really enjoyed it and left half way through her third year to marry Cobus. The chief delight of their two children, Freddie and Elmarie, seven and nine years old, is water-skiing; zooming about behind their father's power boat on the Vyeboom Dam where the family has a two-roomed cottage. It is a few hours' drive away, towards the Swaziland border, and most summer weekends are spent there, usually with friends and their children. In the colder wea-ther they go to their grandfather's small game farm about 300 hectares in extent, at Mica, in the Hoedspruit area, blistering hot in summer, but wonderfully warm for winter weekends.

Another young couple with two young children, con-temporary with Freddie and Elmarie, arrive and stay to supper. The children are very well behaved; when they speak it is in Afrikaans. They sit on carved, high-backed chairs round a very large circular table, covered by a patterned tablecloth. Cobus says grace in Afrikaans, but he and Pauline converse with the visitor in English. There is a dish piled with roast meat, a large bowl of mashed sweet potatoes, another of green beans and a third of mashed pumpkin. This is followed by a pudding and coffee.

Across the narrow dusty road and extending to the stream, hardly a stream until the spring rains, lies the property of his father, Johann Frederick Farrell. A large jacaranda tree shades a parking area. In the garage is a new Mercedes and a 1950

Chevrolet. The way to the bungalow is across thick lawns backed by massed clumps of bougainvillaeas, dusty pink and gaudy cerise. The inspiration is Mexican and it is fronted by a series of arches opening onto a paved patio on which deck chairs and a table are set out.

Johann Frederick Farrell, a spare, desiccated man of fifty-five years, tells you that the name was originally O'Farrell, but the 'O' got lost, probably during the Anglo-Boer War. The Irish origins of the family have faded in the course of marriages which the early Farrell men made with German and Afrikaner women and their absorption into the Afrikaner culture and church. Johann Frederick, or Fred as he is known, was born on a farm, Vlakfontein, in the Bronkhorstspruit district, the youngest of eight children. His father, Jacobus Daniël Farrell, born in 1883, was a stonemason who built many churches, among them the Nederduitse Gereformeerde Kerk in Heidelberg, Transvaal. His grandfather was a carpenter on the railways for the old ZAR, the South African Republic, and made all the doors and window frames in the stations from Komatipoort to Waterval Boven; this last station, no longer in use, has recently been declared a national monument and is being converted into a tourist centre, complete with coffee bar. Fred is proud of the skill of his forebears and appears to accord less importance to the direction taken by some of the new generation. 'The Farrells were, most of them, tradesmen. The younger ones, now, are going to universities and that sort of thing.'

He relates an incident in the Anglo-Boer War when his father, fighting on the side of the Boers, found himself in a skirmish near Witbank. The victorious Boers pursued the enemy. 'My father was after them too, but he looked back and saw a man lying. It was an Englishman. He turned his horse, and dismounted and asked, "Are you hurt?" (I think he must have spoken in Afrikaans; I don't think my dad could speak English at that time.) He took the saddle off the man's dead horse, put it against an ant heap and made the man comfortable. Then he took his own water bottle and gave it to him. And off he went.' Thirty years later Jacobus Daniël Farrell, known as Koos, was sitting one evening in the club of the colliery where he worked. 'The mine manager, Willie Bowles, sat chatting to him. He said to my father, "Koos, you know it's funny, we English and the Boers fought in the Boer War. I was an English soldier. You know, we weren't enemies, actually. We were in a battle somewhere around here and I was wounded in the stomach. A Boer turned back and he got off his horse . . ." and my dad said, "Yes he gave you his water bottle and made you comfortable against an anthill . . ." They were great pals after that.'

Koos Farrell was captured some time later in the same Witbank area and according to his son, spent eight days, together with other prisoners, in an open cattle truck with no food on the journey to Durban. From there they were shipped to the Shahjhanpur camp at Bhimtal in India where, as prisoners-of-war, they planted trees in the hills. The anecdotes that Fred remembers his father telling of this time were not of the misery, but of the boyish pranks directed at bucking the system. Providentially, he had some sovereigns with him and before returning to South Africa, always a bit of a dandy and tempted by the low cost of tailoring there, had a suit made. 'My dad never wore a suit not tailormade. He was very proud. Even laying bricks or stone, I never saw him work without a tie – he wore a leather tie at work. Even in the heat.'

Susanna Dirkie Els, born in 1894, the fifth in her line of that name which had originated with the family in Holland, was to be Frederick Farrell's mother. During the Anglo-Boer War, in order to escape the concentration camps to which the British consigned the Boer women and children, her mother hid herself and all the children in a cave in the *koppies* on their farm. Family servants brought them provisions from the farm; discretion was necessary not only to preserve the white family, but themselves, for blacks, in many cases, fared hardly better than the Afrikaners. Less resourceful relatives found themselves in the concentration camps where more than 26,000 women and children died. Fred recounts some of the stories of hardship and suffering that he remembers hearing, of the poison that women believed was being put in their food, of the death of his aunts, only two of the many whose graves may be seen at Balmoral and at other sites. The scorched earth strategy of the British meant that most Boer homesteads were burnt and farm buildings destroyed. 'After the war, when they went back, there were no houses. Only two things were not touched: that was the *boerevolk* and religion.' *Boerevolk* means literally the Boer, or Afrikaner, people; but the word *volk* has powerful, deeply emotional, almost religious connotations. 'Lots of churches were burnt down. Religion was still there and the land was still there. But they were as poor as lice. They had no money, nothing.' He views with suspicion the loans that were made to the returning farmers. Certainly some prospered and paid back their loans, but in other cases, he points out, the land reverted to 'the magnates' who had loaned the money.

By 1913 Koos Farrell had prospered sufficiently to be able to buy a farm in the Lake Chrissie district. Farming in those earlier days was generally a casual affair, often combined with other pursuits. Ten years later he sold the farm and bought another, Vlakfontein, in the Bronkhorstspruit district. In the winter when grazing was depleted he would move his livestock to the lowveld where heat and disease prevented summer grazing. In 1933 disaster struck. He had trekked with his animals into the Groblersdal district where, in one night, he lost thirty-seven cattle from *spons-siekte*, 'spongy sickness'. Fred was only two years old at the time, but it was a story that he heard again and again. 'He nearly went off his head! He lost his whole herd!' The disaster was compounded when, some days later, he turned his sheep into apparently verdant pastures, unaware of the dangers of the poison grasses in the area. 'Every single sheep died. That broke him completely.' Koos found work at the Clydesdale Colliery near Witbank, leaving his wife to manage the farm.

It was at Vlakfontein that Frederick Farrell grew up. His father came home from the colliery only at weekends. The Els family from which his mother, Susanna Dirkie, came was a hard-working one, so she buckled down to the realities of their reduced circumstances. She sold milk, butter and eggs, but somehow managed to indulge her love of gardening in a patch of roses and perennials. The children were expected to do their share of the work: 'After school you went onto the lands to cultivate, plough or do whatever else was necessary. Then you had to milk. You did your homework by candlelight. At four in the morning you got up, made the fire, brewed coffee – there was no electricity, so you had first to make the fire in the stove.'

The staple diet of the blacks on the farm was *putu*, maize-meal porridge, cooked in a large iron three-legged pot over an open fire. Fred recollects with salivating relish, 'You can smell it a long way off.' He would scoop a fistful and carry it off to the dairy where, first making sure that his mother was not about, stolen cream would be added. 'Ooh! it was fantastic! Occasionally I cook it for the kids on a Sunday afternoon; they like it, too, and say, "Pa, come cook us some *putu*." Very nice and healthy.'

Selective memory sometimes converts the pleasanter childhood experiences into what amounts almost to a golden age. Fred dwells on how he grew up with blacks and ate (or seized) porridge out of the same pot, which experiences he views as giving him some authority to speak on their behalf. He idealizes their way of life as he observed it. 'The women saw to everything in the home; they saw that there was sufficient beer, sufficient porridge and everything for the men. They were happy. They earned a certain amount of mealies, some wages and they built the houses themselves; they kept cattle.

'My father was always very strict, but was always highly respected. The blacks respected him very, very highly and he had very great respect for them. We, as kids, had very great respect for the older blacks. We called the old men *outa* and the women *aia* and the blacks always called me *kleinbaas* [little master].' Wrongdoers were whipped with the *sjambok*, a leather-thonged whip. 'If they did something wrong my father used to *sjambok* the blacks: that was the best medicine out; not to cut him to pieces, but give him a good hiding so that he must feel it; about five or six strokes.' Such punishment was not confined to the blacks. 'One Sunday my father told me I mustn't swim; the old people were very strict about not doing those things on the sabbath. And then after lunch my brother and I and two little blacks went into the dam and we swam there. Next thing we see the old man there with a *sjambok* and each and every one, the blacks and us, all of us, we were all *sjambokked*, every one, with no clothes on. It was very sore, I remember it clearly. It hurt like hell. You feel it. You remember it very well. You never forget that.' It would be a good thing, he believes, if today instead of being gaoled for three or four months, wayward youngsters were given the cane. 'They're getting five star treatment in gaols today. Some of them steal to be in gaol because they know that's where they'll get food three times a day, proper food and they've got a roof and a bed to sleep on. Everything. The gaols of today are five star hotels with fish twice a week, meat every day, beans, porridge, bread, margarine, coffee.'

He remembers going with his father to visit one of his old labourers who was dying. 'We drove there in the horse and cart and when we got there the man said, "*Oubaas* [old master], I'm very sick," and my old man kneeled down and prayed for him; it was one of the best prayers I've ever heard. About an hour later he was gone. So that's missionary: he brought the Word into his house and he prayed for him there.'

When the time came for Fred, the youngest and most indulged member of the family, to go to school in Witbank, 30 miles distant, he boarded with people there: 'Wasn't very easy for a small kid. It was a three-mile walk to school, too. I had shoes occasionally, sometimes not.' Eventually there was a school bus which stopped at the farm gate at half-past six in the morning, taking Frederick and his brothers to the school recently established in Kendal and returning them in the afternoons. In those days, under the United Party government, there was school feeding. 'I think it was an excellent idea because in the thirties and forties there were very poor people in this country. Lots of people didn't have food to eat.' The Farrell family, even if not always able to afford shoes, was never short of food. 'My mother used to bake twenty huge loaves in the outside oven; an ordinary bread knife couldn't cut them. She would give bread and vegetables to our poor neighbours.'

The family never took formal holidays, but a change in routine and an opportunity to enjoy some high jinks occurred when the parents journeyed to *nagmaal* services. It being impossible for farmers to attend a weekly communion, the *nagmaal* services, spread over several days, were held in Bronkhorstspruit at three-monthly intervals. The tarpaulin cover would be erected over the arched framework on the Farrells' ox-wagon and his mother and father, together with Fred's only sister, would leave for the church in Bronkhorstspruit. Tents were erected on the town square. While piety might have been the central purpose, it was also a time to meet family and friends, a time for catching up on news, for there were no telephones in the country districts and the poor dirt roads did not encourage travel. Women would exchange recipes, admire babies and compare their handwork. Men would gather to smoke pipes and perhaps, on occasion, surreptitiously enjoy a *sopie* of peach brandy for there could be no drinking in front of the *kerk*. It was a time, too, for courting.

The responsibility of looking after the farm while their parents were away was not one that weighed too heavily upon the boys, for after all, it was the black servants who attended to all the routine affairs. 'Our cousins came to stay with us and that is the time when we were really naughty, swimming in the dam, catching barbel, shooting birds. We had a marvellous time! We had a whole soccer team with my cousins and the black children. There were lots of little piccanins on our farm and on the neighbours' farms. Each team was made up of blacks and whites.'

In 1946 Fred's father and mother, having sold their farm, retired to one of the solid square single-storeyed houses in the village of Bronkhorstspruit. Susanna Farrell had an acre in which to cultivate her garden. Koos Farrell served on the Town Council and also became a *koster* or churchwarden in the Nederduitse Gereformeerde Kerk, a position of responsibility and status which he took seriously, for he was a deeply religious man. Congregants generally lived on far-flung farms, reached by dubious roads. The minister was often absent on church business and it fell to Koos Farrell to conduct services or funerals and give Holy Communion.

At fourteen Fred, never an enthusiastic scholar, left school and was apprenticed as a motor mechanic to the General Motors agent in the village. From his earliest childhood, engines had fascinated him and he had learned, by trial and error, to repair his father's DKW car. 'To be a master craftsman you had to pass examinations and practical and technical tests. Not much time for studying. I used to work till eleven or twelve at night in the garage. My journeyman was hard, a bloke called Bouwer. But he was highly skilled. We used to make or repair; there was no such thing as replacing in those days.' His pay was 40s.10d. a week. No overtime pay. 'On Saturdays, after twelve, I get home, have a bit of food, get into a clean overall and go back down to the garage and sell petrol with the old hand pumps. So I was selling petrol and was paid half a crown for the afternoon and that night I'd go to the bioscope [cinema]. Sixpence for bioscope and tickey [threepence] for a coke. Sometimes, if I got tips in the afternoon, I took a girl.' Electricity was a rarity and not laid on at the bioscope. Before long Frederick, with his aptitude for engines, was in charge of the generator which ran the projector. There was some small payment and the ecstasy of 'free bioscope'.

During the five years of his apprenticeship Frederick studied correspondence courses at night, eventually passing his National Technical Certificate 3, 'something a bit past matric; your next step will be a diploma engineer.' Once qualified he joined the roads department where, at the time, pay was somewhat higher than in the private sector. He embarked on a correspondence course for an engineering degree and studied in the evenings. On Christmas Eve 1952, aged twenty-one, he married Magdalena Henriette Elizabeth Boshoff, known as Lena. Her father was a cartage contractor in the little Transvaal town of Belfast near which he had been working. With his pay of £52.10s. a month and that of his wife who was a senior in the local telephone exchange, the young couple bought a house and furniture and even, Frederick adds, paid insurance.

In 1965 Mr Boshoff, his father-in-law, became ill and was ordered by his doctor to leave Belfast for the warmer lowveld. Lena, their only daughter, was deeply attached to her parents, so she and Frederick sold their house and with Cobus, their ten-year-old son, moved with them to Nelspruit. Frederick bought land, 24 morgen in extent (he refers to it as a plot), on the Burnside road, some 20 kilometres outside the town. Here their fortunes changed dramatically, for in 1966 Fred found a job as inspector of workshop production at Osken Engineering. It was financed by Bonuskor, an investment corporation offshoot of SANLAM, the powerful financial group of companies developed by Afrikaners. His pay was 2,400 rand a month. Questioned as to how he gained such a highly remunerative appointment, Fred Farrell gives a little deprecating laugh, 'Well, I was skilled and workmen of my quality were very, very scarce, that I can tell you. The management had a lot of faith in me. I was quality controller, a very senior position. When I took over the work-shop of Osken Engineering they were in a bit of a mess, lots of drama with comebacks. Within my first two months there were no more comebacks. It's a question of management.' The roads department paid him his pension which, for fifteen years of ser-vice, amounted to 1,180 rand, 'peanuts', he calls it. 'So I nearly sent that cheque back to them, but I put it in a savings account. We're not people who spend money recklessly, my wife and I. We know where money comes from. She gives piano lessons, she's a very good musician. We saved quite a lot, a little bit of a nest egg.'

Nelspruit is a park-like town, its streets lined with jacarandas and spreading poinciana trees with their scarlet midsummer blos-soms. The Crocodile River meanders through the farms in the fertile valley that extends from before and far beyond the town, supplying water for the irrigation of tropical fruit, vegetables, tobacco and cotton. It is not only the richness of such resources that generates prosperity, but the fact that Nelspruit is the centre of vast labour pools. Men in neighbouring Mozambique, in the largely poverty-stricken homelands of Lebowa, Kangwane and a little further away, Gazankulu, are eager and often desperate for jobs. The more affluent blacks from these areas shop in Nelspruit and buy their bedroom or kitchen suites on hire purchase from the chain stores.

The Farrell nest egg came in handy in 1969 when a small sheet-metal business, chiefly involved in the manufacture of galvanized water tanks, was offered to him for 3,000 rand. He seized the opportunity and bought it. 'I started this business under the mulberry tree,' he recounts. 'When I came here, not much more than twenty years ago, there was only one European shop, "Nelspruit Winkels", and only one café. There were three Indian shops, a post office, a police station and that was about all.' Nelspruit is unusual in that the Indian traders were not, upon the introduction of the Group Areas Act, removed beyond the periphery of the town. 'I think that the properties were given to them by Paul Kruger. They're still in the same place, but they've built beautiful shops now. They live in the Indian township called Nel India; you must go and see the houses some of them have built – palaces! They've really spent, make no mistake.' His thoughts turn to the tricameral parliament, introduced in 1984 and in which the Indian and Coloured people have, for the first time, been given representation. 'To me it's unfair, giving the Indians seats in Parliament and not the blacks.'

Today there are ten- and twelve-storeyed buildings and branches of all the main chain stores in Nelspruit. The value of property has risen more than tenfold. Mr Farrell is disinclined to boast, yet is proud of his achievements. 'We've built up quite a concern. I think there are very few businesses in town which have made the progress we have made. I think it's due to management – management and hard work. When my son Cobus was still a kid I had various contracts from the government for pollution-free kitchens, canopies over the stoves. I've done most of the hostels in the Transvaal. I worked day and night.'

Cobus grew up in the valley between the mountains where the plaintive cry of the hadedas echoes in the mornings and evenings. His playmate was a young black boy, the child of one of his father's servants. In his adult years he recalls that time: 'It was a beautiful experience which I had with him. And referring to their rollicking fun, 'We really *jolled*, and the blacks can do that! They can play, they can play with nothing. They taught me to play because they really can play! That is a blessing which

I'm thankful for. There's lots of fields where they can teach me a lot of things: like veldcraft and bushcraft and music, they're very good at music, they sing beautifully. I don't want to give myself out as an expert on black people, but growing up with a black gives a good background of their traditions, their ways of doing things.

'At the moment my little boy is growing up and he's also got a piccanin that he's playing with. My piccanin's still in town; he comes in here regularly, comes and greets me. Petrus is his name. We're still good friends, but we went our separate ways; we've divorced, sort of.' Asked whether, when Petrus came to visit him in his office, he would sit down, Cobus's face closed: 'He would *never* try *that!*'

He matriculated at the local Afrikaans-medium school and did his compulsory Army service. 'I was terrible at English at school, nearly failed, but in the Army I learned a lot of English. One month it's English and one month Afrikaans. That's the rule – they don't stick to the rules, but that is the rule. And then in business you're forced to speak English because that is the business language. I was just thrown in the deep end and I had to swim. That's where I learned English.'

After three months basic training at Kimberley he was sent to Rundu, a South African military centre in northern Namibia, just south of the Angolan border, and from which the South African troops launch some of their attacks into Angola. 'It was super! I had a good time, a very good time. You're forced to mix. I like English people and it's easy for me to mix with them; but there are some English people who don't want to mix with Afrikaans people for some or other reason and some Afrikaans people who don't want to mix with English people. But I don't think it's a major problem. Everything was actually very quiet up there; that was 1973. There were a few border crossings from the other side, SWAPO terrorists.'

When Cobus married Pauline Fick in October 1976 they moved into a flat in town. He hankered for the land. 'And dad's neighbour got into financial trouble and they came to ask if I want to buy the property, 17 hectares, which I did for 18,000 rand, with the house, everything laid on. I borrowed the capital from my dad and I've paid it all back. There are some mango and avocado trees. We're just living here, not farming. I've got a tractor for cutting the grass. It's very nice, the whole family together,' referring to his sister and her husband living on the adjoining land and his father and mother across the road. 'Though', and he laughs, 'sometimes it's not so nice. But we can sort out our differences.'

The Farrells employ fifty-seven blacks and seventeen whites at their factory and when they move into the new premises they are building the numbers will be increased. The salaries and working conditions which they provide are competitive 'with everybody in town'. 'All we want out of a man is a day's work.' At the end of each financial year workers are paid a bonus which, for the blacks, amounted in 1986 to about 200 rand each. 'It's very handy and they really appreciate it.'

The three men, two Swazis and a Shangaan, who worked for Fred Farrell at the outset are with him still, though two of them will soon be pensioned off. John Mathabula is one of a number of employees who have been helped to build their own houses in the adjoining black township of Kanyamazane. Cobus explains how the firm's loan scheme operates: 'We give him 500 rand at a time which he will pay back to us, interest free. We must help him, but we mustn't help him into the deep end; that's why we only make the loan of 500 rand at a time. He pays us back and then he can borrow another 500 rand.' Siza Ndawo has been with the firm for fourteen years; unlike the rest of the employees who are black, he is a man of mixed race, a coloured man. 'He's a very gifted black, one of the few who can do three-dimensional work – with our type of work you must be able to work in all three dimensions. He's built himself a very nice house with a bathroom, toilet, shower, carpets – the works! He's got electricity now, with a geyser.' The firm has helped some of the workers by advancing the deposits on cars they buy. 'They pay off so much a week. I'm not a credit corporation so I don't charge them interest.'

Fred Farrell has introduced a private pension scheme for his staff. Referring to his workmen he pronounces, somewhat biblically, 'They're also reaping. I'm not pocketing everything I can and just getting everything out of them. Every year they get a bonus and good leave. We look after them. We've helped them to build houses in the location; they've got some of the best houses in the Bantu Trust.' He believes that they are happy. Cobus encourages the workmen to make their own decisions wherever possible: 'You cannot make decisions for them, because then they're becoming puppets and we don't want that. Like Siza Ndawo; I can give him a drawing, tell him the customer's requirements, the thickness of the material to be used and let him get on with it. There are lots of different ways the job could be done, but I leave it to him to decide. If he's done a good job I'll tell him so and praise him.'

The foundations of the unpretentious little factory under the mulberry tree were laid in what is now the industrial area of Nelspruit. Cobus's insistence upon increased mechanization has enhanced productivity. The machinery in the two small factories is worth three-quarters of a million rand; nothing is owing on it. 'I wouldn't put things on account; everything was strictly cash,' says Fred. Their turnover is a quarter of a million a month, but money is tight and Cobus spends a good deal of his time collecting debts. One of their businesses manufactures sheet iron for building, another the corrugated iron sheeting extensively used in the black areas for roofing and sometimes for the entire house. A third venture is devoted to heavy engineering and builds truck bodies and trailers. Fred Farrell keenly awaits the completion of the large premises, 3,000 square metres, which they are building. All three businesses will then be under one roof.

The Farrells' most recently completed contract was the installation of a water purification scheme in Mauritius. Their membership of the Conservative and Herstigte Nasionale Parties does not seem to interfere with their getting government contracts. Cobus laughs and says, 'You'd be surprised how many government employees are CP or HNP.' There are also contracts from the homeland governments, the most recent one being for 400 water tanks to be raised on stands.

There are now two black welders working for them, 'very productive and I respect them. They are paid 5.20 rand an hour, which works out at 234 rand a week. That's good pay, but they work for that money. We're very happy with them.' The six white welders are paid 8.50 rand an hour. Fred explains the disparity in terms of National Industrial Council regulations and upon being questioned, claims that they have a better output than the blacks. 'You can give the white man a job and you go and check it and it'll be all right. The black, you can give him a job and one day it'll be 100 per cent and the next day there's something that isn't right. The fact is, and it's been proved through the whole history, that a black can do so much, but you can't give him full responsibility. I've got one here, been work- ing for me for the past eighteen years, he's a very skilled man. I can give him a job and tell him to carry on with it, but you have to check continuously to make sure.' Blacks, he maintains, cannot read a plan, cannot work in three dimensions. Upon it being suggested to him that educated blacks do not have these problems, he agrees.

'My biggest worry is this . . . I've got nothing against education; I should give them matric, give them even a degree, and believe me, they're all going for that. But who's going to do the work?' He answers his own question, 'Actually as far as building is concerned, they've taken over. For many years I haven't seen a white man on the scaffold, laying bricks.' White bricklayers have now become foremen. He refers to the new premises they are building: 'There's not a single white bricklayer and they're doing a fine job. They've got a black there and he's laying bricks with both hands; left hand when he goes to the left and right hand when he goes to the right. I've never seen it before in my life. He's laying up to 3,000 bricks a day and that's a record. He gets a certain salary up to, I think, 2,000 bricks a day, and each one he lays after that he gets a bonus.'

Trade unions have grown in size and strength throughout South Africa in recent years, a trend Cobus hardly welcomes. 'I see the unions and the government interfering with my freedom and in my private affairs. They are making it difficult for me to manage my own business.' The company is registered with the

Metal and Allied Workers Union which has representatives on the National Industrial Council, the body which negotiates wages and working conditions. But the Farrells' workers have joined the Forestry and Allied Workers Union, probably because there are extensive forestry companies in the area and the union has zealous local representatives. Cobus is baffled as to how this has come about and can only think that the union is keen to increase its membership, irrespective of whether or not they work in forestry. He is worried about 'agitators' infiltrating his staff.

Cobus would prefer the trade unions not to have a place in his organization 'I feel that my management is such that if my people have a problem they can talk to me about it. I see no reason for a third person to interfere with our relationship. It's definitely a fact that 90 per cent of the trade unions are militant at this stage and we know that the UDF [United Democratic Front] is playing a major part in COSATU [Congress of South African Trade Unions]. There is definitely political involvement. I think that the trade unions ought to be there to look after the rights of the worker in the labour context: it shouldn't have anything to do with politics.'

Father and son concur on the matter of trade unions. Fred relates, 'When they started off with this union business about 50 per cent of them joined the union and after about two weeks they came to borrow some money. I said, "Sorry, go to the union and borrow money from them." So the whole lot have resigned. They've dumped it. I wouldn't like to see them as members of a union and it's unfair for me to support the union, and the big brass of the unions are getting big salaries and my poor people must starve and struggle. They've made all sorts of promises that they'll help with the schools but all they've done is to advocate strikes.'

In April 1986 black leaders nationwide called for a week-long stayaway. Despite reprisals threatened against anyone who went to work, several of his workmen turned up on the first morning of the strike. They explained to him that the strike leaders in the township had threatened that the houses of those who went to work were to be burnt and they asked to be excused from work. Both Farrells immediately urged them to return to protect themselves and their houses and agreed to their staying away for the rest of the week. On the following Monday the full workforce reported for duty. Cobus maintains that management learnt a good lesson during the stayway. 'We realized that we were overstaffed.' Asked why he kept unnecessary labourers, his reply was not without a degree of ambiguity: 'Ach, I don't know – a lot of sentiment in it. The thing is that you get times when you use them and it's a semi-skilled job which we're doing and in fact if you take somebody from the street it takes three weeks to train them and by that time you're rushing. So we keep them and we keep them busy, that's for sure! They don't stand around doing nothing.' Staff cannot, the Farrells believe, lightly be dismissed at a time of such exceptionally high unemployment; but should there be a downturn in the business then the workers might have to be put on 'short time'. 'You must keep them in your service and provide for them because you are actually liable for their families. You must take care of their families. Everybody's happy with the work; he's happy with his pay packet; he's happy with his bonus; he's happy with his three weeks' leave a year.'

Cobus speaks with zest of his business, 'We're making a good living and we're enjoying it. That's the main thing: we must *enjoy* it. You must love the things you do there. And you must love the people you work with; love what they create and what you create. In love there's respect, and I must respect the people I'm working with and in turn, they'll respect me and they'll love me.'

In the Farrell business colour is not a factor. Black customers are welcomed, 'Daily they walk in here with a couple of thousand rand in cash – they buy in cash; they're good customers of mine and I admire them.' Fred continues, 'You get the white man, buying with a cheque book, and the cheque bounces. That's the usual thing. But as I say, the sun isn't just here to shine over the white people, it's also for them.' Most of the black customers are shopkeepers in the government-created homelands around Nelspruit; the greatest demand is for galvanized roof sheeting, corrugated iron. 'There is a Swazi and when he comes to pay his account it's usually at least 7,000 rand,' Cobus relates. 'There's a lot of blacks whom I will trust and there are whites I wouldn't trust.' He is more guarded concerning his business dealings with Indians with whom he has had some unfortunate experiences. Jews are good businessmen in his opinion; he doesn't like them, but he likes doing business with them 'because they really test your skill – I'm talking now about the "*regte ou Boerejood*", the proper old Jew who went round the farms in the old days, peddling goods and buying skins – they were making fortunes, those guys, some of them! If you do business with Jews there's no place for fooling around. You must be sharp if you deal with them because they're good businessmen. They got a gift.' With regard to Afrikaners, Cobus feels that although formerly they appeared to meet with little success in business, they have been forced to become more astute, or be taken over. 'I don't say we're the smartest, but we do business.'

'I'm proud of my heritage. I feel you must draw the line somewhere and the place where I draw the line is on starting to socialize with people. And although I've got nothing against blacks – I work nicely with them, we've got a good relationship in our workshop here – I feel we must stop at some point. I stop it on social grounds.' Reminded of his relationship with 'his piccanin' Cobus agrees that that was 'socializing' but puts it firmly in another compartment of his understanding, a compartment which he shut when he was fourteen years old. 'As soon as we start socializing with them it's not right because you are awakening some sort of expectations with the people: you won't be able to fulfil these expectations at this stage. You'll have to disappoint the people.'

Questioned as to the nature of the expectations that might be awakened by an excess of friendliness, Cobus responded, 'I'd hate it . . . one day I'd hate to see my daughter, Elmarie, marrying a black. Now I know that people say that you are responsible for the upbringing of your daughter and your son and you should see that it mustn't happen, which is very, very true. But because there are people who don't do that I would hate to see it happen to other people's children.' Blacks, he believes, view mixed marriages with a distaste that matches his own. He returns to his preoccupation. 'Once you start letting them into your church or into your lounge, you are opening the door and soon they'll bring their kids and the kids will play together and next time they'll grow up and next time little Jimmy will come and say, "Please I want to take Elmarie to the movies tonight," or to a dance, and you know I've got no grounds to say no. I am being pushed into a corner and I must say yes. You can't really say to somebody, "Look I don't like you. You don't take my daughter out." I know there are some people who do it, but I don't feel that's the right way. You can't give them half your hand and then pull it back again. Rather keep it back from them all the way. Don't do something that you won't be able to carry through.'

The Farrell family for many generations belonged to the Nederduitse Gereformeerde Kerk. Fred Farrell will tell you, 'I'm a very big religious man. I know why I've made a success of my business: my main partner is our almighty Lord. And I pray every morning and every night that he must lead us.' When, in October 1986, the synod of the NG Kerk stated that its past support for apartheid had been a scriptural error and that the doors of the Church should be open to worshippers of all races, the Farrells were confused and unhappy. Cobus, who had been a member of the *Kerkraad*, or Church Council, says, 'I think that you'll find all conservative Afrikaners have got a problem with the NG Kerk at the moment. It's going a bit left.' He speaks of occasions when blacks have been present at services in his church: 'I know that some people do not mind and that there are people who have strong arguments, backed by biblical authority, that say this is right – but there are also people who use biblical arguments to prove that it is wrong.' In former times blacks who were allowed to attend the occasional wedding or funeral sat discreetly at the back of the church, but more recently a black person has been known to sit boldly up in the middle, among the whites. Cobus is troubled, 'I think there are cultural differences that make it very difficult to go to church with them.

You cannot listen to what you should listen to; your attention is divided. We're giving thousands of rand at the moment for blacks to build their own churches. There is no reason in my mind why they should mix with us in our churches. I know there are a lot of arguments, but I'm a racist. Everybody else is: everybody is proud of their heritage and I'm proud of my heritage, too. And I feel that you must draw the line somewhere.' Although he is attending the Evangeliese Gereformeerde Kerk (the Evangelical Reformed Church), he has not formally resigned from the NG Kerk. 'I've got a big thing to clear up in my own mind before I join any church; something I must sort out for myself.' There are aspects of the church's new policy, in addition to that of admission of blacks to the church, with which he is not in agreement. 'There's a tendency in the NG Kerk to become a financial institution instead of a church. They're pushing finances all the time. They built this massive office complex building in Pretoria. The synod is in it, but it was built for prestige, I can't see any other reason for building it. They've incurred a *massive* debt. We can talk a long time about the reasons why I'm leaving the NG Kerk.'

Fred Farrell and his wife have joined the Evangeliese Gereformeerde Kerk. 'That's like the old Dutch Reformed Church; they're still singing hymns and making use of the previous Bible; not the new Bible [of 1983], because some of the things there don't correspond with the old Bible. They're very conservative. On the front door they've got a board up: Right of Admission Reserved. We do missionary work, but the missionary work must stay where it belongs and let them stay there where they belong. They don't want to be involved in a gathering where all colours and everybody goes in, like in the NG Kerk. I've got nothing against doing religious work, but I would never like the other colour in the same church that I'm going to, and the blacks wouldn't like a white person to visit their congregation.' He has heard that one of the members of the local NG Kerk brought a black man, an announcer on the black television service, to the church, 'And I think', there are ominous undertones, 'that he stayed over with one of the ministers.'

All white male South African citizens who are medically fit are liable for military service, an initial and continuous period of two years, followed by 720 days over twelve years. After that they are liable to be called up for commando duty. Cobus is required to do twelve days duty and three weekend camps each year. He is a navigator and in July 1986 did thirty hours of flying time, considerably in excess of his obligations. 'We've got four flights in our squadron and each flight gets a standby month. With these landmine incidents and so on that are happening here, the people are going voluntarily. I think some people are not so keen to go, but because they see their neighbour go, they feel they must go too.' The pay is of little account and so the members of the squadron pool it and use it, from time to time, for everyone to take his family on a weekend flying jaunt.

Cobus describes a recent experience when he was flying over the surrounding country. 'On the one side of the river there are white farms, irrigated, beautiful lands, green as a lawn. The other side, which is a black area, there's nothing. And I know what went into that black area in the form of agricultural support. Millions of taxpayers' money, and those people weren't prepared to absorb that knowledge and that tremendous amount of support, they just sort of rejected it.' The suggestion that the problem might lie in the overcrowding in the black areas, where after all, the blacks who constitute over 70 per cent of the population may occupy only 13 per cent of the land, surprised him. Wasting no time in considering the implications, he reiterated indignantly that despite the government having, in his view, supplied 'the ways and means to create nice farms', these had been rejected or ignored by the blacks. He gave another example, this time of the government endeavouring to establish a kibbutz system in a black area. 'And it was a total disaster. Not because the blacks are so bad or the whites are so good or whatever, but because the blacks were not ready at that stage to take up the task they were given. I agree with my father that the moment that Verwoerd started with his homelands that's where our troubles started.' The Western system, in his view, has been forced upon the blacks 'too fast, too soon and in too big amounts.'

His thoughts turn to a version of history, to the time, 300 years ago when the white man established himself at the Cape. 'If you look at the black civilization, which is a very respected civilization in my view, you will see that they hadn't even discovered the wheel at that stage. So now we can see that their civilization is *miles* behind ours. And what we did, we tried to force them, with brute force, up to the standard where we are.'

Fred Farrell is equally condemnatory of the way in which he preceives blacks squandering the resources so generously bestowed upon them by the government. 'Today, when the government hands over to blacks fertile farms previously owned by white farmers, they are not capable of maintaining them.' With an assumed magnanimity he pronounces, 'If they cultivate that 13 per cent which they've got and prove they can do something with it, I'll be prepared to give them 50 per cent.'

In common with many South Africans, the Farrells take comfort in their white superiority when they view what they believe to be the sorry state into which black rule has precipitated some black African states. 'If the white man should pull out of South Africa today, you'll see, in six months there won't be any food here. We can go to Mozambique, next door, and see what's happening there.' Fred attributes the plight in which Mozambique finds itself to the fact that the whites fled. Reluctantly he accepts that Zimbabwe appears to be doing well, but attributes this to the good rains in the past season. Mugabe, he has been told, is a clever man and has made rich slaves out of the whites there. 'The whites have a good time in Zimbabwe, but they cannot go even an inch out of Zimbabwe because everything is tied up and they're not allowed to take money out.' This is not something on which he is inclined to dwell.

Fred Farrell had been a member of the National Party. His brother, Paul Farrell, is the Nationalist Member of Parliament for Bethlehem in the Orange Free State. Later, however, Fred's allegiance shifted to the HNP, to the right of the government. Cobus joined the HNP immediately after leaving school. Like many HNP members he views the government-controlled television news programmes with disfavour. 'We get people like

Tutu and Boesak and Beyers Naude on TV; they have committed themselves to the other side; committed themselves to violence in the way of sanctions. Why do the authorities give them all the time on television and you don't hear about the group that doesn't want them? There are groups in the black areas, too, who are frightened and don't want them. If you look at the viewing time on television that the National Party is getting and then look at the time that the PFP and HNP are getting – it's shocking really! These people are using television for their own benefit!'

Before the May 1987 elections Fred changed his allegiance to the Conservative Party, now the official parliamentary opposition. He regrets the fact that in Nelspruit his own party and the HNP stood separately, thus splitting the right-wing vote and preventing the defeat of the government candidate. Cobus has remained a member of the HNP but guardedly declines at present to give his reasons for doing so. 'Talk to me in three months' time.' He is pessimistic about the future. 'Smuts said, correct me if I'm wrong, that you mustn't awaken the animal of nationalism among the black people, because that can ruin Africa – and it has ruined Africa. Kissinger, when he came to South Africa, said that the country would have to choose between integration and segregation. If the people choose integration I would have to accept it. I love my country and I'll *never* leave it. I can't see a way out. I'll just have to side with my group and stay with my group and teach my children to stay with their group. I'd like to see white schools and black schools; the blacks must have everything, but still be separate. They can go to *their* church and *their* schools. The only thing I hope for my son is that he can have the chances in life that my dad gave me. That's the wish out of my heart for him. It would be nice to have him carry on our family business, but whatever he does, I hope he enjoys it.'

The AWB, led by the demagogic Eugene Terre'Blanche, has a considerable following in Nelspruit despite its not having held any public meetings there. Neither of the Farrells has joined the movement; Fred feels that it is perhaps too right-wing: 'It's like the Ossewa-Brandwag.' He lunched with Terre'Blanche on his recent visit to Nelspruit. 'He's got a very strong personality and he's a strong speaker. He said he didn't want to get into politics as a political party. They will sit back until this government capitulates and then they'll climb in and really show their colours. But I can tell you this much, they're very strong and they're working underground at the moment. As far as I can understand it seems that 90 per cent of the police force and 99 per cent of the Army – they're not members of the AWB, but they're with him in spirit.'

The government, although anxiously alert to right-wing reaction, has begun tinkering with the Group Areas Act, one of the cornerstones of apartheid, an Act which confines racial groups to strictly demarcated areas. Fred Farrell thinks that there is a possibility of it being scrapped, adding, 'From what I can make out there are lots of Nationalist Members of Parliament who are going to walk to the right when they do that. As far as the Group Areas Act is concerned, it's just a word now, like apartheid: it's gone. Our towns will be taken over. The sun is there to shine on everybody. They've got the buying power nowadays, these blacks.' He would be quite agreeable to a black man opening a business next door to his but the possibility of blacks moving onto the plot next door to his evokes a different response. 'The blacks come and buy the house and there's not just one family moving in there; there's about ten families moving into the one house. They park all their old motor cars around and make a noise so that the only way out is to sell.' It is pointed out to him that those living in black townships near the cities live in much the same way as white people of a similar income level; he agrees to the possibility, but relates his fears to the ramshackle dwellings in little villages at Bushbuckridge, a poverty stricken area that he passes on his way to his game farm.

'And another thing that makes me worried – I'm driving along this road at least three times a month at various times of the day and night, and especially at coming-out-of-school time you're passing *thousands* of black kids. My biggest worry is what is going to happen in five years' time. Who is going to employ these people? Who's going to feed them? I think it's come to the time now when the white man can't feed the whole of South Africa any more. He'll only be able to feed the whites and some of the blacks.'

Fred Farrell, when asked how he saw the future of his country, uses the metaphor close to the heart of the trekkers from whom he is descended through the female line: 'The white must put his shoulder to the wheel and *push* the wagon. Let the blacks develop in their own territory. They can come in and sell their labour. I got nothing against them. I don't hate them, but sure God, I don't love them.'

TONY ARDINGTON

THE COASTAL ROAD winds northwards from Durban, passing Umhlanga Rocks, with its hotels, tall time-share buildings and condominiums. Further on, towards and beyond Tongaat, gaps in the coastal bush reveal the breakers crashing onto rocks or sandy beaches. On the other side of the road tall green sugar-cane, bearing in July its smoky floral plumes, extends away over the gently rolling hills. Some 100 kilometres from Durban a dirt road curls among the cane fields, past turnoffs bearing the names of farms. That to the Ardington farm leads up a hill, ending in a circular driveway, verdant with indigenous trees and shrubs which partly conceal the low creeper-covered house. Beyond ranges the limitless vista of the sugar-cane, undulating to the horizon. Tony Ardington (christened Anthony John), tall, blond and sturdily built, wears shorts, a long-sleeved shirt, knee-length socks and lace-up shoes. He was born in March 1940 on his maternal grandfather's farm, Elderslie, in the Karkloof valley, half an hour's run from what was then the little Natal village of Howick. His father, John Christopher (Jack) Ardington, serving in North Africa with the South African troops at the time, was later to be captured at Tobruk. He spent the rest of the war in prisoner-of-war camps, first in Italy and later in Germany. His mother, Muriel Lynette Shaw, was born on the same family farm in 1911. The Shaws had been among the 5,000 English and Scots brought to South Africa in 1849 under the Byrne

Settlers scheme. According to Tony, the Shaw family originally 'farmed trees, robbing nature; later they turned to general farming and dairying. The men were polo players and over the years there was nearly always one of the Shaws in the Natal polo team.'

Frank Ardington, Tony's paternal grandfather, was a Londoner, a captain in the merchant marine. On his way to settle in South Africa which had seemed to him, when he called at its ports, to be a land of opportunities, he met Annie Dobson, a Yorkshirewoman. They married in 1904, travelling immediately up to the Transvaal goldfields where he became a mine manager and where Jack, their second child, was born in 1906. Frank Ardington's health did not measure up to the standards set by the authorities of those days for men going underground where the fine dust often damaged the lungs. He maintained that he could not remain a mine manager without being able to keep in touch with conditions underground and so left the mines and went to Natal where he bought a sugar farm, Blairbeth. Jack, in due course, was sent to Michaelhouse, the private boarding-school for boys at Balgowan in the Natal midlands. After matriculating he managed a farm his father had acquired north of Pretoria. In 1936, as the result of a prolonged drought, the farm was sold and he came to Natal where he bought Cranburn, a sugar farm just south of Gingindlovu. In 1937 he married Muriel Lynette Shaw at the Karkloof Anglican Church, not far from the Shaw family farms.

World War II broke out in September 1939 and a year later almost every one of the younger white men in the district had joined the Army or the Air Force and were away fighting. The Indian and black staff were generally able to continue with the day-to-day running of the farms and in many cases the wives took over the management. In 1944 Frank Ardington, Tony's grandfather, died. There was no one to run his farm and it was sold on a very depressed market. The four Shaw brothers farmed on adjacent areas in the Karkloof and it was among this large family community that Tony spent much of his early childhood which he regards as being particularly happy. His memories are of Elderslie where there were always cousins about, of rambling through the forests and playing in the mountain streams.

Tony's father came home from the prisoner-of-war camp in Germany in late 1945 and the family returned to Cranburn. The house they lived in was built by the original settler out of wood and iron, there being no bricks available in that region in the early days. 'You imported the plan and all the materials from England and then built it up, like a Meccano set. It had ceilings, but it was jolly hot.' Tony enjoyed traipsing around the farm behind his father, or travelling beside him in his van. 'From an early age I was doing little jobs. If there was anything to fix he would try and allocate some part of it for me to do; when there was trouble with a tractor he would say, "You do that part and I'll do this." If he was using a theodolite to put in a contour I would be expected to hold the staff. I can remember, when I was ten or twelve, helping him in his workshop and learning to weld. I'd be his constant companion until my friends arrived and we'd find better things to do.

'After the war, from the time I was about five, Mark Bell, a cousin of mine from Johannesburg, used to come down and stay with us and later he started bringing friends with him. We represented a terrible bunch of little boys who quickly formed a gang that got up to all sorts of mischief. The gang consisted of whoever arrived for the game which could be cops and robbers, cowboys and Indians, or Robin Hood and his merry men. There would be Mark and me and another friend who'd come down, so there were never more than two or three whites and perhaps ten Zulus, children of people who worked on the farm.

'My father was continually involved in a whole lot of engineering projects in his workshop and he was always building something the whole of his life. He was very creative in the engineering field and built new contraptions to mechanize this or that operation. He built one of the first cranes, used to tranship sugarcane; it became known as the Zulu crane.' Jack Ardington's crane, once it was on wheels, helped to circumvent the laborious processes involved in conveying the cane to the sugar mills. Prior to its introduction sugar-cane, cut by hand (as it is to this day), was carried by labourers up a ladder, to be placed in an ox-wagon and held together by chains. It was conveyed to the railway siding where the chains were released and it tumbled out onto the ground. Once more it had to be picked up and carried by a different group of men up another ladder and placed in the railway truck. 'Incredibly laborious. One of the first jobs my father did once he had his crane was to use it to tranship the cane from the road vehicles into the railway trucks. In those days,' Tony continues, 'in order to produce 1,000 tons of sugar-cane twenty people were employed. Today, to produce the same thousand tons four people are employed. It all goes in bulk containers now from the farm direct to the sugar mill.'

Tony and his sister, fifteen months older than himself, rode on their ponies to their preschool at his uncle's house in the Karkloof bush. Returning to Zululand after the war, aged five, he graduated to a private school at Amatikulu adjacent to a sugar mill. Two teachers dealt with seven classes, 'a situation that meant that you acquired the knowledge not only of your own class, but a good deal of that of the higher ones'. Thus, when in 1948 he went, aged seven, as a boarder to his preparatory school, Cordwalles, in Pietermaritzburg, he found he was ahead of his peers. The transition from home to boarding-school was something he had been brought up to expect and was made easier both by his having an older cousin at the school and the fact that he was good at games. In his final year he was put in a special scholarship group: 'I was the only one not to be successful, but I managed', he remarks wryly, 'to survive that as well.'

At thirteen he went on to Michaelhouse, his father's old school. In his final years there he played cricket, tennis, squash and hockey for the school. A knee injury at rugby had relegated him to coaching the teams of younger players. Boys were free to go wherever they chose on Sundays and Tony, interested in natural history, rambled with friends through the surrounding farms, spotting birds in their various habitats, and revelling in the countryside which undulated towards the foothills of the Drakensberg Mountains whose peaks in winter would occasionally be capped with snow. 'We were given packed lunches, but also bought food in the tuck-shop and tried out our culinary arts. Various people would pool together and we'd have exotic stews cooked out in the bush on a little primus stove.' He recalls the storms that so often came up on summer afternoons, round about two or three o'clock; their violence spent, the sun would shine in a crystal clear sky.

Whereas today some 12 per cent of the boys at Michaelhouse are black, in Tony's time the only boys of other races were a few Chinese. There was, however, a day school for black children on the Michaelhouse farm. Tony, who relates how he always tended to be 'laughed off as too liberal, a *kaffir-boetie*' (a term meaning literally a *kaffir*-brother, and generally used mockingly, if not pejoratively), was one of those who helped to build a soccer field on which, afterwards, boys from both schools used to play. 'I was quite politically aware as a boy. We also started a society that tried to get involved with the boys at the school, starting with the soccer field and then going up there and playing other games and getting a vegetable garden started. It helped that I spoke Zulu. I seemed to spend most of my energy trying to charge up the other guys in our society, to get them really committed and enthusiastic. Breaking down barriers in our society has always required such an enormous effort and that was my first lesson of how long it was going to take in any barrier-breaking-down operation.' The boys at Michaelhouse tended to come from the privileged and richer English-speaking families. In retrospect Tony fears that they might, at times, have been somewhat paternalistic or condescending.

He is now on the board of governors of Michaelhouse and expresses hopes that they might one day be able to do 'something substantial' for the farm school. Through succeeding years other boys have built additional class-rooms for the school and in 1986 Michaelhouse gave the first scholarship to a boy from the farm school. There are now nearly 400 children attending the school and where there are suitable candidates further scholarships may be awarded. The effect, he believes, upon the teachers and the other pupils cannot fail to be stimulating and the privileged whites might well gain a different kind of benefit. Some concern had been felt as to the possibly overwhelming effects of the Michaelhouse environment upon a young peasant boy, but Tony reports, 'Far from being cowed and timid, he's apparently an extraordinarily happy and cheeky child, playing rugby for the first team in his age group.'

In the late 1950s, when Tony left school, only about four out of every ten young white men were being conscripted. Tony, having matriculated and stayed on for a post-matric year, was one of those called up for the Army, but was exempted on account of his knee injury. In 1959 he went to Rhodes University in Grahamstown, a little city founded in 1812 and therefore old by South African standards. It lies in a hollow of the hills, encompassing its many churches, schools, training colleges and the university. He read for a B.Sc. degree, majoring in maths, chemistry and geology. Quick to view himself critically, Tony wonders whether the experience, enriching though it was from the point of view of its corporate life-style, was not somewhat limiting. 'I went there with some of my closest friends and did a course which I found easiest to do, so I probably wasn't as extended as I might have been had I done some other course, or if I had gone to a place where I didn't know many people.'

During the holidays he worked on the farm, 'not only because I wanted to, but because I was expected to do so. I was paid, and paid generously, with the object that I would learn something about money by paying for my own education and providing my own pocket money at university.' He played a good deal of sport, cricket for the first team and squash and tennis for the second teams. He became chairman of the Students' Union, a member of the Students' Representative Council and joined the light opera society. 'We did *The Boy Friend* and Gilbert and Sullivan. I would have loved to have been a great opera singer. I enjoy singing: apparently those who've got to listen don't enjoy it that much.' His life, up to this time, had been circumscribed by the farm and his boarding-school, so that he had almost no experience of the larger world, or of girls. 'I'd lived a totally sheltered, almost monastic life. My only experience of towns had been Durban, which I had found rather inhibiting in the little time I had spent there. The only girls I knew well were my sister and my cousins and those I'd met at various country dances and tennis tournaments. So at university I was also learning about girls and had a lot of friends who happened to be girls, as distinct from girlfriends.

'My father had always had a strong liberal streak in him; he was a person who tended to have sympathy for, and to back the underdog. He seemed to be extraordinarily free of prejudice. For instance, despite having been a prisoner of war in Germany he had a very considerable respect for those Germans he'd come in contact with. He was extremely concerned that he was on a farm that was labour intensive, that we were, in a way, battling on many occasions to make ends meet and simultaneously paying pretty appalling wages to most of the people on the farm. It was a matter of deep personal concern to him. He felt that he was exploiting his workers but that he had to pay what the market would bear. In his opinion society exploited farmers and used farmers to exploit blacks. These beliefs and sentiments had a big impact on my whole life.'

At Rhodes Tony met liberals of a different kind. 'They were limousine liberals. For them it was all nice and theoretical; they had never actually had to take any hard decisions like I'd seen my father, for example, having to take. You see, he had bought the farm in 1937 and built it up to produce 6,000 or 7,000 tons annually, to find, when he returned from the war, an alarming fall in production. He had the responsibility of a young, growing family, a farm to develop and no resources whatsoever.

'It struck me that some of these people I met at university at that time, motivated by the terrible injustices of South African society, were suggesting that if you redistributed all the wealth everything would be wonderful; you would have a system of social justice.' They failed, he thought, to take account of the inadequacy of the economy in relation to such expectations. 'You would have had to have a very significant economic growth to achieve that.' Such areas of disagreement did not affect his fundamental views about what was right and wrong, about the inequalities and inequities, and the sheer gross lack of social justice that existed in the society, but it made him suspicious of some of the people who appeared to share his deep concern about these issues. He denies any implication that there might, in such cases, have been a mere payment of lip-service. 'Some of them really had a lot of steel in their beings and were prepared to make very considerable sacrifices for what they believed. Some even got locked up. But I don't believe that they were fully aware of what they were actually asking of themselves and of other people, of actual economic realities; they were not facing the fact that we were, indeed, a Third World country then, as now.' Today some of those who expressed quite radical views at university are 'comfortable captains of business, industry and commerce; very conservative'.

In 1962, having gained an Honours degree in Geology, he and one of his close friends applied for Rhodes Scholarships. 'He got the Natal one and I got the Cape one. We heard the good news just as we were about to leave for England by ship, both of us having just been awarded Abe Bailey Travel Scholarships. The two months in Europe were very exciting, but for me the prospect of going to Oxford was rather terrifying. Such an honour: I was afraid I wouldn't be able to live up to it.' Sixty or seventy Rhodes Scholars are elected every year and as most are reading for a two- or three-year degree there might be over 150 Rhodes Scholars at Oxford at any one time. 'We had the privilege of being members of Rhodes House as well as our individual colleges. The Warden administered the Rhodes Trust and was responsible for overseeing our academic performances.' Before leaving for Oxford in September 1963 Tony spent six months working on the farm. His father reacted to his son's award of a Rhodes Scholarship by announcing to those whom he met, 'Take that bloody fool son of mine, he's just got a Rhodes Scholarship.' At the time this discomfited Tony somewhat, for he heard the 'bloody fool' part, not realizing that this was his father's way of dealing with his pride without apparent ostentation.

At his Oxford college, Corpus Christi, he launched into an obscure branch of science, X-ray crystallography, but recognizing that he was on the threshold of a wonderful opportunity in an international environment and should be studying the broadest possible course, he abandoned it and changed to PPE, Politics, Philosophy and Economics, specializing in economics. He played cricket for the university's first team and squash and tennis for the second. Whenever possible, he travelled.

After graduating with a first he was tempted to become an academic but, 'I'd always intended to come back and felt a very strong obligation to do so, although I'd got some very interesting possibilities.' Moreover, 'I was also strongly of the opinion that if everybody had the chance that I'd had and then said, "What the hell! I'm going to do what *I* want to do", rather than come back and try to do something in South Africa,' Tony hesitates, anxious not to inflate his motives, 'well, I just felt that if everybody adopted the attitude of saying, "I've been out of the country and I've had all these chances, thank you very much South Africa and my parents and everybody else for giving me this nice, happy childhood and upbringing and nice education, I am now going to wash my hands of you and off I'm going to do what *I* want to do." Somehow, to use a farmer's expression, there must be a ploughing back of the manure. That and my deep emotional ties with South Africa and my family meant there really was never any question about coming back.'

He returned to the family farm in July 1966. 'In a way, these were difficult years because I was worried that I wasn't going to be fully extended, worried that I was going to be bored. Everybody, other than my father, told me that I was a total fool and what a waste that I'd gone back onto the farm.' He contrived a complicated system of payment incentives for workers on the farm which he thought would increase productivity. 'And all that I created was a whole host of suspicion in what had previously been a relatively happy community under my father. I created suspicion because I was new and secondly, because I came and changed things and thirdly because I thought I knew everything.' He introduced a system he termed 'carrots and sticks'; the carrots were bonuses and the reverse side was deprivation of the bonus. His hope had been that this would result in a substantial increase in productivity which would enable him to pay higher wages. 'This shining-eyed liberal that had just come from Oxford was going to be able to double everybody's wages: this was the new society into which we were going to move. And all that I created was an enormous amount of suspicion. And productivity', he recounts, with a grim little laugh, 'went down. Fortunately I picked up, just by chance, a magazine called *Management*. On the cover it had a pile of sticks, a plus sign (a bunch of carrots) and it had an equals sign – and it equalled a donkey. I realized that if my management consisted of sticks and carrots I was actually treating all the people with whom I was working as donkeys and that if that's the extent of your motivation – sticks and carrots – then you're not really a manager.' Since that time Tony has simplified the wage structure, and made sure that it is fully understood. Productivity has gone up, not only on the Ardington farms, but throughout the sugar industry, chiefly as a result of the new technology. 'If, for instance, someone is distributing a couple of hundred rands' worth of chemicals a day, you can afford to pay him quite well in order to see that those are correctly applied.'

He has endeavoured to build close and trusting relationships with his workers. The success of the savings scheme instituted on the farms, whereby interest is paid on money being saved, would seem to be indicative of the trust in which the management is held. 'We have about fifty or sixty workers on this farm and at any one time we've got as much as 7,000 rand saved: they wouldn't do that if they weren't totally confident that I was trustworthy. They're actually treating me as a bank.'

The relative absence of intellectual challenge left an uncomfortable void which he sought to fill by extending his farming activities. At the outset there had been two family farms and one that his father was managing for someone else. Tony bought a fourth farm. 'Running four farms might have been improving my management challenges, but hardly helped with the intellectual challenges. I got myself very thinly stretched over a number of enterprises and in addition was getting increasingly involved in the sugar industry and directorates of various companies.' His father had left the management to him and was involved in cattle development. There were some Indian farm managers, and some fairly senior blacks, but none seemed of the calibre to assume responsibility. Neither did the appointment of two white managers significantly ease his position.

Then one of the Indian managers died. Tony, recognizing the imperative need for a competent replacement, turned his attention to the chief clerk on the farm, a matriculated Zulu, about twenty-eight years of age. Quite a number of sugar farms were managed by Indians, but at that time almost none by blacks. 'The more I thought about it, the more I realized that if, in the late seventies, I couldn't appoint a black as a manager in Zululand, well then, we'd really got the thing screwed up much worse than everybody thought.' The young Zulu man had a clever, logical mind. Tony took the leap and appointed him, a step he has not regretted. 'He lives rent free in a pretty big house, has the private use of a vehicle and all the perks that go with management such as two domestic servants, one for indoors and one for the garden, paid for by the farm. His much higher salary, 1,000 rand a month, and status has isolated him from the people with whom he had previously been fraternizing, leaving him in a somewhat lonely predicament. It was evident that what the young man especially needed, and unfortunately lacked, was emotional support. He needed a few really good friends when he came home from work in the evening. And he didn't have them.' He lacked colleagues with whom to discuss farming problems, cane varieties, what should be planted where, new chemicals, new systems, what fertilizer to use. 'I don't think that, apart from myself, he would easily have got into conversation with any of his white neighbours who were doing a similar job to him. He would tend to be too deferential towards them.' Since then a second Zulu manager has been appointed on one of the nearby farms and Tony hopes the two men will enjoy a relationship of colleagues.

In May 1980 Tony represented the sugar industry on the Buthelezi Commission, named after the Chief Minister of KwaZulu, Chief Mangosuthu Buthelezi (not present at their deliberations). KwaZulu is composed of forty-six fragments of territory within

Natal which, on a map, look like odd pieces of a jigsaw puzzle. 'The Commission set the scene for the type of regional administration and legislative body that could be established in the Natal region. There's something like four billion rand that is spent annually by the Natal and KwaZulu governments on services for the people there; basically on education, health care, roads and housing – that represents about 85 per cent of both budgets. I think that there were those who were saying that this money is being spent very inefficiently and the people themselves are getting very poor services, not because of any intention on the part of the administrators who are in charge, but because of the structures that exist. For instance, you would have empty white schools and empty white teacher training establishments cheek by jowl with grossly overcrowded facilities for people of other races, sometimes just across the street. It was felt that something should be done at local level.

'Moreover, at the time this was one of the few places in the country where one could speak with blacks who had credibility with significant communities. If, for example, one had tried to set up any type of negotiation in the eastern Cape I don't think that any black leaders would have emerged. There are huge suspicions among black communities with respect to their various leadership groups.'

Tony became chairman of the economic development committee which consisted of representatives of agriculture, commerce, industry, the administration, trade unions and academics. 'In March 1982 we got a unanimous report, largely due to Jill Nattrass, who now heads the Economic Development Unit of the Centre for Applied Social Sciences at the University of Natal, and who was on the committee. She made the bullets and I fired them. The government rejected the Commission's proposal that multiracial political and constitutional structures, based on a recognition of the interdependence of Natal and KwaZulu, be established. The report of the Commission continued to be a very significant reference document and indeed a springboard from which various ideas, including the Bill of Rights, that were later put to the Indaba came.'

The KwaZulu Natal Indaba was an event of great historical significance, the first inter-racial constitutional conference held in South Africa's history. It was convened in April 1986 by the KwaZulu administration and the Natal provincial council with a view to reaching consensus on proposals to be put to the government for the creation of a single legislative body to govern the combined area of KwaZulu and Natal as part of South Africa.

Once more heading the economic committee, Tony explained, 'Natal generates something like 15 per cent of the Gross National Product of South Africa, but it houses over 20 per cent of the population, so its needs are greater than its resources.' His fear was that the people of Natal might, in their enthusiasm, accept (if it were offered to them) the responsibilities of local government, or regional government, without simultaneously securing the resources with which to deliver improved services for the vast majority of the people in the fields of education, health care, housing and land availability. 'And that's not going to come from the resources of Natal alone. The Indaba would have to be seen by the central government as a valuable political initiative that shouldn't be allowed to fail. In other words, there needed to be an inflow of resources in order to establish an initial stepping-stone which, it was hoped, would represent the eventual model from which a one-man-one-vote non-racial federation for the whole of South Africa could be formed.

'The danger, to me, is that the government is grudgingly going to accept what the Indaba has come up with . . . so you're going to get the local leadership once again involved in a situation where they've accepted responsibility, but they haven't got the resources to meet this responsibility.' This he termed the Verwoerdian trap; precisely the kind of impasse into which Prime Minister Verwoerd precipitated the *bantustans*, or homelands, that were created in 1959.

'I don't see the KwaZulu Natal Indaba as competitive with one-man-one-vote. I see it as a technique, a constitutional technique to start removing the power from the office of the State President, because you will be establishing round the country regional centres of power. These centres would have a real job to do, big responsibilities in terms of distributing the services of government, and access to substantial resources. In concept I think it is marvellous.'

One of the first steps the education committee would have to take would be to abolish the existing system where there are six education departments in Natal: that of KwaZulu (for blacks); the Natal Education Department (for whites); the Indian Education Department; the Coloured Education Department; the Department of Education and Training (which is responsible for educating blacks in white Natal as distinct from KwaZulu); and the Department of National Education which is responsible for tertiary education. 'All this,' Tony explains, 'with six budgets. There are probably sixteen or seventeen education departments in the whole country if you include the so-called independent states of Bophuthatswana, Transkei, Ciskei and Venda. And all that is duplicated with health care; we've got four authorities administering health care in Natal.'

'The most savage thing about our South African society is that we have taxed everybody and given to the rich. For instance the annual State expenditure for the education of each black child is only 200 rand and that for a white child is 2,300 rand. It's just the thing that sticks in my craw. The ultimate iniquity in this country, as far as I'm concerned, is that the whites, who are generally much richer, should get free education for their children, and the blacks have to pay so much for it. The schools get built free in Durban, but not free in KwaZulu. That, to me, is the most savage and vicious thing. Of the 3,000 schools in KwaZulu, those in the main townships have been built by the government; the rest have been built by the community. There might be a subsidy from the KwaZulu administration, once the class-rooms have been built, and they fund the operation of the school.'

The delegates of the KwaNatal Indaba have signed an agreement as to what sort of constitution and Bill of Rights should apply to this region. 'They have taken the first step in trying to establish a non-racial federal government in South Africa. There would be one-man-one-vote and there are various constitutional mechanisms to try to protect the language and cultural rights of minorities who identify themselves voluntarily. For instance, right now I have no choice about being a white South African: I'm forced to be it, and likewise all Indians, coloureds and blacks are obliged to be categorized with the racial group to which they are designated. Under the Indaba constitutional proposals, if the Afrikaans-speaking community, for instance, consider themselves to be a minority that's threatened, they would have the opportunity to voluntarily identify themselves and thereby seek protection of their legitimate rights.

'I don't think that the Indaba has ever purported to be coming up with a national solution. It was intended to light a path down which other regions could follow and which could eventually result in a national reconciliation between all parties.'

Market research and opinion surveys in the early part of 1987 had indicated that the white people of Natal held positive attitudes concerning the Indaba and yet the expected strong vote for the Progressive Federal Party which supported the Indaba did not materialize in the May 1987 general election. 'There is a view that many whites in Natal said, 'We are happy to go into the Indaba, but we would wish the Nationalists to negotiate us into it.' Also people were petrified by the huge scare propaganda put out just before the elections.

'In the event, the Indaba proposals were rejected entirely by the government. I think it's an absolute disaster if the opportunity it presented isn't picked up by South Africa because the options further down the road to create a prosperous and happy society get increasingly bleak. The government is under a great deal of pressure at the moment to come up with something that will swim and I don't think they've got anything that looks like doing so. It looks as though whites are not ready to negotiate a transfer of power and that before they do become ready to do so the harrow's going to go over us. What sort of society emerges once you've had really tragic events taking place, where the terrible experiences of those in the townships is replicated right across the country and violence takes over in the society on a large scale? The biggest danger is this office of executive president with all this power concentrated in the centre; to leave that office as the prize after you've had a civil war is a really frightening prospect.'

Wages, Tony believes, are determined by the market-place. 'If you have a skill and there's a shortage of that skill you'll find that reflected in the market-place. We might not like that; we might find it offensive, but if you have got a relatively free economy in the labour market, that is going to happen.' Various codes, or sets of principles, have been drawn up over the past fifteen or so years by the European Economic Community, by the Reverend Leon Sullivan and by some others and have been directed towards improving labour conditions in South Africa, particularly with regard to blacks, in the factory and workplace. He does not see these as helpful. 'I have seen a lot of companies here that are very concerned about the conditions of the people working in their company and in order to be able to improve the conditions, they have gone more and more capital-intensive, and have been encouraged to do so by the tax laws here. They replaced people with capital.' The result, he points out, is that you end up, inside the factory gate, with a First World environment. If you've got to find somebody to clean the office and working areas, what you do is contract out the job to some office cleaning organization. Thus within the company itself you can stand scrutiny from anybody, from the European Economic Community, Reverend Leon Sullivan and his people – they'll find that you're absolutely perfect. Meantime there's a sea of unemployed at the factory gate, all very happy to work for 10 rand a day. And many of them happy to work for 5 rand a day.

'Another thing that makes employment more expensive is that we have tended to export people who are living in so-called 'white areas', adjacent to their places of employment, to distant points. Take District Six in Cape Town where people used to walk to work, or Cato Manor in Durban. The people who lived in these places are now beyond the fringes of the city so that in Durban it costs the average worker 60 or 70 rand a month to get to work – either directly out of his own pocket, or indirectly in terms of subsidies. And this economy is competing with the economies of Singapore, Hong Kong and Tai Pei, all the burgeoning economies of the Far East where people walk to work. So that is another thing that has tended to increase the cost of employment and enables people to say the capital-intensive option is the cheaper one.

'What's best for society is not going to be determined by philanthropic or altruistic businessmen. Companies are going to try to make a profit and they will choose the cheapest way of doing a particular job. They will always follow their own best interest. It's up to the authorities to determine whether to subsidize down the cost of capital and increase the cost of labour (in which case you're liable to have high unemployment) or alternatively, subsidize down the cost of employment and increase the cost of capital, in which case the techniques of production are liable to be more labour-intensive and you tend to reduce unemployment. The artificial barriers that have been created in this country limit the migration of people to areas of economic opportunity, limit competition in the labour market and raise the cost of employment. In addition the authorities have subsidized down the cost of capital and we have steadily introduced very capital-intensive, First-World-type industrial production techniques. The consequence of these policies has been to exacerbate the level of unemployment.

'We've fouled up the whole thing. Between 1960 and 1987 this economy has been absolutely appallingly managed. The criterion of economic efficiency has not been a part of the policies of our country. The major criteria determining the policies of South Africa have been to secure the privileged position of the whites and if this involves taking people who are living in District Six or Cato Manor, adjacent to their place of work, and pushing them 35 kilometres away, without adequate transport amenities to get themselves to their work, so be it. People planning our society haven't had economic growth in mind; they've been securing whites' perception of what will be best for them. We also spend a large amount of our money on control functions in society as distinct from welfare functions. Our society is very controlled and regulated and all the rules and regulations have to be administered and policed (in both official languages) and that costs a lot of money. If you got rid of all that you could use the money for education and health care.

'Sugar-cane farming in South Africa is labour-intensive; this means that a high proportion of the total proceeds generated by the industry are going to flow to the people employed. You're not servicing a large amount of capital; you're servicing a large number of people and you're going to find relatively low wages in that environment. If you don't have low wage rates, you're going to pack up: you're not going to compete.' Most farm employees get board and housing and generally live with their families, several members of whom might also be income earners. Labourers on his farm get a basic wage of about 180 rand a month and in addition probably earn bonuses of 50 to 80 rand a month. Tractor drivers and other more skilled workers are paid at higher levels. Married men have free housing for themselves and their families and are issued with a weekly food ration which includes meat. Unmarried men live in the hostel, rent free, and have free meals. Wages are higher in the towns, but this advantage is often negated by the fact that so much of the income has to be spent on rent, transport, buying lunches and the more expensive clothes that are generally needed.

The discussion turns to management techniques. In order to illustrate his point, Tony uses the metaphor of a rugby team whose coach is concerned with motivation of his players. 'He is part of the team and he'll bust his butt for them; he will do anything for them and they know it. That is one model of employment in the sugar industry. The other is, "There are a whole lot of poverty-stricken people out there and they're *bloody* lucky that I've given them a job. They happen to be very, very lazy types who don't appear to be grateful to me for what I've done for them and I'm going to try to get as much as I can out of them for as little as possible." Such an employer has, living on his farm, thirty or forty workers and their families in a state of perpetual confrontation. The fellow who's leading the team actually enjoys farming. The other fellow, after twenty years says, "I can't take it any longer," and he gets out.

'What I'm basically saying is that if a major concern of the company or firm is the people who are working there (or, in the case of the farmer, the people who are also living there) then the opportunity to increase the productivity of everybody in that organization is greatly enhanced. You generally find that in an exploitative environment productivity is low, while in the supportive environment productivity can increase quite considerably.'

The provision of adequate housing on farms is an essential component of good labour relations. The aim on the Ardington farms has been to provide a house for every man who wishes to stay there with his wife and family. An employee with a record of long service can live on the farm until he dies, when his widow may remain. Nevertheless, there must inevitably be a degree of insecurity in the man's tenure of his house which he would lose were he to give notice, or be obliged to leave. Tony favours the development of farm villages, a concept propounded by the noted anthropologist, the late Monica Wilson. In such villages farm workers would be able to own homes and be totally independent of the farmer. 'It would also give an opportunity to have a larger community which could aggregate its income. Money would tend to be spent in the village, starting the rands going round within their own community and possibly creating new employment.' Such a plan would absolve the farmer from the moral dilemma in which he may find himself when he has to dismiss a worker, knowing that the man and his family will thus be homeless. 'I think that the idea would be substantially resisted by some people in agriculture because they like the dependency relationship; it gives them greater control. It also, of course, distorts the relationship.'

Most workers have tended to make sure that they've always got a second home, in the Transkei or in KwaZulu where the tribal authorities allocate to them a piece of land on which to build. But there are Shangaans who have migrated from Mozambique: 'They've never, for the past thirty years, known any home other than that on the farm. They've long since lost any connection with Mozambique. The attitude of the government is to export these people back to where they've come from, back into the arms of FRELIMO or RENAMO. We allow Mozambicans who've worked for us to retire on the farm.'

While visiting Lima some few years ago, Tony noticed, because a bus had run into it and damaged the exterior surface, that Lima's huge cathedral, which appears to be built of solid stone and is over 150 years old, was built of bamboo and daub. This has persuaded him that the next batch of houses on his farm will be of wattle and daub, in the old African style. 'If you speak to any architects that have been involved, they'll tell you that it's marvellous material and that there's nothing to stop you building a wattle and daub house with water-borne sewerage, showers, electric lights, the whole lot. You just make a little concrete slab and you put in all your water, electricity and plumbing and then you build the wattle and daub house round it.' These new houses will be both cheaper and, he believes, superior in every way to the old brick ones, a view he is convinced will be endorsed by those who are going to live in them.

Is he considering joining the stream of well-qualified, mainly English-speaking South Africans leaving the country? 'We did have a bad thought about it just after the elections, but basically we have taken a decision that we will stay here unless life becomes intolerable for any member of our family.' Nevertheless, Tony admits, 'I wouldn't like to take the moral decisions that some of those young people have to take, being involved in an Army that's defending apartheid.' Tony sits on the Rhodes Scholarship Selection Committee where he frequently encounters extremely bright young men who have completed, for instance, a five-year law degree, then their articles and have, as he describes it, 'run out of options' in their endeavour to stay out of the Army. Some say that if they are called up they will refuse to serve; that they will go, instead, to prison. 'And these are bright, bright youngsters, absolutely outstanding people. That takes a lot of guts! There's no way that I could see myself spending six years in prison, because that's what it is now. That's a hell of a price to pay!'

Turning to the case of his son who, at the time he was speaking did not appear to be unduly concerned about the issue of his Army service, Tony continued, 'With his background, his upbringing and education I think he would feel pretty strongly about it by the time that he's got to go into the Army. If he decided he would go into the Army, either because he felt he should, or because he felt neutral about it, or because he felt there was something that had to be done and the sooner you got rid of it the better, I would live with all those reasons. But if *he* says that he's unable to go into the Army, I've got to support him. Because that person really needs support in our society. I believe they are placed in an unacceptably difficult position. The penalty for refusing to serve is, as I've already said, six years in gaol. It's really very, very difficult for me to expect him to have to take a decision like that. Maybe we've got to move. But I don't know. That's probably five years down the road and things will have happened and that particular problem could well have passed.'

Most South Africans are uneasy about the future. Many whites, particularly the younger ones, consider emigration, creating currents of unease in their communities. Not a few feel bitter concerning those who have scuttled off. Some have pointed to Tony's privileged education which would enable him, if he found life under any government especially distasteful, to leave the country with his family. His retort is, 'Educational qualifications are not much good in the job market when you're aged forty-seven.

'Everybody has an option to get up and leave. The totally democratic government that I advocate and hope for might not arrive. Following a civil war some monster could take power and might make life for a lot of people intolerable. The chances are, indeed, that if we keep the existing constitutional structures, then the person who gets hold of that presidential office is going to make life pretty unpleasant for a lot of people. Just as the present incumbent leads a government that has made life pretty unpleasant for a lot of people.' He reiterates his faith in a federal solution, with regional leaders who have a genuine power base that cannot be eroded by 'some potentate at the centre'. 'That's why I support the Natal Indaba concept. I'm not hopeful though that a new system of government would make this country any more wonderful to live in. We're probably going to have the harrow go over us.'

GLOSSARY

baas: 'master'. Term for white boss used by black workers, usually farm-workers. Also *kleinbaas* (little master) and *oubaas* (old master).

bakkie: a light truck or van with a cabin or an open back for conveying goods, animals or people.

biltong: strips of lean meat, preserved by salting and drying.

boerevolk: literally the *boer* or Afrikaner people. Emotive term conveying the idea of Afrikaner unity and tradition.

boerewors: literally 'farm sausage'. A type of sausage, often home-made, generally *braaied* (cooked over an open fire) and which might spring to the mind of a white South African asked to name his national food.

bondeldraers: travelling merchants who carried their wares in bundles from village to village in country districts.

bowser: a petrol pump. The name derives from the American firm, Bowser, which supplied the first pumps in South Africa.

braaivleis: meat cooked over an open fire and often eaten with *putu*, chunks of stiff maize-meal porridge.

bywoner: a white tenant farmer who was given a portion of the farm-land to work for himself in return for assisting the farmer on his land. Sometimes he farmed the owner's land and the crop was shared.

commando: an armed party called out for military purposes.

dominee: a pastor in the Nederduitse Gereformeerde Kerk.

dorp: a small country town.

droëwors: dried sausage.

fanakalo: the word means literally 'do it like this'. *Fanakalo* was developed by blacks working in southern Africa in the mines and in industry and was later formalized and used by mine management as a means of communication with different African language groups. It is based chiefly on Zulu.

homelands: areas of South Africa set aside for blacks, each one for a specific language group. Several of the homelands consist of fragmented pieces, sometimes widely separated. The area of the homelands is roughly 13 per cent of the Republic: blacks (not including Indians and coloureds) constitute 74 per cent of the total population of the whole of the Republic of South Africa. Four of the homelands are theoretically self-governing: Transkei, Venda, Bophuthatswana and Ciskei. The remainder are KwaZulu, Gazankulu, Lebowa, KwaNdebele, QwaQwa and KaNgwane.

hotnot: a derogatory term, generally used in the Cape Province, applied to people of mixed blood.

impis: Zulu regiments.

jol: to have boisterous fun.

kerkhuis: church house.

kerkraad: church council.

kloof: chasm.

koppie: hill.

kraal: an enclosure, pen, or fold for farm animals.

location: general term for a designated, segregated area for black people, bordering a town or city.

mealies, mealie-meal: maize, maize-meal.

meid: used to refer to a black servant-girl; conveys a sense of racial inferiority and is generally resented by black women.

morgen: a land measurement. Originally the area of land which could be ploughed in one morning, it has been standardized to 2.11 acres. No longer in use, having been replaced by the hectare (2.47 acres).

morogo: a type of wild spinach.

nagmaal: the three-monthly communion service held in town, which would be attended by Dutch Reformed Church members from isolated country areas. Historically almost as much a social as a religious occasion.

ouma, oupa: grandma, grandpa.

piccanin: term used by whites to refer to young black boys.

pocket: a sack or bag, generally made of jute, to contain vegetables or fruit.

putu-pap: a stiff maize-meal porridge.

rooinek: 'red-neck'. Used pejoratively by Afrikaners about English-speakers. It originated in the South African War where exposed areas of the English soldiers' skins were observed to redden in the sun.

sjambok: a leather-thonged whip.

smous: a travelling pedlar, usually Jewish.

sopie: a drink, tot.

stoep: a terraced veranda running the length of a house.

tickey: threepence in old South African currency.

townships: segregated areas on fringes of white towns and cities where blacks are required by law to live.

trekboer: nomadic pastoralist.

tsotsis: black urban gangsters, generally under the age of thirty.

verlig: enlightened.

Voortrekker: the men and women who undertook the Great Trek in 1834–8. About 10,000 men, women and children left Cape Colony to escape from British control after the abolition of slavery and establish independent Boer Republics. The *Voortrekkers* are now potent elements of Afrikaner mythology.

Political and Institutional

African National Congress: Founded in 1912 by Dr Pixley Seme and Reverend John Dube to promote African unity and African interests. Banned in 1960, but still operates in exile and within the country. Most popular and widely supported African political organization inside and outside South Africa. It has a small number of white members. The nominal leader is Nelson Mandela who has been imprisoned on Robben Island, and more recently at Pollsmoor, since 1963.

Afrikaner Weerstandsbeweging [AWB]: African Resistance Organization. An extreme right-wing paramilitary resistance group for whites only, led by Eugene Terre'Blanche.

Conservative Party [CP]: Formed in 1982 by the breaking away of the more right-wing members of the National Party, led by Dr Andries Treurnicht. It is now the official opposition.

FRELIMO: Front for the Liberation of Mozambique. Ruling force in Mozambique since 1974 after the downfall of the Portuguese regime.

Herstigte Nasionale Party [HNP]: An extreme right-wing political party founded in 1969 by the late Dr Albert Hertzog. It aims at the Afrikanerization of the English-speaking sector.

National Party [NP]: formed in 1914. In June 1934 the majority of its members, led by General Hertzog, fused with the South African Party, led by General Smuts, to form the United Party. A relatively small number of dissenting Nationalists, led by Dr Malan, formed the Gesuiwerde (Purified) National Party. This is the party (the word 'gesuiwerde' was dropped) that came to power and has remained in power since 1948.

Nederduitse Gereformeerde Kerk [NG Kerk]: Dutch Reformed Church.

Ossewa-Brandwag [OB]: It was founded in 1939. The name means literally 'sentinels of the ox-wagon'. It was an illegal, secret, paramilitary organization whose aim was the establishment of an Afrikaner Republic. During World War II its members committed some acts of sabotage.

Pan Africanist Congress [PAC]: A breakaway movement from the ANC, formed in 1959 and led by the late Robert Sobukwe; Africanist as opposed to the non-racial ANC.

Progressive Federal Party [PFP]: Established in 1959 by the breaking away of some of the more liberally inclined United Party members. Until May 1987 the official parliamentary opposition, its membership is chiefly middle-class and English-speaking.

RENAMO: Resistençia Naçional Moçambicana (Mozambican

National Resistance Movement) founded by the Rhodesian government, headed by Ian Smith, and, after the liberation of Mozambique, supported by Mozambican exiles in Portugal and the South African government.

Sappe: Supporters of the old South African Party led by Generals Louis Botha and Jan Smuts.

Sendingkerk: The missionary arm of the Dutch Reformed Church. It is involved in providing and funding churches for the black and coloured population.

SWAPO: South-West African People's Organization.

United Party [UP]: Formed in 1933 when General Hertzog's National Party fused with General Smuts's South African Party.

Note on the South African Education System for Whites

The medium of education in South Africa is either English or Afrikaans. Afrikaans-medium schools teach English as a second language and all other subjects are taught in Afrikaans. In English-medium schools the situation is reversed. In dual-medium schools both languages are used more or less equally. In parallel-medium schools there is an Afrikaans and an English class for each standard. When the National Party came to power in 1948 they drastically reduced the number of dual-medium and parallel-medium schools. The Standards, or classes, run from Standard 1 (for 8- to 9-year olds) to Standard 10 (for 17- to 18-year olds). Matriculation is the Standard 10 or university entrance examination in which one of the official languages must be sat at a higher level and the other at a lower level.